Alex's Wake

A Voyage of Betrayal
and a Journey of Remembrance

Martin Goldsmith

Da Capo Press
A Member of the Perseus Books Group

Epigraph on page vii: From THE THEATRE OF TENNESSEE WILLIAMS VOL. VIII, copyright ©1977, 1979 by The University of the South. Reprinted by permission of New Directions Publishing Corp.

Design and composition by Eclipse Publishing Services
Set in 12-point Adobe Jenson Pro Light

Cataloging-in-Publication data for this book is available from the Library of Congress.
First Da Capo Press edition 2014

ISBN: 978-0-306-82322-0 (hardcover)
ISBN: 978-0-306-82323-7 (e-book)

Published by Da Capo Press
A Member of the Perseus Books Group
www.dacapopress.com

Da Capo Press books are available at special discounts for bulk purchases in the U.S. by corporations, institutions, and other organizations. For more information, please contact the Special Markets Department at the Perseus Books Group, 2300 Chestnut Street, Suite 200, Philadelphia, PA 19103, or call (800) 810-4145, ext. 5000, or e-mail special.markets@perseusbooks.com.

10 9 8 7 6 5 4 3 2 1

*To the memory of my brother, Peter,
and, once again, to Amy*

Contents

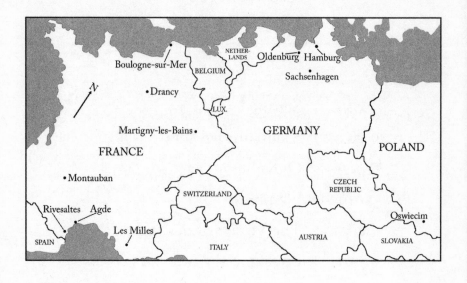

And I only am escaped alone to tell thee.

—Job

All right, I've told you my story. Now I want you to do something for me. Take me out to Cypress Hill and we'll hear the dead people talk. They do talk there. They chatter together like birds on Cypress Hill, but all they say is one word and that word is "live," they say, "Live, live, live, live, live!" It's all they've learned, it's the only advice they can give. Just live.

—Tennessee Williams

I

Setting Forth

THAT TIMELESS AMERICAN TRAVELER, Huckleberry Finn, introduces himself this way: "You don't know about me without you have read a book by the name of *The Adventures of Tom Sawyer*; but that ain't no matter. That book was made by Mr. Mark Twain, and he told the truth, mainly." Some years ago, I made a book by the name of *The Inextinguishable Symphony* and told the story of my father and mother. In that book, my father mostly appeared as a young man named Günther Ludwig Goldschmidt who, by dint of good fortune and dogged persistence, escaped Nazi Germany and arrived on Ellis Island in June 1941. Shortly thereafter, he changed his name to George Gunther Goldsmith, and he and his young wife Rosemary began their lives in The Land of the Free. It's a good book, I think, and I'm proud of it. And, yes, I told the truth, mainly.

I finished writing *The Inextinguishable Symphony* on December 31, 1999, just as the clock crept toward the close of a century as brutal and bloody as any in the history of our glorious and unhappy planet. The book was published in September 2000, and I began what my wife generously calls "The Never-Ending Book Tour." I'm pleased to say that I have made well over a hundred appearances on behalf of the book, speaking from one end of the United States to the other and in such foreign cities as Toronto, Berlin, and St. Petersburg. I mention these facts not in a spirit of self-aggrandizement so much as to give weight to the additional fact that in nearly every city I am asked, "So, after writing this book, what has happened to your Jewish identity? And what was your father's reaction to the book?" I'm not sure I realized it at the time, but my attempts to answer those questions represented the first stirrings of the journey that has resulted in the making of this book.

I think that my father had a rather ambivalent reaction to *The Inextinguishable Symphony*. He was pleased at its favorable reception, happy for my opportunities to discuss it, and honored to have been the subject of the book, but I think it also made him profoundly uncomfortable, and in no small measure ashamed. In many ways, Günther Goldschmidt is the hero of the book. George Goldsmith, however, didn't feel like a hero. Mr. Mark Twain would have called that heroic portrait a "stretcher" of the truth, and, much as it pains me to acknowledge it, he would have been right.

George's father, my grandfather Alex Goldschmidt, and his younger brother, my uncle Klaus Helmut Goldschmidt, were two of the more than nine hundred Jewish refugees who attempted to flee Nazi Germany in May 1939 on board an ocean liner called the *St. Louis*. The fate of that ship commanded global attention for a few weeks that spring—the *New York Times* declared it "the saddest ship afloat today"—as it attempted to find safe harbor in an unwelcoming world. After more than a month at sea, my grandfather and uncle found themselves in France, where they would remain for the next three years. They spent time in a number of different settlements, each less hospitable than the last, before being shipped to their deaths at Auschwitz in August 1942.

Alex had spent four years fighting in the muddy, ghastly trenches of the First World War, achieving the distinction of the Iron Cross, First Class from a presumably grateful German government. In the uneasy peace that followed the Great War, he achieved success as a businessman and parlayed his profitable women's clothing store into a lofty position in the emerging society of his adopted hometown of Oldenburg. Never one to allow life's circumstances to dictate terms to him where he could help it, Alex was a man of forthright action and blunt expression. Even while caught in the snares of his French imprisonment, he wrote impassioned letters to those in charge, stating the case for his freedom and that of his younger son. And he sent letters to his older son, my father, to spur him into action on their behalf.

In his very last letter to George, Grandfather Alex recounted the horrors he and Helmut had endured since boarding the *St. Louis* more than three years earlier. With all the pent-up pain and frustration of his captivity flowing through his pen, Alex concluded, "I have already described our situation for you several times. This will be the last time. If you don't move heaven and earth to help us, that's up to you, but it will be on your conscience."

My father and mother had managed to emigrate to the United States in June 1941. They had survived as Jews in Germany until then because of their status as musicians in an all-Jewish performing arts organization called the *Kulturbund*. Once in America, they both found menial jobs: my mother as a domestic, cooking and cleaning houses for twelve dollars a week, and my father working in a factory where he cut zippers out of discarded pants and polished them on a wheel, reconditioning them so that they could serve again in the flies of new trousers. For this, he was paid fourteen dollars a week. They didn't have much, but they occasionally sent as much as twenty-five dollars, nearly a full week's salary, via Quaker intermediaries to the camps in France to try to ease the burden of Alex and Helmut.

But did my father do as much as he could have on his family's behalf? Did he, as his father had implored him, "move heaven and earth"? Probably not. In the late summer of 1941, my parents landed jobs performing at a music festival in Columbia, South Carolina. They took the train from their home in New York City down to Columbia, passing through Washington, D.C., on their journeys south and north. Neither time did my father disembark in the capital to visit the halls of Congress, where he might have found an important ally who could have helped him to fill out the proper form or contact the right immigration officer who might have reached the exact authority in France in time to ensure that Alex and Helmut never boarded that fateful train to Auschwitz. There were reasons aplenty why every effort under the sun might have failed to win his family's freedom, but the inescapable fact remains that Alex begged his son to save his life and my father failed to do so.

"It will be on your conscience," wrote Alex, and Alex was right. In 1945, with the end of the war, the grisly newsreels appeared, documenting the full range of the atrocities that the Nazis had perpetrated, unspeakable crimes that included the murders of my father's family as five among the six million. In addition to Alex and Helmut, dead in Auschwitz, there were Toni and Eva, my grandmother and aunt, deported to Riga, and my father's Grandmother Behrens, murdered in Terezin. The next year, my father gave up his flute and the music profession that he loved in favor of a job selling furniture in a department store, an act of penance for his failure to save his family. In a revealing letter, sent late in his life, my father wrote, "The unanswered question which disturbs me most profoundly and which I shall carry to my own death is whether through an enormous last-minute effort I could have saved my father and brother from their horrible end."

The guilt that my father carried he passed on to my brother, Peter, and me as our emotional inheritance. The violent fates of their families (my mother, an only child, lost her mother to the camp at Trawniki) were a subject my parents assiduously avoided in my early years. No doubt they wished to protect Peter and me from the truth, for fear that we might have trouble sleeping at night or developing a sense of trust. How little they suspected that, even without words, we could feel and absorb the unspoken pain that circulated like dust in the air of our home, and how much we were aware of the darkness, the enormous unknown yet deeply felt secret that obscured the light of the truth.

My parents' way of dealing with their guilt and sadness was to deny it and keep it hidden. But secrets derive a significant part of their power from silence and shame. "They died in the war," was my father's curt reply to my brother's direct question about why, unlike all our friends, we couldn't visit our grandparents at Christmas or birthdays. There was nothing more, no stories, no reassurances that their fate would not be ours. And there was no acknowledgment that we were Jews, despite that being the singular reason for our family's violent dismemberment. When I, as a teenager, discovered our religious roots, my father dismissed it all by declaring that we were, at most, "so-called Jews." He did not choose to regard himself as a Jew, despite the unavoidable fact that he'd been bar mitzvahed, that his parents were both Jews, and that he and his wife had both performed in an all-Jewish orchestra. "Adolf Hitler thought I was a Jew, so I had no choice. I choose to exercise that choice now. I am not a Jew," he said.

As I grew to manhood, I became aware of my inherited guilt. In my forties, I began to research the story of my parents' lives in Germany and of their families' lives as well, a tale that I told in *The Inextinguishable Symphony*. But over the years since that book's publication, I have come to see that tale as only the starting point of a journey of self-discovery that I unknowingly began the moment I first asked a question about what happened to my family.

I've come to feel a deep need to connect with that vanished generation, with those members of my family who were murdered a decade before I was born. In one of his letters, my grandfather acknowledged that he was writing on the morning of Rosh Hashanah, the Jewish New Year. He obviously self-identified as a Jew. So I began to explore Judaism, partly as a purely spiritual quest, but mostly as a way to reach back through those vanished years to try to touch my grandfather. When I heard the Kol Nidre prayer intoned on Yom Kippur, my eyes would fill with tears because of the melancholy beauty of the melody, and also because I knew that, once upon a time, my grandfather had heard that same melody on that same holy night. In the autumn of 2006, I began a twenty-month course of study, discussion, and learning that culminated in my becoming a Son of the Commandment, a Bar Mitzvah Boy, at the age of fifty-five.

With the help of my wife and my therapist, I came to recognize a rhetorical question that hung over me like the mist that follows in the wake of an ocean liner. "How can I ever be truly happy, how can I ever deserve happiness," I would say to myself, "when my grandfather was murdered in Auschwitz?"

I realized also that, although my grandmothers and aunt had been murdered as well, it was the story of Alex and Helmut that fully galvanized my interest. I became consumed with a desire to know the facts of their voyage on the *St. Louis* and of their three years' imprisonment in France. Eventually it occurred to me why, beyond a certain spectator's curiosity, that was so. I wanted to learn the facts of their final years on earth because I wanted to save them. My father had failed, and the responsibility had passed to me. I was the backstop, the catcher racing up the first base line to snag an errant throw from an infielder. I couldn't save them, of course. Again, they died ten years before I was born. But my father's burden had become mine and his guilt was mine as well. If I couldn't save them, the least I could do was to place flowers on their graves, to tell the world their story, and to bear witness.

In March 2006, my wife and I visited my father in Tucson, where he and my mother had moved following their retirement, and where George had remained following my mother's death in 1984. George was now ninety-two years old and living alone, and Amy and I thought it was probably time to bring up the subject of assisted living. There is a nice facility nearly across the street from our home in Maryland, and we spent what we thought was a productive Saturday afternoon discussing a possible move east. My father asked several pointed questions but seemed quite interested in the prospect of living so close to Washington, D.C., and all its political and cultural attractions. When we parted that evening, Amy and I breathed sighs of relief, assuming that most of the heavy lifting had been accomplished.

The following morning, when we raised the issue again at breakfast, George became indignant, accusing us of conspiring to take him away from the home he loved. "But yesterday you said that it was such a good idea!" I exclaimed, frustrated by what I took to be the simple querulousness of a cranky old man. We flew back to Maryland that afternoon, unsure what to do.

Within a few weeks our way forward became painfully clear. A neighbor had come to visit George and found him in a heap on the floor, unable to rise. He was taken to a hospital, and several days later a neurologist called me with the news that my father had Alzheimer's disease. What I had taken for a disagreeable refusal to acknowledge a logical plan of action had in reality been my father's simple inability to remember a conversation from one day to the next.

There followed a nightmare of weeks of legal maneuvering attempting to persuade the state of Arizona to declare me George's legal guardian so that I could move him to Arbor Place, an Alzheimer's facility near us in Maryland. The single worst day of my life came in late June, when we somehow got him on an airplane, doing our best to ignore his repeated vehement declarations that I was behaving like a Nazi and that Amy was a willing Nazi *hausfrau*. His use of those epithets was doubtless evidence of his illness, but no less ironic or painful for all of that.

A slow, sad diminuendo marked the last years of George Goldsmith, during which I had frequent opportunities to visit with Günther Goldschmidt, the young man I'd come to know while working on *The Inextinguishable Symphony*. As I sat with him in the fenced-in garden of Arbor Place at twilight, or, increasingly as time went on, by his bedside in his tiny room, on a slippery brown leather chair we'd brought along from his home in Arizona, he would speak lovingly and longingly of his long-lost homeland. At times, his memories would skip across decades, as when he declared that he first heard the news of President Kennedy's assassination from a passerby on Gartenstrasse, where he'd lived as a child in Oldenburg. Mostly, though, he would share with me his happy memories of playing in the Schlossgarten, the elegant park, formerly the ducal gardens, that began just steps from his father's spacious house. Many were the times that we would plan a return visit to his hometown that I knew would never happen; we'd fly to Amsterdam, I told him, and after a day or two take the train (oh, how he loved trains!) to Osnabrück and then to Oldenburg. He would show me all the sights, we'd hear music in the thirteenth-century Lambertikirche, and we'd stroll together through the Schlossgarten, admiring the rhododendrons and throwing bread crumbs to the ducks who swam contentedly in the park's peaceful ponds. Invariably after these fanciful conversations, my visit would end, he would fall into a happy sleep, and I would drive home in tears.

Then, as a gentle spring took hold in 2009, his decline quickened. In the middle of a rainy April night, a phone call summoned me to a suburban hospital where my father had been rushed when a caretaker at Arbor Place discovered him struggling for breath. A few days later, he was returned to his own little bed under hospice care; his doctor, without explicitly saying the words, prepared me for the end. On Wednesday night, April 29, I had the chance to say goodbye. My father, shrunken and shaken by his last struggles, could no longer reply as I told him that I loved him and thanked him for my life and for my love of music. He grasped my hand with what must have remained of his strength and opened his eyes wide before closing them and sinking back into his pillow. The next day, shortly after noon, his long journey ended at last.

Exactly eleven months later, on March 30, 2010, I received the shocking, inexplicable news that my brother had died. A once brilliant student at Stanford University who, like me, had gone into the business of introducing classical music on the radio, Peter had in recent years been struck low by physical ailments and a profound depression that, I am sure, was exacerbated by the long-standing family guilt and shame. Now he was gone, quickly felled by a heart attack. He was sixty. The one person of my generation who understood the issues I'd grown up with, intimately and with no need of explanation, had disappeared. My parents, the other two people who'd known me all my life, were also gone. I was suddenly alone, the last Goldsmith standing.

As I struggled to make sense of my unfamiliar place in the universe and to come to terms with my sorrow, one certainty seemed to wrap itself comfortingly around me, as if I'd slipped on a well-worn flannel shirt on a cold morning. I would once again write a book about my family. The family had been reduced to all but nothing, but I would do my best to see that it lived on. I would tell the story of my Grandfather Alex and Uncle Helmut, of their journey on the *St. Louis* and their unhappy odyssey through France. Having lost my father and my brother, I would write about my father's father and his brother. Perhaps I was trying to cling to what had slipped away forever. But whatever the source of my decision, I told myself that I would write the book so that it could be completed by the day I, too, reached sixty. I didn't have much time.

I began by paying several visits to the United States Holocaust Memorial Museum, the immense building on the National Mall in Washington, solemnly designed to suggest a concentration camp. I knew that Alex and Helmut had landed in France in June 1939 and that they'd arrived in the Rivesaltes concentration camp in January 1941, but where and how they had passed those interim eighteen months remained a mystery.

In 1941, a helpful French functionary filled out these cards that, seventy years later, provided me with invaluable clues regarding my grandfather and uncle's journey through France. Note the handwritten cities listed just below the line marked Nationalite.
(Courtesy of the United States Holocaust Memorial Museum)

But then, while poring over microfilm in the museum's library, I made an intriguing discovery. Examining the information in the section given over to Camp de Rivesaltes, I found the cards that an efficient French functionary had filled out to mark the transference of my grandfather and uncle from that camp to their next destination, Camp des Milles, in July 1941. In addition to noting their names, hometowns, professions, dates of birth, and the names of their nearest relatives, my unknown helper of seven decades earlier had also written in the words "Boulogne," "Montauban," "Agde," and "Rivesaltes." Boulogne and Rivesaltes I knew, respectively, to be the names of the town where Alex and Helmut had landed in France and the hellish camp near the Pyrenees, but what of the other two?

A little breathlessly, I called over a museum staffer. She furrowed her brow and then brightened. "Why, Agde was another camp, also in the south of France, near the Mediterranean. And Montauban . . . that's a town in the south of France, near Toulouse. Those must have been your relatives' last known addresses before their arrival in Rivesaltes!" Montauban was not a concentration or refugee camp, but it was possible that my grandfather and uncle had been held there, maybe hidden there, after the start of the war in September 1939. More mystery.

I went home and confirmed that Montauban is indeed a city in southern France, the capital of the *departement* of Tarn-et-Garonne, located about thirty miles north of Toulouse. I also learned that it proudly proclaims itself the sister city of Pawhuska, Oklahoma. On a whim, I placed a call the next day to Pawhuska's city hall and asked for the person in charge of the sister-city program. "Oh, that's Jack Shoemate. . . . Here's his number. . . . He'll be happy to talk to you." I hung up, profoundly grateful, and not for the first time, for the easygoing friendliness of small-town American ways.

Mr. Shoemate was eager to talk about Pawhuska's sister city in far-off France, and more than happy to give me the e-mail address of his primary contact in Montauban, Jean-Claude Drouilhet. I immediately wrote to M. Drouilhet to ask him what, if anything, he knew about foreign Jews who might have been held in Montauban in the early days of World War II. I was delighted when M. Drouilhet responded almost immediately, excited when he declared that my subject was of extreme importance to him, and thrilled when he wrote again a few days later to tell me that he'd gone to police headquarters in Montauban and had unearthed some information sure to be of interest to me. He had digitally photographed his discoveries and attached them to his e-mail. I clicked them open . . . and there were two more cards, similar to those filled out at Rivesaltes, these dominated by a large red letter *J* carved in blood, it seemed, in the upper left. Again I read the usual details of Alex and Helmut's birthdays, professions, and the names of their relatives, but here was a line that listed where they'd been prior to their arrival in Montauban. On the line was written clearly "Martigny-les-Bains." Another clue!

Within days, I had confirmed with an archivist at the Holocaust Museum that, yes, a number of *St. Louis* refugees who'd disembarked in France had been taken to Martigny-les-Bains, a village in the northeast that had enjoyed a degree of prosperity at the turn of the twentieth century as a spa town with renowned healing waters. Just why Alex and Helmut had been brought there remained a bit of a mystery, but now the course of their journey through France had become clearer.

Then, as the long winter began to wane and the days began to lengthen, with their promise of another spring and its infinite possibilities, my grandfather and uncle's itinerary began to burn itself into my brain with an improbable urgency. Boulogne-to-Martigny-to-Montauban-to-Agde-to-Rivesaltes-to-Les Milles-to-Drancy-to-Auschwitz. That list of names became as familiar to me as my own address and telephone number. Late one night, it came to me what I must do: I knew that I needed to retrace their steps, to set foot on the earth they trod during those final three years of initial hope and eventual hopelessness, to see what they saw and to breathe the air they breathed before they breathed their last. I would tell their story as a grandson, a nephew, and an eyewitness.

Their stories were more than their last years, however, so I decided to begin my journey where my grandfather started his, the little village of Sachsenhagen in Germany's Lower Saxony. I would then travel to Oldenburg, where Alex established his business and where Günther and Helmut were born, and then to Hamburg, where the *St. Louis* began its unhappy voyage. I would then cross the Low Countries to meet up metaphorically with Alex and Helmut when they landed in Boulogne-sur-Mer, and from there follow them along their winding road to Auschwitz.

Though I share my father's love of trains, it seemed to me that the nature of this journey would require a car. I consulted a map. Adding up the distances I was able to estimate between destinations, I concluded that I would be traveling a minimum of thirty-five hundred miles, more than a drive across the United States from east to west. Given the time I would reasonably need in each city, I decided that the trip would last about six weeks.

The journey began to take on a life of its own, becoming a force that seemed to be willing me onward, dominating my thoughts by day and my dreams by night. I found myself exhilarated by the prospect one minute and then consumed by fears and doubts the next. My greatest fear was that I would fly home from Europe at the end of the six weeks thinking to myself, "Well, *that* was a colossal waste of time!" I also feared coming face to face with the daily record of my family's descent into death, and I wondered just how I would find my way through the heart of Europe with my limited German and my nearly nonexistent French. And I was fully conscious of the immense contrast between Alex and Helmut's journey and mine, how they had been prisoners caught in a Kafkaesque quagmire of bureaucracy, indifference, and cruelty; what they had to endure as their rations were reduced and they lost weight and hope; and how I would be traveling in an air-conditioned car, staying in lovely hotels, with all of France's celebrated cuisine at my fingertips. Was this quest of mine in some fashion a monstrous game of dress-up and make-believe, not so much a tribute to my grandfather and uncle as a mockery of their suffering?

Just weeks before my departure, I asked my wife if she would accompany me on this grand adventure, to temper my fears and also to share in the pleasures of the experience, the new sights, sounds, and tastes we would surely encounter on the road. "Grief can take care of itself," wrote Mr. Twain, "But to get full value of a joy you must have somebody to divide it with." She said yes, bless her.

So, on Tuesday, May 10, 2011, we set forth. I took along small photographs of Alex and Helmut, a single suitcase, and a small box containing my father's ashes, a box that had spent the previous two years in the shadows of an upstairs closet. It was time, I'd decided, for Günther to make his return to his cherished homeland. I also packed the fervent hope that in the coming six weeks, I might learn much about the ordeal of my grandfather and uncle, yet also find a way to set down my family's long-borne burden, to steer my way out of the churning turbulence of Alex's wake into the calm and peaceful waters of my living family, my friends, and my life.

It was a beautiful clear evening as our 757 climbed to thirty-nine thousand feet along the eastern seaboard on its navigational path from Washington to Europe. Gazing down over the sprawling boroughs of New York City, I had an unhindered view of the Statue of Liberty and neighboring Ellis Island. My parents had roused themselves at 4:00 a.m. to catch their first glimpse of Miss Liberty's welcoming torch when they arrived safely in America in 1941. Alex and Helmut had found the golden door shut firmly against them two years earlier. I pondered those two journeys that I could almost see far below me and the fate that had intervened in both, and as we bent our way east into the gathering night and my latest voyage into that land of mystery we call the past, I recalled the words of Martin Buber: "All journeys have secret destinations of which the traveler is unaware."

2

Sachsenhagen

WEDNESDAY, MAY 11, 2011. We land in Switzerland. Writing from Interlachen 120 years earlier, Mr. Twain called Switzerland "the cradle of liberty" and enthused that "it is healing and refreshing to breathe air that has known no taint of slavery for six hundred years." But we grounded our choice of this country as the starting point of our journey more in practicality than idealism. After following my uncle and grandfather for what we assume will be a fairly harrowing venture, we plan to decompress at a splendid old hotel in the Swiss Alps that was a favorite destination of Amy's uncle, so we chose Zürich as our landing site.

At the airport, we wheel our bags through the maze of corridors and duty-free shops to the rental car counter, where we are given possession of a sleek silver Opel Meriva. My first order of business is to borrow a single strip of adhesive tape from the rental desk, which I use to affix the small photos of Alex and Helmut to a space just above the Meriva's rearview mirror. With this physical reminder of our journey's purpose set firmly before us, we are now ready to begin. I note the odometer's figure of 1,063 kilometers, and we set out into Zürich's daunting traffic, heading west.

The great Irish writer James Joyce, who left Dublin for good when he was thirty years old, moved to Zürich in 1915 and spent the rest of the Great War there working on his epic retelling of the story of Ulysses, the immortal wanderer. In 1940, Joyce fled Paris in advance of the Nazi invasion and returned to Zürich, where he died in January 1941 of a perforated ulcer. He is buried in Zürich's Fluntern Cemetery, hard by the city's zoo. Joyce's widow, Nora Barnacle, declared of her husband, "He was awfully fond of the lions—I like to think of him lying there and listening to them roar." On this sunny May morning, we see signs for the zoo but, alternately fighting fatigue and pumping adrenaline, we make our determined way to the Swiss expressway A3, which in turn takes us over cow-dotted hills and through long winding tunnels toward Basel. Just east of Basel, we cross the legendary River Rhine and enter my ancestral homeland, speeding north.

Our route skirts the edge of the Black Forest, where Alex would take his family on vacations to such lovely spa towns as Baden-Baden and Eisenbach. Every now and then, we spy castles perched precariously yet triumphantly on the brow of jagged hills, reminding us that we are not rolling along a familiar American interstate. We pass Karlsruhe, where my father lived as a young student and where he received his fateful summons to join the *Kulturbund*, and maneuver our way around Frankfurt, where my parents met and first lived together as young musicians in love. Amy, embracing her navigator duties with vigor, announces that the town of Giessen, about fifty kilometers ahead, appears to be a promising destination. We leave the autobahn, creep our way into Giessen, and on only our second attempt, find a perfectly serviceable inn in which to pass the night. We enjoy a light *Abendbrot*, or evening snack, take a brief walk in the farmland on the edge of town, then return to our inn and fall into bed. It's been a long day and a half since our departure, but we're on the road and very satisfied with our initial progress.

Our first full day in Europe dawns cloudy, and as we resume our way north our view of the countryside occasionally yields to a thick fog. We endure hours of autobahns, with heavy trucks making our plucky little Meriva shiver and vibrate as we maneuver around them and shiny black Audis and Mercedes-Benzes whizzing past us at 150 kph on their hip yet efficient way to Berlin and Leipzig. Finally, a little past noon, we leave the thundering traffic for a more peaceful two-lane highway, which takes us gently to the lovely town of Bückeburg, the site of the official archives of the German state of Lower Saxony. We have arrived in the land of my forebears.

Lower Saxony is the second largest and fourth most populous of the sixteen states of Germany. It covers much of the territory of the ancient Kingdom of Hannover, which has supplied royalty to both Germany and, since the eighteenth century, England. Lower Saxony appeals to me geographically because it borders more neighboring states (nine) than any other German state, in much the same way that my birth state of Missouri borders more states (eight) than any other American state. It's largely agricultural land, producing wheat, potatoes, rye, and poultry, and featuring the sort of sandy soil that fosters grasslands, the raising of cattle, and the breeding of horses. Indeed, the Lower Saxony coat of arms is a red shield on which rears a white Saxon steed. Horses played a large role in my family throughout the nineteenth century, and I've come to Bückeburg, a town about fifteen miles southwest of Alex's birthplace of Sachsenhagen, to learn what I can about how the Goldschmidts lived.

Once the capital city of the tiny municipality of Schaumburg-Lippe, Bückeburg today is within the borders of Schaumburg, a district of Lower Saxony. In 1750, the year Johann Sebastian Bach died, Prince Wilhelm von Schaumburg-Lippe recruited the great man's ninth son, Johann Christoph Friedrich Bach, to come to Bückeburg as court harpsichordist, where he stayed, writing keyboard sonatas, chamber music, symphonies, and oratorios, until his death in 1795. Present-day Bückeburg boasts a helicopter museum containing early drawings of flying machines by Leonardo da Vinci, in addition to forty working helicopters. But our destination on this still-overcast Thursday after-noon is the ornate Bückeburg Palace, a yellow castle with turrets and fountains and gently manicured gardens that for over seven hundred years has been the official residence of the princes of Schaumburg-Lippe. We enter a side tower of the palace, climb stairs past royal red walls hung with portraits of generations of Schaumburg-Lippe royalty, until we come to the archive reading room.

Dr. Hendrick Weingarten of the Bückeburg Archives, with whom I struck up an Internet correspondence some weeks ago, meets us here.

He arranges for several immense leather-bound tomes to be brought to us from the dusty depths of the castle holdings. We all stand silently when three aides enter the reading room bearing their burden of books and the many years, lives, and events contained within them. When the hands that wrote these documents passed over the pages and left their trails of ink, human beings still measured distances by how far a horse could pull a carriage in a day, flight was reserved for the winged creatures of the air, the telegraph was the new means of communication, and at night people lit their lives with fire. I am holding a folder of yellowing but still stoutly legible papers contained in a soft blue binder tied together by a forest-green ribbon. And there before me, on a page dated 10 January 1879, is the notice that in the hamlet of Sachsenhagen, on the first day of January in the year one thousand eight hundred seventy-nine at six o'clock in the morning, was delivered to Moses and Auguste Goldschmidt a male baby whose first name was Alexander.

My grandfather, whom I have come all this way to save, has been born.

THE HISTORY OF SACHSENHAGEN goes back to the thirteenth century, when it was a lonely cluster of houses and barns existing in the shadow of a grand moated castle built by the reigning duke of Saxony to secure the countryside from thieves, cutpurses, highwaymen, and other lowlifes of those Dark Ages. It was then a swampy region located along an old trading route running southwest to northeast, roughly the same path as today's B65 federal highway. Both castle and hamlet are first mentioned in local chronicles in the year 1253; forty-four years later, in 1297, the castle changed hands as the result of a dispute over an unpaid dowry.

By the beginning of the seventeenth century, Sachsenhagen had become a rural center for farmers, merchants, traders, and craftsmen. A great fire swept through its thatched-roofed wooden buildings in 1619, nearly destroying the entire village, sparing only the *Rathaus*, or city hall, and a single tower from the medieval castle. But the town persevered, rebuilt, and on March 1, 1650, was granted the honor of being designated an official *Stadt*, or city, rather than a mere hamlet.

It must have been a gala day, full of pomp and pageantry, when Her Highness the Countess Amalie Elizabeth von Hessen, daughter of His Highness Philip Ludwig II, Count of Hanau-Münzenberg, swept into Sachsenhagen to sign the royal decree allowing the newly minted city to build its own church, hold three grand market fairs each year, and design and maintain its own coat of arms.

For years, Sachsenhagen belonged to the holdings of Schaumburg-Lippe; then in the mid-seventeenth century, it was annexed by the Hessian principality. Finally, in 1974, it became part of the district of Schaumburg. Today it can boast the honor of being the second-smallest city in all of Lower Saxony, with a population of about two thousand souls.

In the year 1601, while it still languished in hamlet status, Sachsenhagen welcomed into its midst, though admittedly on the outskirts of the settlement, a family by the name of Leffmann, the first recorded Jews to make Sachsenhagen their home. Over time, a small, steady stream of Jewish families flowed into the village, provided that they followed a few regulations. In order to live in Sachsenhagen, at least for the next century, a Jew was required to purchase a letter of safe conduct from the sovereign—a prince of Schaumberg-Lippe or a Hessian count— a letter that had to be renewed regularly. These letters of safe conduct amounted to nothing less than a protection racket for the rulers, providing them a steady income from a population that had learned hard lessons of the perils of an unprotected existence. A Jewish household also considered it prudent to supplement its safe-conduct fee with the occasional additional gift, perhaps a finely wrought saddle or the fruits of a plentiful harvest.

By the middle of the nineteenth century, Jews made up about 7 percent of the population of Sachsenhagen; in the census of 1861, of the 695 people living in the village, 52 were Jewish. In 1855, after years of sending their children to Jewish schools in the nearby towns of Rehburg, Hagenburg, and Rodenberg, the elders of Sachsenhagen decided that the distances traveled to those places were too demanding and established their own school. That same 1861 census reveals that the Jewish school in Sachsenhagen taught fourteen young scholars and that they huddled together in a building that measured only twenty feet long, nine feet wide, and ten feet high. The dimensions of the salary the Jewish community was able to offer its teachers were meager as well: fifty thalers per year, though room and board were generously included. Not surprisingly, it proved difficult over the years to attract and retain competent, highly motivated teachers at such wages.

On July 28, 1869, the local newspaper reported on a joyous ceremony in Sachsenhagen, blessed with fine weather and attended by a large and festive crowd, which featured the laying of the foundation stone for the city synagogue. The building was completed and consecrated the following year and was commodious enough to offer space to the Jewish school and living quarters for the teacher. Life in Sachsenhagen was good for the Jews.

Death had also been provided for. In 1823, the electorate of Hessen issued the following ordinance: "Each synagogue is permitted to have its own cemetery but its layout, enclosure, the time of its burials and the depths of its graves must follow the regulations established by the police. With regard to Jewish cemeteries that already exist, it is expected that their future use will conform as much as possible to this order."

A Jewish cemetery had already existed in Sachsenhagen for nearly a century prior to 1823. Though a map of the village dated 1714 shows no sign of one, it appears that within a couple of decades, a graveyard for the Jews had been acquired. Such an acquisition was no routine matter. Land had to be purchased, and for many years European authorities had frowned on selling land to Jews; even when such transactions were allowed, the land that changed hands was often of substandard value, perhaps swampy or riddled with stones, making it unsuitable for agriculture. But the Jews of Sachsenhagen were fortunate: the land purchased for their cemetery, though outside the boundaries of the village, was flat and arable. Hops grew along the edges of the cemetery, and the soil produced sturdy oaks and elms and a healthy hazelnut bush. The oldest surviving headstone in the Jewish cemetery dates from 1787. But the oldest headstone that is marked by both German and Hebrew inscriptions belongs to Levi Goldschmidt. In Hebrew, the text reads, "Here lies a decent and God-fearing man. He was honest and just. He died at age 60." He was my great-great-grandfather.

The former house number 17, now number 9 Oberestrasse, where my great-great-grandfather Levi lived with his wife Johanna and their "poor man's cow."

Levi Goldschmidt was born on July 18, 1799, the son of Jehuda Goldschmidt. Where he was born remains a mystery, although some evidence points south about twenty miles from Sachsenhagen to the town of Hameln. Known as Hamelin in English, it's the site of the legendary Pied Piper, who rid the town of its plague of mice and rats and then, in revenge for not being paid for his services, rid the town of all its children. When Levi moved to Sachsenhagen is also unclear, but he bought a house there in 1834, at age thirty-five, and married Johanna Frank. Within a very short time, the Goldschmidts were among the most prominent of the Jewish families of Sachsenhagen.

In a registry of assets for the year 1841, Levi and Johanna are listed as living in house number 17 in Sachsenhagen. (At the time, all the town's houses were simply given numbers, regardless of the street. Today, the address is 9 Oberestrasse, the main thoroughfare through town.) In 1841, the Goldschmidt family's assets were modest: two fruit trees and a single goat, considered in those days to be "the poor man's cow." By comparison, 108 of the 128 families living in Sachsenhagen had at least one cow, including all three of the other Jewish families. By the end of the decade, however, the Goldschmidt family fortune had soared; Levi had become a *Pferdehändler*, a dealer of horses.

As far back as the Middle Ages, European laws prevented Jews from owning land and encouraged them to practice professions that Christians largely avoided. Scriptural strictures against lending money and charging interest led Christians to shun the financial vocations, and thus it fell to the Jews to become bankers and moneylenders. In the nineteenth century, Jews were still barred from journalism, most professorships, and the law. As late as 1905 in Europe, there was little chance that a Jew could become a judge, and even then only if he renounced his faith and converted to Christianity. Although excluded from certain professions, Jews often flourished in those they were allowed to practice, and in the European countryside, they embraced the horse business. In Russia and the Austro-Hungarian Empire, the horse trade was largely a Jewish enterprise, and in Germany, most of the prominent suppliers of horses to the well-born and well-connected were Jews. So identified were Jews with the buying and selling of horses that by the 1930s, the rise of National Socialism was accompanied by municipal attempts to expel and ban Jews from the profession.

In much the same way that the automobile dominates our lives in the early twenty-first century, horses were nearly indispensable in the nineteenth. Urban dwellers depended on horse-drawn conveyances for transportation and commerce. In the countryside, farmers relied on horses to plow the earth and transport goods to and from market. In the 1840s, Levi Goldschmidt recognized that there was no dealer of horses in Sachsenhagen, so he stepped into the breach. Within a few years, he had established himself as a reliable judge of horseflesh and a shrewd businessman and was accepted as one of the trusted elders of the village's Jewish community.

Levi was called upon to speak for the community in a dispute involving the Jewish cemetery and a local wheelwright named Georg Buschmann. Not until 1908 was a fence erected around the perimeter of the cemetery, and in 1845 Herr Buschmann began taking a shortcut through the cemetery on his way home. Because the path between the graves was so narrow, the heavy wooden wheels of Buschmann's wagon would often rumble over a gravesite. Naturally enough, the Jewish families considered Buschmann's shortcut an act of desecration and demanded a hearing of the district authorities to force the wheelwright to use the common path around the cemetery. Levi was chosen to represent the Jewish side in the dispute, but after more than two months of arguing and proposing several solutions to the problem, the authorities simply threw up their hands and walked away, leaving the matter as it was. Buschmann's wheels continued to roll through the cemetery.

Within a few years, however, Levi achieved a healthy measure of satisfaction. Herr Buschmann died and, with his business booming, Levi sold his house number 17 and bought the wheelwright's much larger house from Buschmann's widow in 1848. The more spacious home, number 35 on the market square, was a necessary investment; Levi and Johanna had eight children. The eldest was Moses, my great-grandfather, followed by Marianne, Samuel, Ruben, Emma, Hermann, Friederike, and Helene. When he died, Levi's household comprised his wife, their eight children, a maid, and two servants.

The Goldschmidts had achieved remarkable wealth in a short time. The profession of *Pferdehändler* had been good to them, and in turn Great-Great-Grandfather Levi had been good to Sachsenhagen. At the time of his death, on September 17, 1859, in addition to being remembered as decent, honest, and just on his headstone, Levi had acquired a reputation for magnanimity. He had made gifts to the community that amounted to more than the value of his considerable property, which included the market square house and several fields in the countryside.

His widow, Johanna, known also as Hanna or Chana, lived nearly another thirty years. She died in Sachsenhagen on October 15, 1887. The inscription on her headstone in the Jewish cemetery reads, in Hebrew, "Here rests a decent and kind woman. Her path was just and charitable. She taught her children the Torah."

The eldest child, Moses, was born on February 18, 1835, in the house on Oberestrasse. As the first male offspring, Moses was perhaps fated to take over the family business, but he took to it enthusiastically and with quite spectacular results. Demand for horses increased throughout the nineteenth century; in 1850, there were about 2.7 million horses in Germany, and by the end of the century, at the dawn of the age of the horseless carriage, that number had risen to around 4.2 million. Moses's customers were his neighbors in Sachsenhagen and the surrounding rural communities who needed horses for transportation and farm work, and he also sold horses to the hotels and hackney cab companies in Stadthagen, Bückeburg, and Hameln that required fine horses for their elegant carriages, and to the military for its elite cavalry troops. A good horse might fetch a price of 800 marks, roughly the annual starting salary for an average worker. Several times a year, Moses would travel to Hannover and Hamburg to purchase horses from north German breeders, and occasionally he'd even go abroad in search of a fine steed at a good price. On one such journey, he went north to Denmark, where he not only bought three horses but also found a reliable worker named David Larsen whom he brought back to Sachsenhagen as his assistant and right-hand man.

In 1859, the year he turned twenty-four and lost his father, Moses married Auguste Philippsohn, four years his junior and a member of perhaps the most prominent Jewish family in Sachsenhagen. Auguste's father, Joseph Philippsohn, a successful merchant, had been born in Sachsenhagen in 1813 and could trace his ancestry back to Itzhak Philippsohn, born in the village in 1761. Like his father before him, Moses sired eight children, seven boys and a girl, Bertha, who died in infancy. In time for the birth of their first child, Albert, in 1860, Moses and Auguste moved from the house on the marketplace to a grand house at 94 Mittelstrasse, a place that could boast something only a few other homes could claim, a baker's oven. On the roof of the house, there were two wooden planks on which, early every spring, a pair of storks would build a nest and care for their young throughout the languid days of summer until the whole family would depart in September in search of a winter refuge farther south.

My great-grandfather was a pillar of his community, remembered by his neighbors as a kind, generous man and also something of a character, a "Sachsenhagen original." Julius Geweke, who was born in

Sachsenhagen in 1902, asked his father, a saddler, to recall life in the village in his day: "The horse dealer Moses Goldschmidt lived behind our house, over on Mittelstrasse. Whenever Goldschmidt received a shipment of horses he'd place a notice in the newspaper. And when a potential buyer came by to look at the horses, Goldschmidt would have the animals pranced through the streets of Sachsenhagen, his work-hand Larsen trotting along keeping pace. Goldschmidt himself would stand in front of his house, smiling, smoking a big cigar, and cracking his whip smartly. The buyer would watch this parade of horses and then pick one out for closer inspection, looking into its mouth to verify that the animal was of the age advertised. After a bit of wrangling, the deal was sealed with a hearty handshake."

The family business was not without its conflicts. On January 28, 1884, a dispute between Moses Goldschmidt and a carter named Heine was formally entered into the proceedings of the law courts of Stadthagen. There is no evidence today indicating what the dispute was about, but it took a long time to be resolved. Not until November 5 was a decision rendered, but for Moses, it was apparently worth the wait. The judge ruled in his favor and awarded him the not-inconsiderable sum of 350 marks.

The grand house at 94 Mittelstrasse was filled with not only the children of Moses and Auguste but four servants as well, who slept next door at 93 Mittelstrasse. They were the butler Fritz Wiebe, the valet Johann Wiltgreve, the housekeeper Fanny Schwarz, and the maid Luise Meuter. There was nearly always a fire burning in the big oven, keeping the house comfortably warm in the winter. And the Jewish holidays were always observed.

Into these secure and prosperous surroundings my grandfather, Alex, was delivered on New Year's Day 1879, the seventh of Moses and Auguste's children. On the same day, in London, the noted writer E. M. Forster was born. That year would also witness the births of Albert Einstein, Wallace Stevens, Ethel Barrymore, Will Rogers, and Joseph Stalin. And on the very last day of 1879, in Menlo Park, New Jersey, Thomas Edison would demonstrate incandescent lighting to the public for the first time.

Thirteen months later, on February 2, 1880, Auguste gave birth to her eighth child and seventh son, Carl Goldschmidt. He may have been one child too many. On November 7, 1881, Auguste died, at age forty-two. On her headstone in the Jewish cemetery in Sachsenhagen are the words, in Hebrew, "Here rests an admired woman, the crown of her husband and children. She was modest and traveled the way of peace."

So my grandfather lost his mother when he was only two. I like to think that his large family cushioned the blow somewhat, even though his oldest sibling, brother Albert, was nineteen years his senior. Alex was quite close to his two immediate brothers, Max, four years older, and Carl, and the three of them attended classes every day at the Jewish school in the synagogue. In 1889, when Alex was ten, a superintendent from Kassel, one of the largest cities in the Hessian principality, paid a visit and filed a report stating that the Jewish school in Sachsenhagen currently was teaching only five pupils and that three of them were Goldschmidts: Max, Alex, and Carl. The superintendent declared that with such minuscule attendance, there was little reason to keep the school open. Within two years, it closed its doors and the three young Goldschmidts began to attend the main public school in Sachsenhagen, arriving immediately after the morning religious class.

Despite the success of his father's business, Alex had no desire to be a horse dealer. Instead, after staying in Sachsenhagen long enough to earn his *Abitur* degree (roughly equivalent to two years of college), he turned his back on his rural upbringing and moved northwest to Lower Saxony's fourth-largest city, Oldenburg, in 1906. He was twenty-seven years old. Perhaps it was just a coincidence that his first apartment in Oldenburg looked out on the city's *Pferdemarkt*, or horse market.

Two years later, just before midnight on April 15, 1908, Moses Goldschmidt died, at the age of seventy-three. Alex and his six brothers gathered for the funeral. Given the resources at hand, it could have been a lavish affair. At the time of his death, *Pferdehändler* Goldschmidt's assets were estimated at 76,500 German marks. It's not an exact reckoning, but in 1913, just five years later, a mark was valued at around four American dollars, making his estate worth approximately $306,000 . . .

in 1908. Given the rate of inflation over the past century, when Moses Goldschmidt died, his total net worth exceeded 7 million in today's dollars. He was by far the wealthiest man in Sachsenhagen and possibly for miles around. The equine occupation had been a runaway, some might say galloping, success.

But death comes for rich and poor alike. His headstone reads, in Hebrew, "Here lies Moses Goldschmidt, a god-fearing man. He loved justice and followed the road of righteousness. He fed the hungry. He died on a Thursday, the first day of Pesach 5668."

THURSDAY, MAY 12, 2011. "*Hier ruht unser lieber Vater Moses Gold-schmidt, geb. d. 18. Febr. 1835 gest. d. 15. April 1908,*" I read aloud to Amy. "Here rests our dear Father Moses Goldschmidt . . . ," I translate from the German side of the headstone. We are standing beneath two tall, graceful trees within the boundaries of the Jewish cemetery in Sachsenhagen on a late afternoon that is turning windy and increasingly cloudy.

Earlier today, after several fruitful hours in the archives of Bückeburg Palace, we returned to our little Meriva and motored across the flat farmland of Lower Saxony along the ancient trade thoroughfare that is now federal highway B65. We drove into the city of Stadthagen and thence on country road L445 through fields of rye and over a small canal, until we reached the southern edge of Sachsenhagen. I was here once before, twelve years ago, on the dire date of November 9 in the company of my brother. We'd had the devil's own time finding the cemetery, which is tucked off the road, securely away from view, but with my memory of its location clear in my mind's unshakable GPS system, I was confident I could find it this time. But there was a glitch in the wiring, and finding the humble graveyard again took several attempts.

Now that we've found it, I note that, as in 1999, the cemetery looks ragged, overgrown, and somewhat neglected. The iron fence that surrounds the place sags here and there, the grass is high, and weeds flourish amid the graves, which seem randomly scattered about. The exceptions, however, are the families Philippsohn and Goldschmidt. My family's headstones are standing side by side, with Levi on the far left and Moses on the far right, with Johanna and Auguste resting between them.

It is a profound and unsettling place, and as the wind freshens and the clouds thicken in the late afternoon sky, I am deeply conscious of my vastly diminished family, the loss of Peter is still keen and aching, and yet here are sturdy and lasting memorials to what was once a thriving, prosperous clan of Goldschmidts on whom fortune smiled. As linden branches toss overhead, I try to imagine these long-dead family members, conjuring with the concept that, should the impossible occur and should we somehow meet face to face, there would be a moment akin to looking into a mirror, of noticing with a start a familiar feature, an eyebrow, an ear, the curve of a lip or the curl of hair, a "Hey, don't I know you?" moment of mysterious yet joyful recognition that I find at this time and in this place overwhelming. I miss my family terribly, those both recently and long departed, and I hug my remaining family, Amy, tightly.

As we turn to leave the cemetery, we notice amid the ragged grass two long parallel depressions in the ground running the length of the graveyard from south to north. They are, we learn later, the ghostly tracks of the heavy wooden wheels of that cart driven so long ago by Georg Buschmann.

Sachsenhagen is too small to sustain a proper hotel, so we drive our Meriva back to Stadthagen, where we've reserved a room in the Gerbergasse, a former tannery. By now the clouds have produced a steady rain, which adds its note of solemnity to the atmosphere. But the next morning arrives with abundant sunshine, and we return to Sachsenhagen eagerly anticipating new discoveries.

For weeks, ever since plans for my journey began to take solid shape, I have been in e-mail contact with Theodor Beckmann, a member of Sachsenhagen's historical society. He has sent me a great deal of information, always in the kindest manner imaginable. I am grateful for his assistance and also for his excellent English. Despite several years of high school German and many trips to the country, my German has never advanced beyond the barely serviceable stage. So I was sorry to learn a week or so ago that on this particular Friday the 13th,

Herr Beckmann would be in France with his wife. His very able colleague, Erika Sembdner, would meet us instead; alas, her English proves to be no better than my German.

But her pleasure at our arrival seems unbounded. We ask for her at the *Rathaus*, and she immediately hurries from her house to greet us. For the next ninety minutes, Erika leads us on a sentimental journey through Sachsenhagen. First she shows us 9 Oberestrasse, the house where Great-Great-Grandfather Levi lived with Johanna, their two fruit trees, and a single goat. The imposing white house with its high sloping roof is situated directly on the main road that leads south toward the cemetery. We then visit the grand house on Mittelstrasse where Great-Grandfather Moses lived from 1864 until his death in 1908. Erika tells us that it's among the oldest houses in Sachsenhagen and has been expertly restored. Built by a master carpenter in the seventeenth century, not long after the great fire, it's a stunning example of the traditional *fachwerk* style, in which heavy wooden beams are fastened together by mortise and tenon joints. Such ancient grandeur. And it belonged to my family. Amy and I stand silently, amazed.

Erika then leads us to a small building just off the market square. Here the Sachsenhagen synagogue and Jewish school once stood, from its gladsome dedication in 1870 until the night of November 9, 1938, when it and countless other *shuls* across Germany were plundered and set afire during the orgy of violence known as *Kristallnacht*. Today the land is occupied by a private house and garden. In 1885, when Grandfather Alex was six years old and attending the Jewish school, there were 58 Jews living in Sachsenhagen, a number that represented 7 percent of the total population of 840. In 1939, in the wake of *Kristallnacht*, the Jewish percentage of the citizenry still measured 8 percent, 88 of 1,089. But then on July 20, 1942, the Gestapo ordered Jewish citizens of Sachsenhagen out of their homes and told them to assemble in the market square. They were rounded up, placed in secure trucks, and deported to the East. None of them returned. Today, the Jewish population of Sachsenhagen is zero.

As I sadly ponder this grim statistic, Erika says brightly, *"Jetzt besuchen wir die Schule,"* and herds us back to our car. Following her

Today there are no more Jews living in my ancestral home of Sachsenhagen, but the village school is named for a Jewish girl who was murdered at Auschwitz in 1942. Amy and I were welcomed as near celebrities.

directions, we drive about a mile to Sachsenhagen's one primary school. We arrive shortly after lunchtime and the grounds and play areas are nearly empty. Erika walks with us into a cheerful red-brick entranceway that declares in brass letters that we have arrived at the Gerda Philippsohn School.

Gerda Philippsohn, born in Sachsenhagen in 1927, began attending school in 1933. She was an eager learner and bright student. On the afternoon of November 15, 1938, six days after *Kristallnacht*, she was summarily dismissed from the school because she was a Jew. On March 28, 1942, Gerda, her parents, and eleven other Sachsenhagen Jews were deported. At age fifteen, Gerda was murdered at Auschwitz.

In 2000, at the urging of former teacher Rita Schewe, the school changed its name to the Gerda Philippsohn School. The entranceway bears a memorial plaque to Gerda, exhibiting her picture and a brief explanation of her fate.

The school's principal, Frau Herrmann, comes out eagerly to shake our hands, take our picture as we pose in front of the little memorial to

Gerda, and present us with a pen and pencil set embossed with the school's name. We feel a bit like visiting celebrities as we are escorted through the school, looking into a few classes, and are introduced as descendants of people who lived in Sachsenhagen many years ago. I feel deeply touched by the decision to rename the village's single school for a long-dead victim of the country's villainous past, yet also curious as to what prompted the decision, seeing that none of the children currently attending the Gerda Philippsohn School shares the one characteristic that marked its innocent namesake for murder.

Perhaps by way of an answer, Erika announces that the final stop on our tour will be a visit with Rita Schewe, the teacher and local historian who led the effort to rename the school. We drive out into the country, where Rita lives with her husband and dog. Erika has phoned ahead, and when we knock, Rita throws open the front door and envelopes me in a mighty bear hug. "Herr Goldschmidt!" she keeps exclaiming, and when she finally releases me, I see tears in her eyes.

For an hour, we sit on her patio and enjoy fruit and lemonade and a conversation that rises above its poor practitioners of English and German to achieve an unexpected warmth. Rita has made Jewish Sachsenhagen a private passion and has researched its past and tried to create a new present. How did she come upon the idea to rename the school? She shrugs, smiles, and says that it has fallen to her generation to try to right the wrongs of the previous generation, even if that proves to be an impossible task. I ask her if I am related to Gerda Philippsohn, since my great-grandmother was a Philippsohn. Very likely, she tells me, although the Philippsohn family is a large one; Gerda may well have been a third or fourth cousin.

Eventually I explain that we must be on our way, that we are expected elsewhere that night. At the door, there are more hugs and tears. We promise to return one day. They promise to welcome us. We drive Erika back to her home and thank her profusely for her time, patience, knowledge, and understanding of the many emotions that have colored this memorable day.

As a final goodbye to Sachsenhagen, we return to the cemetery. I place small stones on the graves of Levi and Johanna, of Moses and

Auguste. I gaze across the fields and try to imagine our family living on this land with horses as our livelihood. Then I recall my father, as the shadows deepened on an Arbor Place afternoon, telling me about the few times he had visited his grandfather's house and how every spring the family would eagerly await the return of the storks to their snug nest on the roof. There was peace in my father's eyes as he shared this precious memory and, leaning on the cemetery fence under a cloudless May sky, I begin to understand that there is more to my family's story than murder, loss, sorrow, and shame. There is honor and respect for a job well done; there is a certain standing in a single community over multiple generations; there is success, wealth, and a large, well-cared-for family; and there is a pair of storks that return in the spring, bringing forth precious new life.

What might have happened had Grandfather Alex chosen to stay in this sweet little town? His fate would likely not have altered much, as the Nazi noose tightened around urban and rural regions alike. But perhaps my father would have absorbed a bit more of the happy portions of his heritage and passed them on to his sons. He might not have been inspired by his surroundings to become a professional musician, but maybe . . .

To stop my thoughts from curling around each other in endless serpentine speculation, I take Amy by the hand and walk slowly past my family plot and out of the graveyard. We settle into the Meriva; I smile at the faces of Alex and Helmut and turn the car north to follow my grandfather to the city where prosperity and sorrow awaited him.

3

Oldenburg

Friday, May 13, 2011. In broad afternoon, under a full and friendly sun, we drive through the flat farmland of Lower Saxony. Our route takes us north and west, through the towns of Wölpinghausen, Nienburg, Lemke, and Syke, but mostly past fields of rye, soybeans, and wheat that stretch their still-new shoots upward through the warm May air toward the sapphire sky. Occasionally we spy open pastures in which the white Saxon horses of the state coat of arms graze, rest, or trot. I think of Great-Grandfather Moses, smoking his fat cigar and smartly cracking his whip as he shows off his latest equine acquisitions to a potential buyer, and I smile so fully and wistfully, it brings a prickle to the corners of my eyes.

Slowly the fields give way to more concentrated clusters of homes and businesses as we approach the outer suburbs of Bremen. We leave the pastoral byways and join the heavy westward traffic of another German autobahn. The suburbs of Delmenhorst slip past our windows and we're once more in the countryside, speeding past farms and fields and the occasional insubstantial forest, as the brilliant sun sinks before us. The blue waters of the Tweelbäker See appear on our right and then the first houses and industrial parks that herald our arrival in Oldenburg. We cross the Hunte River, which flows north to merge with the Weser on its passage to the North Sea, and then exit the autobahn at Marschweg, a pretty, urban thoroughfare that leads us past the campus of Carl von Ossietzky University.

A pacifist and anti-Nazi, Carl von Ossietzky was arrested in 1933 just weeks after Adolf Hitler assumed the German chancellorship. He spent time in Berlin's notorious Spandau Prison and also in the Esterwegen concentration camp near Oldenburg. Ossietzky was awarded the 1935 Nobel Peace Prize, but Hermann Göring ordered him to refuse the honor or risk being cast outside the community of the German people. But from the hospital where he was being treated for tuberculosis, Ossietzky wrote a note declaring that he would accept the prize as a means to "encourage understanding between peoples." He was denied permission to travel to Oslo to accept the award, the Nazi press suppressed any mention of the honor, and the government issued a decree forbidding any German citizen from ever again accepting a Nobel Prize. On May 4, 1938, Carl von Ossietzky died in a Berlin hospital while under Gestapo surveillance. In 1991, the University of Oldenburg changed its name in his honor.

Leaving the campus behind, we drive along peaceful lanes to the home of our Oldenburg hosts, Roland and Hiltrud Neidhardt. I have known the Neidhardts since 1998, when I first came to this city in search of my past. Roland, a retired academic who turns seventy this year, has silver-white hair and beard and sparkling blue eyes. Hiltrud has been an active member of Germany's burgeoning Green Party for nearly thirty years. Twenty years ago, she was elected to the Oldenburg city council and, beginning in 1996, served five years as the city's vice mayor. They own no car and get around town by bicycle, which partly accounts for their superb health. Their home is light and airy, full of books, paintings, and the joy of an active life.

In the evening, after a savory meal of bread and pasta served in their garden amid irises, rhododendrons, and an enormous fir tree through which flit an array of swallows, swifts, and magpies, the Neidhardts welcome several old friends who wish to see us. Among them are two people whom I've known for years and to whom I owe a debt of the deepest gratitude. Farschid Ali Zahedi, an Iranian-born filmmaker, has uncovered so many traces of Oldenburg's Nazi past that some in the city's hierarchy have accused him of unnecessarily stirring up old enmities and opening old wounds. He has also done invaluable research into the story of the Goldschmidts. And Dietgard Jacoby, a Lutheran pastor who offered me cherished words of comfort at the end of a memorial march in Oldenburg in 1999, once more reminds me that there are a few rare human spirits in our midst who bring the word "saintly" to mind.

Roland and Hiltrud (Hilu to her friends) have also invited Jörg Witte, an English and geography teacher at Oldenburg's Altes Gymnasium, the high school that both my father and uncle attended. He invites me to address the gymnasium students on Monday morning, an offer I eagerly accept. Last to arrive this evening is the remarkable Mrs. Annemarie Boyken, ninety-three years old, who pulls up to the house in her automobile, which she drives only at night. During the day she, like the Neidhardts and so many other Oldenburgers, commutes by bicycle.

Mrs. Boyken grasps my hands and beams, then embraces me vigorously. She insists on sitting across from me in the living room, the better to gaze at me without any interference. Naturally, I'm eager to learn the source of this rapturous attention. She speaks almost no English, and my German remains under construction, but through the translations provided by the Neidhardts, I learn her story.

As a girl, she lived just down the street from the magnificent house owned by Alex Goldschmidt at 34 Gartenstrasse. My father was four years older than Annemarie, my uncle was four years younger, and she had a crush on both of them. She had hoped to catch Günther's eye and wanted to play marbles with Helmut, but she somehow struck out on both attempts. On this soft May evening so many decades later, she tells me that I remind her of both my relatives and that seeing my face makes her feel years younger.

Then she tells another story. It was spring, sometime in the mid-1920s. Annemarie was eight years old, maybe ten. She went with her mother to shop for an Easter dress at Alex Goldschmidt's *Haus der Mode*, where all fashion-conscious Oldenburg ladies bought their clothes and accessories. She found the perfect frock, but her mother took one look at the price tag and declared it too expensive. Heartbroken at the prospect of having to choose another dress in its place, Annemarie began to cry. At that point, Alex Goldschmidt came over to see what was wrong. He knelt down beside her, took her hand, and asked, "Aren't you the little girl who lives on Taubenstrasse, the little girl who is such a fine marbles player?" Annemarie sniffled and nodded.

"And what has made you so unhappy this fine morning?"

"I love this dress, but my mother says it's too expensive for us."

At that, Mrs. Boyken recalls today, Alex looked at the price tag and exclaimed in a shocked voice, "But there has been some mistake! One of my employees has marked the wrong price on this item. Here is the correct price," and named a figure that was considerably lower. And just like that, his children's playmate got the dress she really wanted.

Annemarie Boyken takes my hand, beams at me again, and says to me, in English, "That is exactly the kind of man your grandfather was."

ONE HUNDRED YEARS AGO, in January 1911, Grandfather Alex purchased the property that would enable him, a decade and a half later, to so delight young Annemarie. His *Haus der Mode*, or "House of Fashion," occupied the ground floor of a three-story building that gracefully followed the curve at the intersection of Schüttingstrasse and Achternstrasse in the maze of narrow cobblestone streets in downtown Oldenburg. As long ago as that seems to a visiting American, a century is less than a tenth of the time that this city has existed.

According to archeological digs, there has been a settlement here on the banks of the Hunte as far back as the seventh or eighth century. The city's modern history dates back to the year 1108, when it was known as Aldenburg and was the most convenient spot to ford the river. As was the case with Sachsenhagen, Oldenburg prospered in the shadow of an enormous moated castle that would house dukes of Oldenburg for generations to come. Toward the end of the twelfth century, work was begun on the soaring church that still dominates the city skyline, a church dedicated to St. Lambert—martyred for his defense of marital fidelity—known as the Lambertikirche.

At the beginning of the seventeenth century, due to several complicated conjugal relationships, the city came under the control of the king of Denmark. Oldenburg grew in size and wealth, much of its income deriving from the same horse trade that would in later years enrich the Goldschmidt family. A breed of horse known as the *Oldenburger Pferde* was soon renowned across Europe. But the good times came to an abrupt end in 1676 when the Great Plague struck the city; at its height, the disease carried off thirty to forty people a week. That same star-crossed year, in another echo of Sachsenhagen, a fire begun by three lightning strikes from a single storm became a conflagration that nearly destroyed the entire town. The Danish crown, initially so eager to reap the benefits of a prosperous Oldenburg, now essentially turned its back on its southern holdings. With very little support from Copenhagen, the reconstruction of Oldenburg took nearly one hundred years.

In 1773, the city returned to German hands in the form of a duchy in the house of Holstein. This next succession of dukes rebuilt Oldenburg with gleaming classical architecture, reserving for themselves a grand palace and spacious royal gardens. The reign of the very last grand duke of Oldenburg, Friedrich August, ended in 1918 with the arrival of republican government in Germany. In the following year, the city of Oldenburg became the capital of the Free State of Oldenburg and the ducal castle was converted into a museum. The beautiful gardens became the public Schlossgarten, where every common citizen could admire its carefully tended flower beds, its stately old trees, its placid pond; where they could stroll on its gracefully curving paths, or rest and dream on its sturdy benches.

Grand Duke Friedrich August von Oldenburg was already in the sixth year of his reign when Alex Goldschmidt arrived in town in 1906, determined to fashion a life for himself far beyond the stables and pastures of Sachsenhagen. From his base in Oldenburg, he made business inquiries in the Lower Saxony cities of Hildesheim, Delmenhorst, and the Free Hanseatic City of Bremen, about thirty miles to the east of Oldenburg. Alex began spending more time in Bremen after making the acquaintance of Toni Behrens, the daughter of the well-to-do coffee importer Ludwig Behrens. Toni was nearly nine years younger than Alex and a few inches taller, a slender woman with short dark hair and a love for books, art, and music. She must have seemed to Alex the very antithesis of his former rural existence, a civilized and stable foundation on which to establish a happy marriage and a secure, prosperous home. Alex and Toni were married in Bremen on March 6, 1908. They took the train to Oldenburg and moved together into Alex's apartment overlooking the *Pferdemarkt*, Oldenburg's horse market.

A month later, Moses died and Alex and Toni traveled to Sachsenhagen for the funeral. Alex returned home determined to acquire larger living quarters, a desire that only quickened after Toni gave birth to their first child, Bertha, in October 1909. In a little over a year, he made his move, purchasing the property at the corner of Schüttingstrasse and Achternstrasse that would house his *Haus der Mode*. Alex moved his family into the two floors above the store. There, on November 17, 1913, my father was born. He was named Günther Ludwig Goldschmidt, in honor of Toni's father.

Only three photographs of my grandfather have survived; the earliest one dates from this period in his life. Taken in the spring of 1914, shortly after Alex's thirty-fifth birthday and about six months after the birth of my father, the photo shows the young family posing in front of a window in an unknown interior. The beginnings of a smile seem to play around my grandmother's lips, my aunt's face is nearly beaming with a five-year-old's joy, and even my father looks moderately pleased with his circumstances. But Alex, in stiff high collar and proper suit, is solemn, serious, dignified; this sitting for the photographer represents to him a formal declaration of what he has achieved: his wife, his children, his hearth. I see pride in his face and in the set of his mouth and strong chin, a confidence that he will be able to meet and overcome whatever challenges life may send his way. He may need to shake an extra hand to make a sale or treat a city council member to a schnapps to get a favorable ruling on an expansion plan, but for Alex Goldschmidt every problem has a solution, if you think about it long and creatively enough and then take action.

Just a few months later, Alex joined the German army to participate in that hideous blunder known as the Great War. He fought for more than four years, first on the Belgian front and later in Russia. Miraculously, given the unspeakable carnage all around him, he was never

The young Goldschmidt family—Alex, Toni, Bertha, and Günther—in 1914.

wounded. For his bravery, or perhaps just for surviving, he was awarded the Iron Cross, First Class. He returned to his home above the shop in January 1919, just days after his fortieth birthday. Toni had run the *Haus der Mode* in his absence and run it well. Their men might have been up to their knees in the mud of the trenches, but the women of Oldenburg had continued to shop for clothes and accessories during the war. With the resumption of peace, Alex decided to add a line of wedding furnishings to his offerings, and business really boomed. By the autumn of 1919, things were going so well financially that he felt comfortable acquiring one of Oldenburg's prime pieces of real estate. In October, he purchased from Friedrich Otto Graepel, a minister in the new republican government, a splendid house at 34 Gartenstrasse. It came equipped with a cook and a housekeeper. By any measure of material success, the Goldschmidt family had arrived.

The house was grand, a dream of well-crafted beauty and security. The main floor contained a large living room, a formal dining room, an expansive library, an enormous kitchen, exposed wooden beams

The magnificent house at 34 Gartenstrasse that Alex purchased in 1919, as seen from across the street.

on the ceiling, and a cozy glassed-in veranda looking out to the green gardens in back. Upstairs were five bedrooms and a spacious bathroom with gleaming fixtures of polished nickel. Downstairs were the servants' quarters and a room kept pleasantly chilled for the bottles of wine that lay neatly in wooden racks. A gardener appeared once a week in spring and summer to care for the apple and peach trees, rosebushes, and rhododendrons, and to tend the spacious lawn. And there was a spot in the backyard given over to a strawberry patch, the special province of Alex himself. Tending it was a singular pleasure: preparing the bed in springtime, tending to the earth in the growing season, and gathering in the rich red berries at harvest time.

My father's chief domestic responsibility was a chicken house and run that extended along the north side of the house, a realm inhabited by a rooster and a dozen hens that provided the family with fresh eggs every morning. But Günther's dearest memories from those happy days on Gartenstrasse stem from the many hours he spent playing with his sister Bertha and a family friend named Elsa Boschen. They would gather at the chicken run after school and then scurry the few hundred yards to the entrance of the glorious Schlossgarten. There they established an imaginary country called the *Anemonen Reich*, or "Anemone Kingdom." The children took turns serving as the country's monarch, issuing decrees, ordering executions, granting pardons, and launching fierce wars against the enemies of the Anemones. But the kingdom had its pacific side as well, and Günther, Bertha, and Elsa spent many idle hours together in the park reading their storybooks or lying on their backs at the edge of the pond, looking up into the blue skies and wondering where the clouds came from and where they went.

Perhaps encouraged by their splendid and spacious new home, Alex and Toni decided to enlarge their family. A second daughter, Eva, was born in June 1920, and then fifteen months later, on September 14, 1921, came a second son, Klaus Helmut. Eva entered the world with a club foot and had to undergo surgery, a delicate operation that was performed at the university hospital in Göttingen, about 170 miles away. The operation was considered a success, but Eva continued to walk with a slight limp for the rest of her life. My father remembered his younger sister as a quiet and sensitive girl, "full of poetry and dreams." Both Eva and Helmut began their schooling at home under Toni's tutelage, but after each turned ten, they entered Oldenburg's school system, Eva at a girls' academy, the Cecilia School, and Helmut at the prestigious Altes Gymnasium.

As the 1920s neared their end, Alex Goldschmidt's fortunes continued to grow. The economic shocks of the early '20s, many stemming from the severe financial penalties imposed upon Germany as part of the Treaty of Versailles, gave way to a sustained recovery. After years of deprivation, the women of Oldenburg were once again able to indulge their desire for attractive clothing, and the *Haus der Mode* was eager to assist them. Business was so good that in 1927, Alex unveiled the first outdoor neon sign ever seen in the narrow winding streets of downtown

The prosperous Goldschmidt and Behrens clans gather for the sixtieth birthday of my great grandmother Jeanette Behrens on March 24, 1923. Grandfather Alex, resplendent in evening wear, stands at the top left. My grandmother Toni stands four persons to his left; Jeanette sits at the center of the photo; and my father Günther, aged nine, sits to her immediate right.

Oldenburg. It read: "Alex Goldschmidt *Spezialhaus für Damenkonfektion und Kleiderstoffe*," or "Specialty House for Women's Ready-to-Wear and Dress Material." The *Haus der Mode* had become a retail landmark, like Macy's or Starbucks. C. A. Will, who ran a shoe store, put an advertisement in the newspaper identifying his store's location as 47 Achternstrasse and added, as a helpful hint, that it was right next door to Goldschmidt's.

At the end of the decade, either by design or by happenstance, Alex entered into negotiations with Oldenburg's city council to alter the dimensions of his store just as the city's chief engineer began to advise the council of the need to widen Achternstrasse at the corner of Schüttingstrasse. In early February 1930, the Oldenburg *Nachrichten* published the minutes of a discussion held during the council's most recent meeting.

The topic was the Goldschmidt company's building plans and a related proposal for the relief of traffic congestion in the inner city. The council debated a recommendation that "the merchant Goldschmidt shall cede about twenty-one square meters of his property in order to widen the Achternstrasse" and that "the merchant Goldschmidt shall receive compensation amounting to twelve thousand Reichmarks [RM] and a mortgage of twenty thousand Reichmarks at 8½% interest." The properties at 48 Achternstrasse and 34 Gartenstrasse would be held as collateral for the mortgage.

One member of the council complained that the figure of 12,000 RM was too generous. Another member agreed and proposed reopening negotiations with Herr Goldschmidt. At that point, the mayor rose and declared that several planning sessions had already taken place and that Herr Goldschmidt had acceded several times to the city's requests. Furthermore, said the mayor, building materials are expensive, the 12,000 RM figure had been painfully arrived at, and he was convinced that Herr Goldschmidt would not profit from the exchange. The city engineer testified that widening Achternstrasse was critical to the effort of easing downtown traffic, and two other council members declared their support for the recommendation, agreeing that traffic congestion had become an urgent matter. With that, the council voted, and the recommendation passed.

Indeed, Alex's planning was already under way. A month earlier, he had taken out an ad in the *Nachrichten* announcing a clearance sale. Suits, dresses, skirts, blouses, silks and other fabrics, decorative arts—all would be emptied from the *Haus der Mode* to make room for an exciting new venture. On February 22, following the approval of the city council's resolution, Alex placed another ad, announcing that soon the Goldschmidt name would be associated exclusively with the purveyance of fine coats. Meanwhile, the special clearance sale would continue with everything sold at rock-bottom prices! During remodeling, the *Haus der Mode* would remain open, although the main entryway would now be "a private entrance" on Schüttingstrasse, the doorway to the family's former apartment above the store. Hurry . . . everything must go!

The Easter-themed advertisement for Alex's House of Coats that ran in the Oldenburg Nachrichten *on April 14, 1930.*

On March 31, another ad declared that remodeling had been finished and that the new store—*Mantelhaus Goldschmidt*, or Goldschmidt's "House of Coats"—would be opening in a few days. Then a week later, on April 7, Alex announced, "The remodeling of my House is complete. My new store will now be a special House of Coats. By concentrating on a single special line, I will be able to be even more competitive. My famous good quality, which was already inexpensive, will become even less expensive. The selection will be even greater! Grand Opening tomorrow, Tuesday, April 8, at 10:00 a.m."

One week later, in an ad framed by images of bunnies, lambs, blooming lilies, hatching chicks, and romping children, Alex announced a "Great Easter Sale At Very Low Prices": "We have received a brand new shipping of the smartest spring and summer coats. The selection surpasses everything you have seen so far ... every size, from Girls' and Teenagers' coats to extra wide and long Ladies' coats in all modern fabrics. Come and see for yourself how competitive we are!"

By June, Alex was proclaiming that his exclusive stock included "Fur coats, light-colored fleece coats, gabardine coats, leather coats, coats of English-style fabrics, Macintoshes, modern coats for travel and sport, practical, comfortable, durable, and inexpensive, in all sizes, extra large and extra long. *Mantelhaus Goldschmidt* is in a class of its own, the premiere house for coats in all of Northwest Germany!"

Alex's customers, many of whom had patronized his House of Fashion for nearly two decades, faithfully followed him to his House of Coats. He encouraged their enthusiasm with a steady stream of hearty advertisements, demonstrating almost daily that here was a man who knew how to move the merchandise. Despite the effects of the worldwide Depression, business remained good.

But buried in the minutes of the same city council meeting that had granted Alex the authority to proceed with his new plan were six lines of testimony offering a chilling preview of the fate that was slouching toward the *Mantelhaus* and, indeed, toward all of Germany and the world beyond. One of the council members complained that Herr Goldschmidt had already been planning his renovations for some time and questioned why the city council should subsidize his business venture. This councilmember was Carl Röver, representing the National Socialist German Workers' Party.

The Nazi Party had emerged from the ruins of German pride in the aftermath of Germany's defeat in 1918 and out of the desperation caused by the economic calamities of the early twenties, when runaway inflation rendered German currency practically worthless. On November 9, 1923, a thirty-four-year-old Austrian who had served as a corporal in the German army during the Great War and who, like Alex Goldschmidt, had been awarded the Iron Cross, First Class, attempted to foment a national revolution from the speaking platform of a beer hall in Munich. The putsch failed and the young revolutionary landed in jail, but Adolf Hitler's campaign for National Socialism had begun.

Within five years, bolstered by a relentless repetition of charges that the German army—and by extension, Germany itself—had been "stabbed in the back" by the "November criminals" who surrendered at the armistice, and by inveighing against the undue influence of Jews and Communists in the economic world order, the Nazi Party had won a small but committed group of followers. In the elections of 1928, the National Socialists attracted 9.8 percent of the vote in the state of Oldenburg, earning them a seat on the Oldenburg city council. The Nazis chose their regional leader, or *Gauleiter*, Herr Röver, to represent them. His vote against Alex's plans in February 1930 was not enough to derail them. But his day would come soon enough.

Seven months later, in the elections of September 1930, the Nazis polled 27.3 percent of the Oldenburg state vote. In the ensuing months, they began to campaign even more heavily in the Northwest, appealing directly to the farmers who had been among the first in Germany to feel the full effects of the Depression. Their platform included calling for cheaper artificial manures, cheaper electricity, higher tariffs on imported corn and wheat, and lower taxes. They bolstered their appeal with mass rallies, fully staged extravaganzas featuring dramatic torchlight parades, dozens of distinctive black-on-red flags, and martial music designed to boil the blood and stiffen the spine. On May 5, 1931, Adolf Hitler himself traveled to Oldenburg for a rally in the *Pferdemarkt*, and a little more than a year later, on May 29, 1932, 48.4 percent of the voters in the state of Oldenburg cast their ballots for the Nazi Party. Though not an absolute majority, that number represented more votes than any other party had achieved. The National Socialists were constitutionally mandated to form a government, making Oldenburg the first state in the country to have duly elected Nazi leaders. The new president of the state ministry was Carl Röver.

Although it would be months before National Socialism would achieve the rule of law over all of Germany, Oldenburg would prove to be an able laboratory in which to cultivate its culture of violence and thuggery, not to mention its long-held antipathy to what it termed "the Jewish race." The Nazi imagination was stimulated by a prurient vision of a Master Race that sprang from the sacred soil of Germany, a race of blond, blue-eyed bodies through which coursed uncorrupted streams of the reddest, purest blood. Years earlier, in 1920, the nascent party had clearly stated its views in its initial twenty-five-point platform. "Only members of the nation may be citizens of the State," it declared. "Only those of German blood, whatever their creed, may be members of the nation. Accordingly, no Jew may be a member of the nation." This need for "racial purity" was at the heart of the Nazis' conviction that they alone possessed the secret and the will to create a superior national culture and a powerful state that would last, in Hitler's boast, for a thousand years.

Hitler spoke of the need to "cleanse" the German body politic of the "corrupt" influence of foreign Jewish forces and "to remove from specified positions important to the state those elements that cannot be entrusted with the life or death of the Reich." Thus was born what came to be known in German as *Arisierung* and in English as Aryanization: a comprehensive expropriation of all social, cultural, and material possessions that belonged to the Jews of Germany, and their redistribution into the hands of the more deserving Master Race.

Aryanization was a fancy five-syllable synonym for state-sponsored theft. Among its earliest examples was the forced sale, in the late autumn of 1932, of Alex Goldschmidt's beautiful house on Oldenburg's Gartenstrasse, to a Nazi functionary named Heinrich Barelmann. The sale price was 26,000 RM, a sum that represented no more than a quarter of what the house was worth. The Goldschmidts sold much of their furniture, dismissed the cook, the housekeeper, and the gardener, and moved into a small apartment at 35 Würzburgerstrasse, near the railroad tracks a bit north and west of the *Pferdemarkt*. Having invested more than twenty years of hard work and determination to reach a level of achievement commensurate with the examples set by Levi and Moses, what must Alex have felt at this humiliating and infuriating confiscation of his house, the very symbol of the safety and security that he thought he possessed?

But it was only the beginning. On Monday, January 30, 1933, Adolf Hitler was sworn in as chancellor of Germany by President Paul von Hindenburg, and the blows began falling one after another. On April 1, 1933, the now fully empowered Nazis staged a boycott of Jewish-owned businesses across the country, with storm troopers dispatched to stand outside stores with signs reading "Germans! Defend Yourselves! Don't Buy From Jews!" Six days later, Hitler's Reichstag passed the Law for the Restoration of Tenure for the Civil Service, legislation stating that "civil servants who are not of Aryan ancestry" were to be immediately dismissed. The response was ruthless, as Jewish government workers, police officers and firefighters, postal workers, librarians, museum curators, and artists who were employed by state-supported cultural institutions were summarily fired.

A month later, on Wednesday, May 10, the National Socialist Student Association staged what it proudly declared to be "the public burning of destructive Jewish writing" in the square in front of the Kroll Opera House in Berlin. The students lit a huge bonfire and hurled an estimated twenty thousand books into the flames, including works by Moses Mendelssohn, Heinrich Heine, Albert Einstein, Sigmund Freud, and Franz Kafka. In their zeal, the student firemen, egged on by a speech from Propaganda Minister Joseph Goebbels, also burned books by non-Jews such as Ernest Hemingway, Jack London, Sinclair Lewis, and Helen Keller.

Over the next two years, more regulations were put in place, from denying Jews entry to public baths and swimming pools across Germany to forbidding Jewish youth groups to wear uniforms or carry banners. But these were mere preludes to the ordinances announced at the annual Nazi Party congress in Nuremberg in September 1935.

From September 11 to 15, the gathering featured high-decibel speeches by day and spectacular torchlight parades by night, faithfully documented by filmmaker Leni Riefenstahl. On the last day of the conference, Adolf Hitler himself made a speech, declaring that the international Jewish conspiracy was growing ever more dangerous and that the German people, filled with righteous outrage, were ready to arise and defend themselves. In order to prevent such confrontations from occurring, and in order for the German *Volk* to enjoy "tolerable relations with the Jewish people," Hitler declared that it was time for a "singular momentous measure," a "legislative solution" to the ongoing, vexing Jewish Problem.

That solution, a codification of the racial theories that formed the basis of so much Nazi ideology, came to be known as the Nuremberg Laws. The Reich Citizenship Law drew a major distinction between Germans and Jews. From then on, there were to be "citizens of the Reich," who enjoyed full political and civic rights, and "subjects of the Reich," who would be entitled to none of those rights. To qualify as a "citizen," one had to prove that one possessed only pure German blood, which led to the next part of the Nuremberg Laws, the Law for the Defense of German Blood and Honor. It prohibited marriage and extramarital sex between Germans and Jews and also protected the flower of German female purity by making it illegal for any Jewish home to employ as a nanny, housekeeper, or maid a German woman under the age of forty-five.

Finally, the Nuremberg Laws codified the Nazi concept of Judaism as a "race" by defining Jews strictly according to their parentage. Keeping kosher, attending synagogue, or holding a particular religious belief had no bearing; the new laws defined a Jew simply as anyone who had three or four Jewish grandparents. And as a Jew, one was no longer a citizen, could no longer vote or hold office, and was subjected to constant and increasing levels of fear and intimidation.

Over the next three years, the Nazis issued more and more edicts, decrees, and regulations. Public parks, libraries, and beaches were closed to Jews. Jews were excluded from the general welfare system. Driver's licenses belonging to Jews were declared invalid. Even if he held a winning ticket, a Jew could not win the national lottery. Jews were forbidden to keep carrier pigeons and other pets. Curfews were announced in German cities; Jews had to be off the streets by 8:00 p.m. in winter and 9:00 p.m. in summer. Jews were only allowed to shop for food after 4:00 p.m., by which time most of the fresh produce had been cleared from the bins. And all Jews were required to adopt a new middle name: "Sara" for women and "Israel" for men.

In these and countless other ways, the Jews of Germany were rendered the Other, stateless strangers in their own land. These decrees represented interim solutions to the Jewish Problem, as the Nazis did their best to convince Jews to emigrate.

Throughout this legal and social onslaught, Alex Goldschmidt remained unconvinced that he and his family were in genuine danger. "I fought for the Kaiser," he declared confidently to anyone who would listen. "Hitler can't touch me." But Alex's certainty and self-assurance were no match for the unrelenting venality of the forces aligned against him. His proud boast about his military service must have rung a little hollow even to him once the Reich Propaganda Ministry ordered the names of Jewish soldiers stricken from the lists of honored dead on World War memorials. Business at "the premiere house for coats in all of Northwest Germany" began a steady decline after the April boycott, and within two years the Goldschmidts had to abandon their apartment on Würzburgerstrasse for an even smaller dwelling at 53 Ofenerstrasse, a large blue apartment building that had become a refuge for many Jewish families.

My father became convinced of the prudence of leaving Germany and made plans to move to Sweden in the spring of 1936, when he was twenty-two years old. He leased an apartment above a milk bar in Stockholm and was days away from leaving his homeland when he met a young violist in Frankfurt and decided to stay in Germany to be with her, a story I have told elsewhere. His older sister, Bertha, immigrated to England and became a gardener. She married late in life and died in 1998, just days before her eighty-ninth birthday. But his younger sister Eva and his brother Klaus Helmut had to navigate their perilous way through the 1930s as schoolchildren in Oldenburg.

I never met my uncle, of course, and my father professed to have retained few if any memories of his younger brother, perhaps because of the passage of time, perhaps due to deep feelings of guilt. He once told me that I bore an unspecified physical resemblance to Helmut, but other than that, he said next to nothing about him. So virtually everything I know about my uncle's childhood I owe to the extraordinary cache of documents unearthed by the filmmaker and longtime Oldenburg resident Farschid Ali Zahedi.

As I mentioned earlier, Klaus Helmut was born on September 14, 1921, during the halcyon days my family spent living in the beautiful house on Gartenstrasse, when business was booming at the *Haus der Mode* and the Goldschmidts were certified *machers* in the affairs of Oldenburg. He spent his first decade in the protective care of his parents, playing in the nearby Schlossgarten and studying at home with his mother. In time for the Easter term of 1931, he left the nest and enrolled in the fourth grade of the city's Wallschule. One year later, on the strength of his performance on an entrance exam, Helmut was admitted as student number 2555 to the fifth grade of the prestigious Altes Gymnasium, which had been founded in the sixteenth century and numbered the psychiatrist and philosopher Karl Jaspers among its graduates.

At the time he matriculated at the Altes Gymnasium Oldenburg (AGO), in the spring of 1932, Helmut was ten-and-a-half years old, stood just under five feet tall, and weighed ninety-one pounds. He was described in a teacher's evaluation as "good-natured, polite, enthusiastic, and conscientious," possessing "the talent and intellectual ability to meet the demands" of the AGO's rigorous curriculum. A year later, in March 1933—two months after Hitler had assumed the chancellorship—a teacher at the AGO described Helmut's "disposition and character" with these words: "talent good, thinking ability good, very good-natured, polite, understands easily, but his effort and attentiveness vary greatly. He is exempt from physical education due to a case of rickets."

Within weeks of that assessment, the Nazi government passed the Law Against Overcrowding of German Schools and Universities, targeting the country's "non-Aryans." The law specified that the number of new Jewish students at any German school must not exceed 1.5 percent of all new applicants and limited the number of Jewish pupils at any one institution to 5 percent of the total student population of that school. As an editorial in a reliable Nazi newspaper explained, "A self-respecting nation cannot leave its higher activities in the hands of people of racially foreign origin. Allowing the presence of too many of these foreigners could be interpreted as an acceptance of other races, something decidedly to be rejected."

Schools across Germany hurried to demonstrate their compliance with this new law. The AGO sent a letter to the Oldenburg State Ministry in early May declaring that, of its 194 students, only 3 were *nichtarisch*, or non-Aryan: Paul Gerson of the fifth grade, Helmut

Goldschmidt of the fifth grade, and Hermann Loewenstein of the fourth. The letter hastened to add that no new *nichtarisch* students had been accepted for the Easter term.

Across town, the all-girl Cecilia School sent its letter to the ministry on May 18, reporting that, of its 543 students, only 6 girls were *nichtarisch*, all of them *israelitisch*. They were first-grader Kathe Gröschler-Jever, second-grader Susanne de Haas, and sixth-graders Inge Cohen, Ingeborg Liepmann, Marianne Schiff, and Eva Goldschmidt. All of the other girls, the Cecilia administrator assured the ministry, were of "Aryan descent."

So it was that my Uncle Helmut and Aunt Eva spent the following five years attending their respective schools as outsiders, an unhappy status for schoolchildren under the best of circumstances. Ottheinrich Hestermann, one of Helmut's schoolmates at the AGO, recalls that Helmut stood apart from the other children during breaks in the day's schedule. Herr Hestermann speculates that Helmut's isolation may have been due to the menacing presence of a brown-shirted official assigned to monitor all free-period activity in the school's courtyard.

Despite being shunned during those periods of official surveillance, Helmut maintained good relationships, especially considering the circumstances, with his teachers and fellow students. Throughout the mid-1930s, even as the outside world grew ever colder for the Jews of Germany, the teachers of the Altes Gymnasium spoke warmly of Helmut Goldschmidt. His evaluation from the fall term of 1935: "His conduct in school is generally praiseworthy; his grades show his good effort and ability." At Christmas 1936: "He achieved good results while his conduct was admirable." At Easter 1937: "His conduct is perfect; application and attentiveness are commendable."

Helmut's grades were also quite commendable, again considering the circumstances of the times. Those circumstances included not only the heightened ostracism and legal discrimination against Jews throughout the country, but also the atmosphere within the hallowed halls of the Altes Gymnasium itself. The school had already existed for five centuries by the 1930s; it had a long, distinguished legacy with a conservative culture that was generally anti-Nazi in nature. But the local leaders installed as AGO headmaster a man named Westhusen, who proudly displayed a golden lapel pin signifying that he had been a member of the National Socialist Party since before Chancellor Hitler assumed office in 1933. As a part of his curriculum, students at the AGO were required to read and discuss a biology textbook that elucidated the tenets of *Rassenkunde*, or "racial knowledge," promoted by a scientist from Leipzig named Otto Steche. According to Dr. Steche, "the Jewish race is foreign to European races" and "mixtures" between Jews and Gentiles are "harmful" and thus to be strenuously avoided. In literature courses, both subtle and overt attacks on the Jews were a regular part of classroom instruction. When an English class studied Shakespeare's *Merchant of Venice*, the teacher made sure his students understood that the character Shylock was proof that the Jew was both inferior and dangerously conniving, unfit to live among and engage in commerce with his Aryan betters. The *Abitur*, the final examination, of 1938, was replete with anti-Semitic slogans and undisguised notions about racial purity.

Through it all, Helmut's grades remained, as his teachers wrote, commendable. The AGO maintained a grading system based on the numbers 1 through 6, wherein a "1" was considered outstanding and a "6" indicated a failing grade. Throughout his years at the AGO, Helmut received only 1s and a single 2 in conduct, and 1s, 2s, and a single 3 in attentiveness. He earned his best grades in language courses, with 1s and 2s in German, 2s and 3s in Latin, 2s and 3s in Greek, and 2s and 3s in French. But his grades in nearly all of his subjects were commendable: 1s, 2s, 3s, and a single 4 in history; 2s and 3s in geography; 2s and 3s and a single 4 in biology, arithmetic, and mathematics. Perhaps surprisingly, given his musical brother, Helmut was a bit less accomplished in his arts classes, receiving a consistent reckoning of 3s and 4s in music and drawing. His handwriting was also judged to be nothing special, with 3s and 4s his usual reward.

Helmut's greatest difficulty at school was physical education, and his most implacable adversary was the teacher of that class. As his early evaluation at the AGO stated, he suffered from rickets, a softening and slight deformity of his leg bones, and was thus exempt from physical education for his first years at the school. Beginning with the autumn term of 1936, however, Helmut's legs had strengthened and he began taking part in the classes. But Helmut was a bookish boy, more at home in the classroom than in the gym or on the playing field, and the results were predictably dismal. His grades in physical education never exceeded a 4, and his written evaluations always made note of his shortcomings. Fall 1937: "In physical education, Helmut needs to make a greater effort." Christmas 1937: "His poor results in physical education have not yet improved." Easter 1938: "It is regrettable that he still has no achievements in physical education." Fall 1938: "In phys. ed. Helmut was without accomplishment, and his physical abilities are generally very low."

Those frank assessments were probably difficult for Helmut to read three times a year, but they were nothing compared to the almost daily abuse he suffered at the hands of his teacher, a committed National Socialist and, apparently, an unreconstructed bully. He made no secret of his contempt for Helmut's weakness and lack of speed and coordination and lost no opportunity to contrast the shortcomings of this miserable human specimen, a representative of the entire Jewish "race," with the strength, endurance, grace, and overall physical beauty of the Aryan Master Race. Helmut's wretched attempts at soccer, swimming, handball, fencing, gymnastics, and track and field were all brass-plated opportunities for the teacher to gleefully spout his racial theories in front of Helmut's schoolmates, most of whom were members of the Hitler Youth and who, even if they had wanted to, had no standing to protest.

Yet it seems that Helmut's classmates did mount a single protest, or perhaps it was no more than a practical joke. The occasion was a school-wide cross-country meet that was held in a local forest known as the Eversten Wald. The runners, including Helmut, gathered at the starting line, the starter's pistol fired, and off they ran, disappearing into the wood. About fifteen minutes later, the lead runner burst out of the trees and raced panting up to the finish line. It was Helmut Goldschmidt. The other boys had conspired to let him win.

The phys. ed. teacher was not amused. Striding up to Helmut, he swung at the boy with such force that his punch knocked my uncle to the ground, unconscious. The rest of the runners, just now arriving, did not dare to intervene but stood silently watching as Helmut, dazed, picked himself up and staggered away, alone.

But my uncle was by no means a completely silent victim, as a famous, or notorious, act of courage and conviction still legendary in the halls of the AGO makes clear. In the early autumn of 1938, the entire school gathered in the venerable assembly hall to hear a lecture by a member of the *Verein für das Deutschtum im Ausland* (VDA), the Society of Germans Living Abroad. Ostensibly, the lecturer was there to promote his organization, to teach the students of the AGO about the many places where Germans lived around the world, and to proclaim proudly that German culture was becoming a global phenomenon. But very soon it became apparent that the speaker had another, darker agenda: to illuminate the growing and menacing worldwide Jewish conspiracy. No matter where in the world an upstanding German citizen might find himself, declared the speaker, there too would exist the Jewish peril. The Jewish banker, the Jewish merchant, the Jewish writer, the Jewish lecher ... all these representatives of the Jewish race threatened traditional German values, German methods of conducting business, and the lovely German women, whose beauty and grace were renowned from pole to pole. The representative of the VDA spelled out an exhaustive list of Jewish atrocities.

Suddenly, in the midst of this vitriol, Helmut Goldschmidt, seventeen, stood up and shouted, *"Das ist alles Lüge!"* ("These are all lies!"). With that, he turned and strode out of the room. Headmaster Westhusen jumped up from his seat, ran after Helmut, caught him by the arm, and forcibly dragged him back into the assembly hall and up onto the stage, next to the red-faced lecturer. There, in full view of more than two hundred students and faculty, Herr Westhusen slapped Helmut across the face and then ordered him to leave. Fellow student Ottheinrich Hestermann, remembered that "we all sat filled with shame as well as sympathy for our courageous comrade. But neither students nor teachers spoke a single word. A touch of pogrom atmosphere had drifted through the hall."

That atmosphere would soon become pervasive and stifling. November 9 was approaching, the fifteenth anniversary of Adolf Hitler's abortive beerhall putsch in Munich, the opening shots fired in the National Socialists' revolution. The date had long been enthusiastically celebrated by the Nazis and warily regarded by the Jews. The writer Karl Heinz Adler recalled, "It was a day for these glorious gangsters to remember their heroes with flags, marches, and songs. You quickly learned that this was not a time for Jews to appear on the streets."

As that date in 1938 approached, the local newspaper wrote an article headlined, "The 9th of November in Oldenburg," heralding the occasion:

> The board of the Oldenburg branch of the National Socialist German Workers' Party has seen to it that the citizens of our city will be able to celebrate the anniversary of the day in 1923 when the Fuehrer marched with his followers to the *Feldherrnhalle* fighting for the re-birth of Germany. In ten events scheduled for the evening of this glorious day of the movement, the comrades of the town will unite in demonstrating their inner closeness to the world view of Adolf Hitler. The dignified ceremonies, carefully adapted for the day, will represent a deeply spiritual experience reaching far into everyday life through their meaningful gravity and their proud devotion to the heroes who sacrificed themselves for and will eternally keep watch over Germany. Over the next few days we will have special reports on these ceremonies and their content.

So a grand celebration had been planned for November 9, but there were signs that more sinister events were in the works as well. Synagogues in Munich and Nuremberg had been set on fire during the summer, and the American ambassador to Germany had cabled his concerns to Washington about increased levels of anti-Jewish violence. There were also reports from Palestine and Slovakia that hinted at the real possibility that Germany would soon stage a "spontaneous" people's action against the Jews.

But whatever had been secretly arranged, real-life events played into the hands of those either wishing for or planning violence. On November 7, a Polish Jew named Herschel Grynszpan, angered by the treatment received by relatives caught up in a border dispute between Germany and Poland, walked into the German Embassy in Paris and shot First Secretary Ernst vom Rath. Rushed to the hospital, vom Rath clung to life for forty-eight hours, but finally succumbed at 5:30 p.m. on November 9.

That night and well into the next morning, supposedly spurred on by righteous anger over the assassination in Paris, gangs of Nazi thugs, many in the brown and black uniforms of the SA and SS, roamed through German cities, looting Jewish homes and businesses. Synagogues and the treasures they held were set on fire. People were dragged from their homes and beaten and stomped, sometimes to death. Thousands more were arrested. The vandals smashed so many windows with clubs, chains, bricks, and stones that the shattered glass lay in heaps, reflecting the glare of spotlights and the flicker of flames. The Nazis christened the action *Kristallnacht*, or the Night of Broken Glass. The Jews simply called it the November Pogrom.

By the time the national spasm of violence was officially called to a halt by Propaganda Minister Joseph Goebbels on November 11, more than two hundred fifty synagogues had been burned, seventy-five hundred Jewish shops and businesses had been looted or destroyed, nearly 100 Jews murdered, and more than twenty-five thousand Jews arrested, among them Alex and Helmut Goldschmidt of Oldenburg.

The knock came on their door at 53 Ofenerstrasse shortly after 5:00 a.m. on Thursday, November 10. By this time, my father was living in Berlin, so only the two remaining men of the household, Alex and Helmut, were ordered to throw on some clothes and accompany their arresting officers to the wide expanse of the *Pferdemarkt*, Oldenburg's old horse market. Once at the market, they joined other Jewish prisoners of both sexes, who were commanded to line up on opposite sides of the square, the men on one side and the women on the other. They remained standing in the bitter wind and slowly breaking dawn until about 9:00. At that point, all of the women and the men under eighteen years of age, including my Uncle Helmut, were dismissed. The remaining prisoners, forty-three men, were then marched through the streets of Oldenburg, past the still smoking remains of the synagogue on Peterstrasse, over the winding cobblestones of the Old City, into the heavily traveled thorough-fare called the Damm, then right onto Elizabethstrasse along the border of the splendid Schlossgarten, and finally left onto Gerichtestrasse and into the courtyard of the squat and ugly Oldenburg Prison. As the dazed and disbelieving men, many of them elderly and leaning on canes, shuffled along the humiliating march past the empty eyes of their fellow citizens, their captors occasionally called out, "These are the criminals, these are the traitors, these are the enemies of the Reich!"

Alex and his 42 fellow "criminals" spent the rest of that day and night in prison. Early the next morning, they were loaded onto a bus and driven to the Oldenburg train station. There they met another 34 Jews who had been rounded up from the surrounding countryside and had spent the previous twelve hours at gunpoint, cleaning up the rubble from the burned synagogue. These 77 men were then loaded onto a train headed east, a train with 938 Jews between the ages of fourteen and eighty-two crammed into a series of cattle cars, a train bound for a concentration camp called Sachsenhausen.

Built during the summer of 1936, the "protective custody" camp of Sachsenhausen was located just outside Oranienburg, a town about twenty miles north of Berlin. Its commandant was Hermann Baranowski; his second in command was a young man who would soon achieve much greater notoriety when he was appointed commandant of the extermination camp at Auschwitz: Rudolf Höss.

When the prisoners arrived from Oldenburg on Friday evening, they were herded, along with hundreds of others, through Sachsenhausen's black iron gates, which proclaimed the infamous and cynical motto of the camps, *Arbeit macht frei*, or "Work makes you free." They lined up at attention in the Appellplatz, or roll-call area, standing in the cold wind with the harsh glare of spotlights trained on them from the nine lookout towers built into the camp's eight-foot-high walls. There they stood until morning, faced with the threat of a beating if they fell or urinated, a need that many yielded to as the dark hours passed. According to a searing report in the *News Chronicle* of London, dozens of the men were severely beaten that night, twelve of them to death, "their skulls smashed, the eyes of some knocked out, their faces flattened and shapeless."

When dawn finally broke, my grandfather, who had managed to remain upright throughout the ordeal, was issued the standard gray-striped prisoner's uniform, given prisoner number 9961, and assigned to barracks number 42. For the next twenty-five days, he arose every morning, lined up for roll call, and then marched to the work zone outside the barracks area, where he assisted in the manufacture of bricks and shoes. Alex Goldschmidt, son and grandson of equine nobility, was fifty-nine years old.

In the days following the November Pogrom the Nazi government acted swiftly to pin responsibility for the violence and destruction on the victims of the assault. The Jews had brought the righteous wrath of the German *Volk* upon themselves. Since Herschel Grynszpan was a Jew, they reasoned, Jews were responsible for cleaning up the mess that had resulted from the "spontaneous demonstrations." Field Marshal Hermann Göring decreed that the Jews were to be fined one billion marks as "reparation" for the death of Secretary vom Rath. And the process of Aryanization, the legal theft of Jewish businesses, was to be promptly accelerated.

A few days later, on November 15, the few Jewish children who remained in German public schools were summarily expelled. The official announcement stated: "After the heinous murder in Paris one cannot demand of any German teacher to continue to teach Jewish children. It is also self-evident that it is unbearable for German schoolchildren to sit in the same classroom with Jewish children. Therefore, effective immediately, attendance at German schools is no longer permitted to Jews. They are allowed to attend only Jewish schools. Insofar as this has not yet happened, all Jewish schoolchildren who at this time are still attending a German school must be dismissed."

Following his outburst at the VDA assembly some weeks before, Helmut must have known that his days at the Altes Gymnasium were numbered. Surely his mother knew as well. Yet on November 14, the day before the official decree that all Jews must be expelled from German schools, Toni sent the following brief note to Headmaster Westhusen: "Herewith I notify you that my son Helmut is leaving school. Kindly send his Leaving Certificate. (signed) Mrs. Toni

Goldschmidt." In effect, she was saying, "You can't dismiss my son . . . he quits!"

The certificate that Toni requested, the *Abgangszeugnis*, duly arrived in a few days, signed by the headmaster and stamped with an official Nazi seal. It included a final rundown of Helmut's grades, including a 2 in German, 3s in Latin, Greek, French, music, mathematics, and biology, and 4s in physics and handwriting. Amusingly his very poor 5 in physical education had been drawn over and turned into a 6, the worst possible grade. It seems his nemesis, the sadistic physical education teacher, had uttered the last laugh.

A bit more than a month later, on December 19, the staff of the Altes Gymnasium, led by Headmaster Westhusen, gathered for a faculty meeting, the last of that tumultuous year of 1938. The second of eight items on the agenda was "Attendance by Jewish Students." The recording secretary for the meeting wrote down a single sentence: *Es befindet sich kein Jude mehr auf der Schule.* "We have determined that there are no more Jews in the school."

In the years since the April boycott of 1933, despite Alex's best efforts, business at the *Mantelhaus* had declined considerably. Money became increasingly tight in the Goldschmidt household. As early as July 6, 1934, Oldenburg's Minister of Churches and Schools had issued a directive to the AGO's headmaster that the salesman Alex Goldschmidt owed 106.80 Reichsmarks in tuition fees for his son Helmut. If those fees were not paid in full by the end of the month, the student would face dismissal from the school.

On August 2, a brief note was sent to the salesman Goldschmidt informing him that, pursuant to the order from the minister dated July 6, his son Helmut was being dismissed from the AGO because his tuition had still not been paid. Alex must have managed to scrape together those 106 marks, as Helmut's tenure at the gymnasium was never interrupted. But the strain on the family's finances must have been acute for the proud businessman to have courted such embarrassment.

In late November 1938, with her husband imprisoned in Sachsenhausen and the *Mantelhaus* shorn of most of its remaining customers, Toni came face to face with impending penury. Desperate for money, she organized a sale of household items, some of them precious family relics, many of them homely everyday effects, from dishes and spoons to hand towels and small paintings. Most of her neighbors were in the same dire straits and couldn't afford to purchase anything, but there were a few meager sales for which Toni was very grateful.

Then came a final blow. In late September, State Ministry President Carl Röver had sent a directive to the minister of finance and the mayor of Oldenburg regarding the ongoing efforts at *Arisierung*, or the Aryanization of Jewish enterprises. President Röver informed them that it was official policy to run all Aryanization applications through him, but that, given the increased pace of the process, such formalities were becoming unnecessarily cumbersome. He was therefore empowering his economic consultant Hermann Fromm to decide on his own all questions of how to "de-Jew" a desired business. In this manner, the desired objective would be more speedily achieved.

On November 26, Herr Fromm reported to his superior on the case of "the Jew salesman Alex Goldschmidt of 53 Ofenerstrasse": "His business has been liquidated and I have added his name to the list of Jewish merchants who have been dealt with." Just like that, my grandfather's store was gone, his inventory confiscated, his livelihood eliminated, his family imperiled, his future bleak.

SATURDAY, MAY 14, 2011. Rain falls softly but steadily from an iron sky. Hilu apologizes profusely for the weather, insisting that this is Oldenburg's first rainy day in almost seven weeks. We don't mind in the least, as it encourages us to stay abed an extra hour to catch up on the sleep our still jet-lagged bodies are demanding. Amy then goes for a run as I use my laptop computer to read about another improbable victory last night by my Cleveland Indians, who have defied expectations by sprinting out to what will soon become a seven-game lead in the American League's Central Division. It won't last, of course (as all true Cleveland fans know), but why question miracles as they are happening?

At noon, the four of us mount bicycles (Hilu and Roland own several bikes in addition to those they use regularly) and, dressed warmly against the rain and chill, pedal into Old Town Oldenburg for lunch and to visit some treasured landmarks. We ride past the grand house on Gartenstrasse that was once the Goldschmidt family home and make our way through a portion of the beautiful Schlossgarten, raindrops dripping from its stately elms and linden trees, the surface of its serpentine lake wrinkled by a stiff steady breeze. We park our bikes by the stately Lambertikirche and walk solemnly through its hushed interior, its gloom brightened by dancing candlelight. Roland tells me that shortly after conducting its premiere in Bremen in 1865, Johannes Brahms came to Oldenburg to lead a performance of his masterful German Requiem in the Lambertikirche.

We find a cozy Italian restaurant on Achternstrasse and then, after lunch, walk down the street to the corner of Schüttingstrasse, the site of Alex's *Haus der Mode* and later his *Mantelhaus*. Though I have been here before, on this occasion I do something I've never done: I find the "private entrance" that Alex mentioned in one of his ads and climb the stairs to the apartment that was my family's living quarters in 1913, the year my father was born. On the second floor, there is now a shop selling LPs from the golden age of rock 'n' roll: the Beatles live in Hamburg, the "Woodstock" soundtrack, and records by the Rolling Stones, Chuck Berry, Johnny Cash, Bob Dylan, and Pink Floyd. On the third floor, a door, shut and locked on this Saturday, announces that within lies an expert tattoo and body piercing parlor. And above that I find an open door that leads into an attic, with creaky, unfinished planks for a floor and holes in the woodwork that let in the rain and provide a view over gabled roofs and down to the wet, winding streets of the town below.

Comfortably numb, I wander slowly through the attic, under the same timber beams my family would have seen each time they climbed the stairs to rummage through a box in storage. I examine each rough surface for signs of their existence, perhaps initials carved into the wood by my father, uncle, or aunts, but I find nothing tangible. There are ghosts hovering in the dark corners, though, of that I am sure, and I pause before descending the stairs to kiss the door jamb and feel its cool, receptive wooden lips convey my love back through the decades.

That evening, Hilu has arranged a public showing of the short film *Farschid Ali Zahedi* made some years ago about me and my family. Given the late hour and the unrelenting rain, we decide to drive to the event in our rented Meriva. I park the car on Peterstrasse, very near the site of the Oldenburg synagogue before its destruction on *Kristallnacht*. Today, the site contains the preserved ruins of the temple, a memorial to the city's sad history. As we cross the street to enter the community center where the film is to be shown, I notice that someone has placed a bouquet of red roses on the memorial.

A crowd of perhaps fifty people has gathered to view the film and hear me answer a few questions. Farschid briefly introduces the film, the lights go down, and we see on the screen images of the store I had visited that afternoon, old footage of the Nazi boycott, and an interview Farschid conducted with me in 1999 as I was working on my first book, when so many discoveries about my family's story were still ahead of me. When the lights come back up, I quickly wipe my eyes and stand to take questions, starting off with one of my own: who was that younger man with the full head of hair pretending to be me twelve years ago?

People ask detailed questions about Alex, about my father and mother, and about the new project that has brought me back to this city for yet another visit. A young woman asks how I feel about being in Oldenburg, where my family was treated so cruelly after their many years of service. I pause and then attempt to explain my very ambivalent feelings about this place, which did indeed betray the Goldschmidts but which has been so warm and kind to me. I mention my dear hosts, Hilu and Roland, Farschid, Pastor Jacoby, and the current faculty of the Altes Gymnasium. I mention the warm, inviting, attractive character of the city, with its lovely park, graceful church, and thriving theater. I conclude by saying that, although I am every inch an American citizen, there is something in my DNA that is decidedly European in general and German in particular and that, the horrors of the past notwithstanding, a part of me feels very much at home in Oldenburg.

The crowd claps politely and, it seems to me, with a certain relief that this particular Jewish descendent of the Holocaust doesn't hold them personally accountable.

At that moment, I see a hand raised at the back of the room, and a man who appears to be a few years my junior slowly gets to his feet. He is carrying a small parcel. He begins speaking haltingly in English and then gives up, asking Hilu to translate his German for me. He says that a few years ago, his great-aunt told him a story about a poor Jewish lady who, down on her luck during the ugly 1930s, had held a sale of household items to raise some badly needed money. His great-aunt had bought some small articles just to be kind; she didn't need them but figured that the money she paid would stand as a loan until the woman was back on her feet and the items could be returned to their rightful owner. But the poor woman disappeared shortly thereafter and the items remained in the great-aunt's possession.

The man swallows, pauses, and then continues in English. "Now I think it is time for these things to go back to their family. Here, Mr. Goldschmidt. . . . I believe these are yours."

With that, he comes forward and hands me his parcel. With trembling fingers, I unwrap it and discover five little oyster shells carved into the shape of fish, each with a tiny, shiny inlaid eye. Hilu excitedly tells me that such fish were part of a smart table setting in German households of the 1920s and '30s; they were placed above the plate when fish was served to hold the bones that the diner discreetly extracted from the creature during the meal. "These belonged to your grandmother! These fish were in your grandparents' house! They have been in this man's family for seventy years and now they are back where they belong!"

I stare at each little fish in wonder and amazement, taking several moments to comprehend Hilu's words. I clasp them to my heart, my eyes flooding with tears. I hand them carefully to Amy and then embrace the man who has so kindly preserved this treasure for me and has tonight brought me such joy. The crowd cheers. I am overcome.

The following day, Sunday, we spend the morning sleeping late, enjoying a splendid breakfast with Hilu and Roland, and taking a walk through a nearby nature preserve. We delight in the day's brilliant sun and puffy white clouds, which race across the sky at the urging of a frisky breeze. As we walk, I prepare myself emotionally for the task I've scheduled for the afternoon: scattering my father's ashes.

Since his death and cremation in the spring of 2009, his ashes have reposed in a heavy cardboard box in an upstairs closet in our home in Maryland. The many tender, though fanciful, conversations my father and I enjoyed in his last years at Arbor Place, during which we planned his return to his hometown and the park where his warmest memories were born, convinced me that it was meet and right to allow his dust to mingle with the rich soil of the Schlossgarten. On Friday night, I told Pastor Jacoby of my plan and asked her to please accompany my father on his homecoming. She readily agreed.

So on this Sunday afternoon, Roland, Amy, and I drive down to Gartenstrasse, Amy holding the box containing the ashes on her lap. We leave the car on a side street and walk solemnly to the Schlossgarten entrance that is nearest the splendid old house where my father grew up, walking the path that he, Bertha, and Elsa undoubtedly took when they visited the happy realm they called the *Anemonen Reich*, their Anemone Kingdom. Dietgard Jacoby is waiting for us.

Our little four-person procession enters the park and turns left onto another of the Schlossgarten's well-tended paths, the weighty box in my arms. My deliberate steps bring me to a grove of rhododendron bushes, ablaze in red and purple blossoms. My father spoke lovingly of the rhododendrons of his youth and I know this to be his proper resting place. But now that the appointed time has come, I find myself frozen, fearful of the finality of what we are about to do.

My loving wife comes to my assistance. She takes the box from me and opens it. I stare at its contents, not comprehending that this grey ash, no different from the substance I recall from countless campfires and cozy fireplaces, was once the man who gave me life.

I look then at the three serious faces gathered around me and try to smile. "Günther Ludwig Goldschmidt was born here in 1913," I say slowly. "George Gunther Goldsmith was my father. May he rest in peace."

The ash is smooth and silky. I grasp a handful and toss it over the nearest rhododendron. I pass the box to Amy, who scatters her handful. Then Dietgard takes her turn, and finally Roland, who accompanies his toss by intoning, *Sh'ma Yisrael Adonai Eloheinu Adonai Ehad*. We continue until the box is nearly empty and the red and purple blossoms have taken on a grayish cast. Dietgard hugs me then and whispers in my ear, "He will always be here. He will always be with you."

I struggle with a trembling voice to proclaim, "The king of the *Anemonen Reich* has returned to reclaim his kingdom." Then, for the second time in twenty-four hours, I am crying, partly because I am saying a final farewell to my father and partly because I suddenly have a vision of Günther as a boy of ten, romping through this magical park with his dear little friends and without a care in the world.

On the way back to the car, I make a detour to 34 Gartenstrasse and sprinkle the remaining ashes over a pink rosebush in the front yard. So even though Alex was forced to sell his beautiful house, Günther will always be there.

That evening, we pay a call on Anneliese Wehrmann, an acquaintance of Hilu and Roland. Now ninety-one, she was a friend and classmate of my Aunt Eva years ago when her name was Anneliese Meyer. The two girls attended the Cecilia School and spent many hours together, at least in the years before the Nazi accession. Anneliese enjoyed the great privilege of "Aryan ancestry."

She invites Amy and me into her snug apartment and offers us tea and cookies. Her nearly white hair is up in a neat bun and her eyes sparkle as she recalls her earliest memories of Eva Goldschmidt. She was a good-natured and good-humored girl, says Frau Wehrmann, although her bad leg made it difficult to run and play with the other girls and she was further isolated by being one of the few Jews in her class. Eva was sometimes mischievous and enjoyed speaking in a hushed voice to lure Anneliese closer and then shaking her head briskly to playfully lash Anneliese with her braids. Eva would then break into such a merry laugh that Anneliese would have no choice but to join in the laughter.

But by 1936 or '37, when the girls were sixteen and seventeen years old, it became increasingly dangerous for non-Jews to associate with Jews. There was no written law, says Frau Wehrmann, but the Nazis had created such a toxic climate of fear that people naturally concluded that spending time with a Jew could bring consequences. There was a time, for instance, that Anneliese wanted to invite Eva to her house to study. Her parents thought it over for a long time and finally gave their consent, but only under certain conditions. When Eva knocked, insisted her parents, Anneliese should open the door immediately and hustle her friend upstairs to her room. When the studying was over, she must usher Eva out herself, without involving them in order that they might maintain a position of plausible deniability should the authorities inquire. Similarly, when Anneliese attended a birthday party at Eva's apartment, Anneliese was to look both ways carefully before knocking, to reduce the chance that anyone would see her entering a Jewish home.

Frau Wehrmann must see the sadness on our faces as she tells these unhappy stories, for she pauses, looks away, and then says softly, "I had no choice, you see. None of us had a choice."

She rises then to get more hot water for our tea. Then settling herself heavily into her chair, she shares her last memory of her long-ago friend. Eva was one of the Jewish children dismissed from her school on November 15, 1938. A few days later, Anneliese saw Eva across the street and waved to her. Eva's eyes widened, she looked around her, then she covered her mouth with her hand to indicate that Anneliese shouldn't call out, that it wasn't safe for her friend to be seen talking to her. Eva then ducked her head and hurried away.

Frau Wehrmann looks at us then and I see tears in her eyes. "That was the last time I ever saw her. To this day I am haunted by that image of her running away from me." She is silent for a long moment. "And . . . I suppose . . . what happened to her?" she asks in the smallest of voices.

I answer far more coldly than I intend to. "She was murdered," I say. "In Riga. Along with her mother. My grandmother. That's what happened."

I rise to leave. "Please don't blame yourself," I say, trying to be kind, but a hardness remains in my voice that I cannot dislodge. "Thank you very much for the tea and for your memories of my aunt." At the door, I turn to her and add, "And thank you for being her friend. Not everyone was."

For the rest of the evening and well into the night, I turn my thoughts and feelings regarding Anneliese Wehrmann around and around in my head. She was my Aunt Eva's friend, she risked her safety and that of her family to see her deep into the 1930s, and yet it doesn't seem right—in fact it makes me clench my fists in frustrated anger—that in the end it was Eva who dragged her afflicted leg and her despised "race" away from Anneliese in order to protect *her*. Dammit, I tell myself, it should have been the other way around: Anneliese should have protected Eva. But how could she have done that in the face of the full force of the brutal gangsterism arrayed against her? As she said, she'd had no choice.

Yet, with no other individual to blame for the violence visited on my family, Anneliese Wehrmann becomes a convenient scapegoat, and I drift off to sleep with malice toward her in my heart.

On Monday morning, the rain has returned. Again, the four of us pile into the Meriva and drive downtown to the Altes Gymnasium for my session with the students. Although the school dates back to 1573, since 1878 it has been in its present prime location, across the street from the Old City and the soaring steeple of the Lambertikirche, just steps from the venerable State Theater, its back bordering the beautiful Schlossgarten. From the outside, it's an imposing building, and yet inside, with students rushing through the corridors, laughing and whistling, greeting friends and teachers, intent on relaying and accepting messages on their cell phones, dropping books and swapping caps, it displays the unmistakable atmosphere of a vibrant school community. We are met by Jörg Witte, the teacher who invited me on Friday evening. He leads us to the site of our gathering: the very assembly hall that was the setting for Helmut's outburst in the autumn of 1938.

As I walk into the room, with its somber black walls bordered by dark wooden carvings, I feel what in the past few days has become a familiar prickling sensation at the corner of my eyes, and the thought rages through my mind, "Can you please stop crying *for five minutes* at least?!" But I cannot rid my imagination of the image of Uncle Helmut staging his hopeless protest against the lies that were being ruthlessly marshaled against his country, his city, his school—lies that he recognized and would not allow to stand. Then my tears give way to a broad smile; I am just so proud of what J. D. Salinger would have called Helmut's "testicularity" at that singular moment.

By way of introducing me, Dr. Witte tells the students, all of them from the tenth and eleventh grades, of the important connection my family has to this auditorium. He points out that Helmut in 1938 was roughly the same age as they are today. "Who among you," he asks, "would have the courage to do what Helmut Goldschmidt did? Who among any of us would?" he asks us, faculty and guests alike. I speak for perhaps ten minutes, telling the story of my family and of the journey I am just beginning. Then I invite their questions, virtually all of which are echoes of the question asked at Saturday night's film screening: how does it feel to be back here at the scene of the crimes committed during what in German is called the *NS Zeit*, the time of National Socialism. Again I try to sort out my complicated feelings and I tell them that the pain of what happened years before I was born is still very present for me but that it has been tempered by the kindnesses shown me by so many Oldenburgers.

But even as I repeat these words, I am reminded of my angry reaction to Anneliese Wehrmann's story and I ask myself just how well-tempered my true feelings have become.

After the students have been dismissed, we spend a few minutes admiring the memorial that stands at the entrance to the auditorium. It is a simple plaque, bordered in green, accompanied by an austere wooden sculpture. The plaque reads, in German, "The murdered Jewish students of this school." The names are Paul Gerson, Helmut Goldschmidt, Ludwig Landsberg, Julius Meyberg, Franz Reyersbach, and Max Wallheimer. The students of the AGO see those names every day. I am very glad to read Uncle Helmut's name and to know that he is celebrated for his courage and mourned as the very last Jewish student at the AGO during the *NS Zeit*. But I am also aware of the deep grief this well-meaning plaque cannot now ease, nor ever will.

That afternoon I try to explain my complicated feelings to Roland and learn that his emotions are no less in turmoil. He has been wrestling with the guilt of his German childhood for all of his adult life.

"It is so tempting," he says, "to think that modern German history has a clear line of demarcation—the year 1945—and that on one side of the line there is National Socialism and on the other side democracy.

But the reality is so much different. I was born in 1941 and in my first fifteen years or so I hardly ever came into contact with people who had not been Nazis—and many still were."

Roland tells me that, with very few exceptions, all of his teachers were former Nazis. In his teenage years—the 1950s—he encountered a wall of silence when he tried to talk about the *NS Zeit* in his hometown. Sometimes, he heard words that were far more painful than silence. "You would think that those few brave souls who had stood up for the Jews, those who sheltered them or brought them food or performed even the simplest acts of charity such as that woman who bought those little fish from your grandmother, that these people would have been lauded and held up as model citizens," Roland says. He shakes his head sadly, and when he resumes speaking, his eyes are blazing. "But no! People here looked upon such people with mistrust or even disgust. They did not want to hear about such heroics. Rather they wished to emphasize that they were being discriminated against by all these efforts to compensate the Jews for the property that had been stolen from them. For instance, my uncle Dieter, a master of figures and statistics, calculated that a certain house had been seized from a Jewish family in 1938 and the owner had been paid about 5 percent of its value. Efforts were underway to make things up to the victim's family. And yet so many people here in Oldenburg were angry about those efforts, saying that the original transaction had been carried out in an orderly and lawful manner. These people would declare loudly, *'Was rechtens war, kann heute nicht Unrecht sein!'* 'What was lawful then cannot be unlawful today!'"

Roland is silent again for several long moments. Then he closes his eyes and tells me about his parents' family doctor. "This man had participated in the euthanasia campaign of the National Socialists in which handicapped and other 'undesirable' people were put to death. Ghastly experiments on human beings this man had also done. He had been sentenced to prison in 1945. And when after ten years he was released from 'internment,' as people called it, in some parts of the Oldenburg population it was considered a matter of honor to choose this man as one's family doctor, just to make a statement."

"It is hard to imagine," Roland says to me sorrowfully, "how hypocritical the established citizens of Oldenburg were."

Roland Neidhardt has spent many decades trying to forge relationships of trust between his German countrymen and the Jews. He has learned to read and speak Hebrew fluently and spends part of every year in Israel. It is obvious that he remains deeply wounded by the same long-ago events that continue to cause me pain and anguish. The past is still very present for Roland, too.

"But things are different today, are they not?" I ask myself. There is that memorial in the AGO, and every year on November 10 the city recreates the march through town of those forty-three Jewish men. There are so many good and decent people in Oldenburg, from Dietgard Jacoby to Jörg Witte to the citizens who attended Farschid's film the other night. And there is the family that kept my grandmother's fish for years until they could be returned to me, their rightful heir.

These people are deeply aware of those events of the 1930s and '40s, I think, and are trying to make amends, even if that proves to be an impossible task. Are my countrymen doing as much to account for the sins of slavery and the annihilation of the Native American population? Is it not eventually up to us, the descendants of the victims, to offer some form of forgiveness?

As I ponder these questions, the phone rings. Hilu answers it in another part of the house and I hear her speaking rapidly, with unmistakable excitement in her voice. After a few minutes, she comes to tell us that a couple who saw a story in Saturday's newspaper about my visit has called with some remarkable news: about ten years ago, they purchased the beautiful house at 34 Gartenstrasse. They want me to visit my grandfather's former home. In mere moments, I register my pleasure at the invitation and ask Hilu to call back with our acceptance.

That evening, the four of us drive to my family's home. We are greeted by Carsten and Monica Meyerbohlen, who usher us inside. He is an architect, tall and silver-haired, whose English is about as accomplished as my German. She is younger, dressed elegantly, born in England to an army officer who was later assigned to postwar Germany.

They welcome us with great kindness and understanding for the welter of emotions they know I am experiencing.

"When we saw our address in the paper in this extraordinary context," Mrs. Meyerbohlen says, "we knew that we had to get in touch with you, to meet you, and to welcome you here. Please, let us show you everything."

Over the next hour, we tour the elegant house from top to bottom. The entrance hallway is lined with bookshelves and adorned with paintings. The living room is spacious, with dark beams high above well-crafted furniture, fronting a glassed-in veranda that overlooks the rear garden. There is an immense dining room and an equally large library, each with twelve-foot ceilings, that look out through tall windows of heavy glass to the traffic that whispers past on Gartenstrasse. The floors of the entrance hall, dining room, and library are finely stained oak; lush woven rugs muffle our steps in the living room. The kitchen has been designed for someone who clearly loves to cook; a big stove with six burners dominates the room, which includes every conceivable culinary gadget.

The floor above boasts four large bedrooms surrounding a central master bathroom. The floor above that has been transformed into a gallery hung with Mr. Meyerbohlen's architectural drawings and sketches, with a balcony that offers a view of the nearby Schlossgarten. The basement includes the former servants' quarters, now converted into cozy guest rooms, and a well-stocked wine cellar.

My head is swirling as I attempt to take it all in. Yes, the mansion has been updated and modernized, but the essential "houseness" of the building is unchanged from when Alex, Toni, Bertha, Günther, Eva, and Helmut lived here in the splendor that Alex's business acumen had won for them, until it was taken away in an instant.

We walk out into the back garden of deep green grass, rhododendrons in bloom, a sunken pool, and a host of fruit trees. One of them, an apple tree, has the wrinkled bark and twisted branches that suggest old age. I conclude that it was probably here in the 1920s, perhaps providing a dappled shade with its springtime blossoms while Alex enjoyed a well-earned Sunday snooze. I picture the peaceful scene, and it is finally too much for me. I lean against its sturdy trunk and weep anew for my lost family. Amy comes to my side and holds me tenderly.

Carsten and Monica, noting my emotion, retreat silently back inside. When we rejoin them a few minutes later, they invite us to the dining room to share a bottle of wine. We tell our stories, and our hosts explain that when they purchased the house in 2001, they had no knowledge of its history. I can see that they are uncomfortable, and I assure them that in no way do I hold them even remotely responsible for the theft of the house in 1932.

Carsten speaks then, and Roland translates. "Ever since we learned from the newspaper story that a Jewish family lived here and was forced out of this house," he says, "we have tried to think of a way to acknowledge what happened. And here is what we would like to do: we would like to erect a plaque on the outside gate, right on Gartenstrasse, that says something like 'This house was owned from 1919 until 1932 by a Jewish businessman, Alex Goldschmidt. He was forced to sell it for far less than it was worth during the time of National Socialism. He was later murdered in Auschwitz.' Carsten pauses. "What do you think of that idea? Would we have your permission to do that?"

I pause for a moment, then quickly say that, although I would have to think about the particulars of the plaque's wording, the idea itself is very welcome, very moving. I tell him and Monica, "*Vielen Dank!* Thank you both very much for your kindness."

We exchange addresses and phone numbers, promise to keep in touch regarding the plaque, say our goodbyes, and silently drive back to the Neidhardts.

That night it takes me forever to fall asleep. Again and again, I move through the beautiful house, admiring this or that aspect of its treasures. I imagine Alex's family celebrating holidays there, birthdays, graduations, and the coming of spring. I remember Alex's strawberry patch and Günther's chicken run. I estimate that the house is probably worth 2, 3, or even 5 million dollars and recall that Alex received a paltry 26,000 marks for it, approximately 10,400 U.S. dollars. I think of the Meyerbohlens' offer of a plaque and my ready acceptance of the offer. As I lie awake, staring upward through the darkness, I find myself wishing that my response had been different. I imagine being back in the elegant dining room with its clinking wine glasses, saying to the Meyerbohlens, "Yes, a plaque would be a nice way to acknowledge the crime that took place here nearly eighty years ago. Or we could do something else. I could give you twenty-six thousand marks and *you could give me back my fucking house!*"

That, of course, would be unreasonable. The Meyerbohlens are completely innocent, as I'd assured them. But those who were guilty have managed to slither away through the broken foundations of history, and who is left to settle up? The deadline for filing a claim with the German government passed long ago. My father never filed such a claim, preferring to wash his hands of all bureaucratic reminders of the murders. So what is left for my generation? Plaques? Memorials? Marches? How do these well-meaning but inadequate gestures compensate for what we have lost? Is restitution many decades after a crime rendered meaningless by the passing of those decades? Would a plaque outside my family's house on Gartenstrasse in the tiniest way make up for the legalized theft of that house, to say nothing of the murders of its owners? And would the placement of a plaque allow the good burghers of Oldenburg to heave a contented sigh and say, "Good. That's taken care of. All better now"? Would it take them off the hook? And yet, is no plaque—the continuation of the silence Roland spoke of this afternoon—a more fitting solution? Might someone passing by 34 Gartenstrasse read about Alex Goldschmidt and recognize the plaque as an eloquent warning not to repeat the crimes of the past—especially if that plaque spawned other plaques throughout Oldenburg and across the country?

I try to silence these thoughts and welcome sleep. My journey recommences in the morning with a train trip to Hamburg, and I need rest. But, as I know so well, this is as much a journey into my family's past as it is a venture of the complicated present. Try as I might, I cannot escape those years of pain and sorrow. And I remember the words of William Faulkner that I quoted as an epigraph in my first book. "The past is never dead. It isn't even past."

4

Hamburg

TUESDAY, MAY 17, 2011. We awaken to find fair May overthrown, her sweet state usurped by an illegitimate and bullying November. Rain falls in sheets, often flung in our faces by sudden squalls, and the mild temperatures of our first week are mere teasing memories. But I enjoy the thought that we will be experiencing Hamburg rather as a sardonic anonymous traveler described its weather back in the eighteenth century, calling it "on the whole somewhat raw, damp and cold most days of the year, just like most of the people." Alex and Helmut had a similar climatological encounter on a May day in 1939 during their one visit to Hamburg, when they thought they were bidding their final farewells to their European lives.

We drive our Meriva to the Oldenburg *Bahnhof*, or train station, and purchase, for twenty-nine euros, a ticket that would allow Amy and me to travel anywhere by train throughout Lower Saxony and as far east as Hamburg, and to take as many rail journeys as we'd like, between 9:00 a.m. today and 3:00 a.m. tomorrow. We are deeply impressed by this evidence of Germany's support for public transportation We consult the bright-yellow schedules that adorn the central waiting area, and learn that we can board a train on Track 7 at 9:46, arrive in Bremen at 10:39, change trains, and pull into Hamburg at 11:42, having traveled a distance of roughly two hundred kilometers. At precisely 9:46, I discover, and not for the first time, that in Germany the trains do indeed run on time.

Our train to Bremen is a local that stops at several hamlets along the way and in the larger community of Delmenhorst. My father used to tell me that, in his day, Delmenhorst was known as a linoleum manufacturing center and that you could always smell the nascent floor covering from the station. So as we roll into town, I lower a window and inhale deeply, but perhaps because of the wind and rain and perhaps because I have no idea what linoleum smells like, I notice nothing out of the ordinary.

I think of my father again during our brief stopover in the bustling train station in Bremen. As a boy, he frequently accompanied his mother on rail journeys to Bremen to visit her family of well-to-do coffee importers. As a child, he made many a visit to the city's thirteenth-century St. Peter's Cathedral and a single visit to the crypt of the eleventh-century Church of Our Lady, where he was so terrorized by its collection of mummified remains that he still shuddered to speak of it in his tenth decade of life.

Our next train leaves promptly—naturally—at 10:50 and pulls into the immense Hamburg *Hauptbahnhof* two minutes early. The Central Station, as it's known in English, opened for business on St. Nicholas Day, 1906, and claims to be the busiest railway station in Germany and, after Paris, the second busiest in all Europe. Today, the hordes of Hamburgers thronging the station are made more imposing by the umbrellas they wield as they stride rapidly through the vast interior, which includes twenty separate tracks and an overhead emporium with restaurants, flower shops, bakeries, and a fully stocked pharmacy.

We find our way to the U-Bahn, or subway, and navigate the underground system for a distance of six stops, emerging at St. Pauli Landungsbrücken, just steps from the River Elbe. The foul weather surprises us anew with its undeniable rudeness. Leaning into a stiff wind, our eyes assaulted by sheets of horizontal rain, we trudge slowly down one of several movable bridges leading to the long landing pier that for more than a century and a half has been an embarkation point for transatlantic voyages. The tide is high, gulls wheel and shriek overhead, and the clouds and mist conspire together to reduce visibility to mere yards. Through the gloom, however, it is possible to see a neon sign on the opposite bank of the Elbe advertising a long-running production of the musical *The Lion King*.

The long pier, more than the length of seven football fields, was heavily bombed during the Second World War and rebuilt during the 1950s and '60s. Despite today's wind and weather, restaurants along the pier are serving English-style fish and chips and traditional German brews. Several hundred yards to the west, a sizable Greek tanker is tied up, and immediately in front of us, a small catamaran is readying for a tour to the island of Helgoland in the North Sea. It is, apparently, just a normal Tuesday on the Hamburg docks.

On such a day as this, I repeat to myself over and over, on a May evening seventy-two years ago, my grandfather and uncle set off on a voyage from this very spot—a voyage that was supposed to end in freedom for them and eventually for the whole Goldschmidt clan. I lean on a railing and squint through the wind and rain, trying to peer past the decades and conjure up a vision of their unfortunate vessel. There is water on my cheeks, the fresh mixing with the salt in the manner of the River Elbe giving way seventy miles downstream to the inexorable pull of the sea.

BEGINNING IN 1847, a new fleet of ships began weighing anchor from the port of Hamburg and sailing to destinations all over the globe. Most of the journeys ended in the New World, in Rio de Janeiro, Buenos Aires, Guayaquil, and Havana; in New Orleans, Baltimore, Boston, Montreal, Halifax, and New York City. These were the ships of the mighty *Hamburg Amerikanische Packetfahrt Actien Gesellschaft*—literally, the Hamburg American Packet-Shipping Joint Stock Company— or HAPAG for short, also known simply as the Hamburg-America Line. In the company's early years, HAPAG ships made the crossing from Hamburg to New York via Southampton in forty days. By the beginning of the twentieth century, the journey had been reduced to less than a week.

Many celebrated ships flew the blue and white HAPAG flag. In September 1858, the SS *Austria* caught fire in the middle of the

North Atlantic and sank, killing 463 of its 538 passengers. Among the survivors was Theodore Eisfeld, the music director of the New York Philharmonic, who had managed to lash himself to a plank and drifted on rough seas for two days and nights without food or water before being rescued. In 1900, the 16,500-ton SS *Deutschland* made history by sailing from Hamburg to New York in just over five days, maintaining a speed of twenty-two knots. Twelve years later, HAPAG's *Amerika* was the first ship to send radio signals warning the luxury liner *Titanic* of icebergs in the vicinity.

But in the storied chronicles of the Hamburg-America Line, which merged in 1970 with Bremen's North German Lloyd to form today's Hapag-Lloyd Corporation, no ship rivals the infamy of the SS *St. Louis*. She was built by the Bremer-Vulkan Shipyards in Bremen, at the time the largest civilian shipbuilding company in the German Empire, and launched on May 6, 1928. Her maiden voyage, with stops in Boulogne-sur-Mer, France, and Southampton, England, en route to New York City, began on March 29, 1929. The *St. Louis* was among the largest ships in the entire HAPAG line, weighing 16,732 tons and measuring 575 feet in length. Diesel powered, gliding through the water on the strength of twin triple-bladed propellers, she regularly reached speeds of sixteen knots as she sailed the trans-Atlantic route from Hamburg to Halifax, Nova Scotia, and New York, and on occasional cruises to the Caribbean. Her cabins and tourist berths were designed to accommodate 973 passengers. She was, in every measure of the phrase, a luxury liner; her gleaming brochures proclaimed, "The *St. Louis* is a ship on which one travels securely and lives in comfort. There is everything one can wish for that makes life on board a pleasure."

By the spring of 1939, the *St. Louis* had been serving its largely well-heeled clientele for ten years. The single voyage for which she remains most famous was about to commence, brought about by the confluence of several interlocking events.

On January 24, 1939, Nazi Field Marshal Hermann Göring appointed Reinhard Heydrich to direct the Central Office for Jewish Emigration. The Final Solution to what the Third Reich termed the Jewish Problem still lay several years in the future; for now the goal was simply to get as many Jews out of Germany as possible. Heydrich knew Claus-Gottfried Holthusen, the director of the Hamburg-America Line, and knew also that, since 1934, the Reich had become the majority shareholder in HAPAG, thus compromising the independence that the shipping company had enjoyed for the past ninety years. And Heydrich was aware that HAPAG had recently been troubled by financial set-backs exacerbated by the uncertain international situation. On its last voyage from New York, for instance, the *St. Louis* had sailed with only about a third of her berths occupied.

Heydrich immediately recognized an opportunity that would be mutually beneficial for the Reich and for HAPAG. He informed Göring and Propaganda Minister Joseph Goebbels about the facts as he saw them, and by the middle of April, they had arranged that the *St. Louis* would sail from Hamburg to Havana, Cuba, on May 13, bearing nearly a thousand Jewish refugees. Everyone involved was satisfied. Göring relished the opportunity to demonstrate to Chancellor Hitler that he was ridding the Reich of Jews. Goebbels perceived the nearly perfect propaganda possibilities: Germans would be pleased that more Jews were leaving the country, while the international community, still shocked from the reports of *Kristallnacht* violence, would observe that Germany was graciously allowing its Jews to leave unharmed and unimpeded—and on a luxury liner, no less. The Hamburg-America Line would turn a profit on a voyage at a time when it sorely needed one. (While the *St. Louis* passengers would be refugees, to be sure, they would be charged the standard fares of 800 Reichsmarks for first class and 600 Reichsmarks for tourist class.) And last, and certainly least, the Jews themselves would surely appreciate this highly civilized manner of being booted out of their own country.

The unmistakable message of the November Pogrom had sunk in for a majority of Germany's Jews, and they began a determined scramble to flee. In 1938, the number of Jewish émigrés from Germany numbered about thirty-five thousand. During the following year, that figure nearly doubled, to sixty-eight thousand. In the days and weeks following *Kristallnacht*, lines were long outside foreign embassies and consulates in all major German cities, as Jews waited to obtain the necessary papers to apply for visas. While every German Jew felt the pressure to leave, some were under more immediate duress than others.

After nearly a month of unspeakably harsh treatment in Sachsenhausen, Alex Goldschmidt was released on December 7, 1938, and informed in no uncertain terms that he had six months to leave the country of his birth or face a second arrest. So my grandfather shakily returned home to Oldenburg and, after spending a week or so recovering from his ordeal and talking matters over with his family, he took the train to Bremen and visited the Cuban consulate. There he applied for permission to emigrate to Cuba in the spring, filling out an application for himself and one for his son Helmut. They planned to establish residency in the New World and to send for the rest of the family a few months later. It must have seemed an eminently logical and sound strategy.

Cuba was among the few places on earth that even considered taking in Jewish refugees during the months following the November Pogrom. In July 1938, delegates from Cuba and thirty other countries gathered in France for the Evian Conference, to discuss what to do about the increasing number of Jews who wanted out of Nazi Germany. Once both the United States and the United Kingdom made it clear that they had no intention of increasing their quota of immigrants from Germany and Austria, the Evian Conference adjourned with most of the countries following the lead of its major players. The conference was ultimately considered a tragic failure, with Chaim Weizman, the future first president of Israel, declaring that "the world now seemed to be divided into two parts: those places where the Jews could not live and those where they could not enter." Cuba, at least, presented itself as a theoretical haven, and Alex, his determination still intact despite his weeks in Sachsenhausen, saw the island nation as a practical solution to his family's latest challenge.

Over the next several months, the Goldschmidt family did all it could to conserve its resources, as Alex knew that many fees, both legal and extralegal, would accompany the emigration process. Now that his business had been officially liquidated, he had no steady source of income. So on December 28, Alex moved his family from the apartment on Ofenerstrasse to a smaller, less expensive apartment on Nordstrasse, just a few blocks from the railroad station.

Alex, Toni, Eva, and Helmut spent the next few months nervously waiting for news from the Cuban consulate in Bremen. Finally, in early March 1939, the family learned that Cuba had granted visas for Alex and Helmut. But the next day, a letter arrived from Manuel Benitez Gonzalez, the director-general of Cuba's Office of Immigration, inform-ing them that Alex and Helmut would each have to purchase a special landing certificate if they intended to disembark in Havana. The price for each certificate was 450 Reichsmarks, a small fortune given the ever more Spartan circumstances of the Goldschmidt family.

Alex realized that they would have to tighten their belts yet again before the journey west. So on March 21, they moved to an even smaller apartment at 17 Staulinie. They were now only a block from the train station, close enough that the constant chug and chuff of engines caused their walls to shiver. A month later, the so-called Benitez certificates arrived. Alex placed the precious documents along with the visas into a cardboard folder, which he stored under his mattress. He checked their safety every night and every morning and several times during the day; other than his wedding ring, he owned nothing of greater value than those four pieces of paper.

The time had now come to secure passage to Cuba. He purchased two tourist class tickets for the May 13 voyage of the *St. Louis*, at a price of 600 Reichmarks (about $240) each. Alex was also obliged to pay an additional 460 Reichsmarks (about $185) for what the Hamburg-America Line termed a "customary contingency fee." This additional expense covered a return voyage to Germany should what HAPAG called "circumstances beyond our control" arise. The line insisted that this "contingency fee" was fully refundable, should the journey proceed as planned.

Alex returned to Oldenburg in triumph, bearing his precious purchases. They had been extremely expensive, but now he had everything he needed—visas, landing certificates, tickets—to apply for a passport. On Monday, May 1, he and Helmut visited the Olden-burg offices of the Emigration Advisory Board to fill out individual

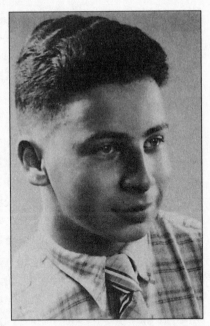

The photos taken of Alex and Helmut that they used for the passports that enabled them to board the St. Louis. *These were also the photos that, attached to the space above our rear-view mirror, accompanied us on our journey.*

applications for the "issuance of a single-family passport for domestic and foreign use."

Father and son completed their forms in much the same manner. On the line marked "profession," Alex wrote "salesman" and Helmut "student." Thanks to this application, I know that my grandfather's eyes were gray and my uncle's were blue. On the line marked destination, they both wrote "Cuba." Both practiced the same small deception: under their address, which they listed as 17 Staulinie, there was a line requesting any previous addresses within the last year. Although the family had in fact moved twice in the past twelve months, they declared that they had lived on Staulinie "for years." Perhaps Alex thought that a history of frequent moves might indicate a troublesome lack of stability. Whatever the reason, their white lie seems to have passed unnoticed.

Under their signatures—both of which included the repulsive required "Israel"—appeared the official assurance that "the applicant is not listed in the register of banned permits" and two questions posed by the Gestapo: "Is it assumed that the applicant wants to use the permit to avoid prosecution or execution?" and "Is it assumed that the permit to travel would endanger the internal or external security or other demands of the Reich?" To each question, on each application, an official wrote, "*Nein!*"

One week later, their applications were approved and their passports issued. The passports cost three Reichsmarks each and were valid from May 9, 1939, to May 9, 1940. With the *St. Louis* scheduled to depart the following week, the family's flight to freedom was about to begin.

Meanwhile, about 450 kilometers southeast of Oldenburg, another family was also preparing to escape from Germany aboard the *St. Louis*. Joseph Karliner owned a general store, which sold groceries, hardware, and fertilizer, in a small town in Silesia, near the German-Polish border. On the night of the November Pogrom, his store was ransacked, and the next morning he was arrested and sent to the Buchenwald concentration camp near the German city of Weimar. Like Alex Goldschmidt, Joseph Karliner was held prisoner for about three weeks and was released on condition that he leave Germany within six months. He, his wife, and their four children initially purchased permits to emigrate to Shanghai, China. But when they learned that the Cuban consulate in Hamburg was selling visas and landing certificates for emigration to Cuba, the Karliners sought refuge in the Caribbean nation instead, hoping it would be a stepping-stone to the United States. They followed much the same procedure as had Alex and Helmut, and by early May 1939, the Karliners set off for Hamburg and the luxury liner *St. Louis*.

The ship was being readied for her voyage to Havana inside shed 76 on the Hamburg waterfront, where she had lain at anchor since her most recent return from New York City. Her captain was Gustav Schroeder, known as "the smallest officer in the German merchant navy"; he stood only five feet, four inches tall. Captain Schroeder may have been short but, at age fifty-three, he was also in superb shape, the result of a twenty-minute regimen of calisthenics every day. He was apparently a real German in his personal habits, bringing to his command the traits of

*The courtly and courageous Gustav
Schroeder, captain of the SS St. Louis
beginning in February 1939.*
(Courtesy of the United States
Holocaust Memorial Museum)

punctuality, order, and precision, as well as a courtliness of manner suggesting an earlier era. Captain Schroeder had thirty-seven years at sea behind him, but in May 1939, he had spent a mere four months at the helm of the *St. Louis*. He was also, despite six years of recruitment efforts by Germany's ruling party, a fervent anti-Nazi.

Captain Schroeder was well aware of the dangers associated with his refusal to join the National Socialists. His predecessor, Captain Friedrich Buch, who had commanded the *St. Louis* since her maiden voyage ten years earlier, had also resisted becoming a party member. Then, in February 1939, Captain Buch was suddenly and summarily dismissed from the bridge at the end of a return voyage to Hamburg, hustled off the ship by agents of the Gestapo, the secret police, and delivered to an unknown fate. Nevertheless, Captain Schroeder was determined to maintain his independence. He politely but firmly declined even to wear an official Nazi lapel pin.

He was unable to ignore the facts, however, that among his crew of 231 were 6 firemen who were in reality undercover Gestapo agents, and that his second-class steward, Otto Schiendick, was a Nazi provocateur connected to the *Abwehr*, or German military intelligence. When Claus-Gottfried Holthusen informed Captain Schroeder of the unusual circumstances of the upcoming voyage to Cuba, the captain realized that the comfort of his passengers could be severely compromised by the political sympathies of his steward and the so-called firemen. He summoned his crew to a stateroom of the *St. Louis* and told them in no uncertain terms that they would, in ten days' time, be expected to serve a full complement of Jewish passengers. He concluded with a stern admonition that any crew member who could not promise to perform his job with professionalism should promptly resign his commission. Neither Schiendick nor the firemen uttered a word.

Over those next ten days, and under the watchful eye of Gustav Schroeder, the crew of the *St. Louis* stocked the ship with all the luxuries of first-class ocean travel: caviar; salmon, both smoked and fresh; the finest cuts of meat; hundreds of cases of robust German beer and mellow Rhine wine; even the highest-quality toilet paper. Often, Captain Schroeder and his purser, Ferdinand Mueller, ignored orders from HAPAG headquarters to substitute cheaper meats or to remove fine cameras from the ship's shop and expensive cosmetics from the hairdressing salon. The captain had decided that since the refugees had paid full fare, they deserved no less than any other *St. Louis* passengers had enjoyed.

The refugees had been purchasing tickets on a first-come, first-served basis since the voyage to Havana had been announced in mid-April. The last of the tickets was sold on Sunday, May 7; the ship was fully booked, all cabins and berths accounted for. By Friday, May 12, more than nine hundred refugees had begun streaming into Hamburg, making their way to the pier below the Landungsbrücken. The city was in the midst of a jubilant observance of its 750th birthday, and the brightly colored bunting and ornate Japanese-style lanterns hanging from streetlights provided a festive appearance. Yet Hamburg's streets were also lined with red-and-black swastika flags, and the banners flew from the masts of nearly every ship in the harbor, the *St. Louis* included.

That afternoon, several dozen passengers made the slow walk up the gangways to board the *St. Louis*. They were Orthodox Jews who were following the Sabbath requirement that no journey can commence between sundown on Friday and dusk on Saturday. Given the extraordinary nature of this voyage, HAPAG officials had waived all usual boarding procedures.

On the following day, May 13, the rest of the passengers, including Alex and Helmut and the four Karliners, passed through shed 76 and made their way on board. It was a cold, raw, rainy day, which must have exacerbated the refugees' feelings that, no matter the ugliness and terror of the previous months and years, today they were leaving their homeland under forced circumstances, very possibly never to return. My father, who traveled from Berlin that day to say goodbye, recalled that the gloomy weather seemed an appropriate backdrop to his feelings of foreboding. Herbert Karliner, Joseph's younger son, remembers that he and his siblings were tremendously excited at the prospect of an ocean voyage, but his parents and the other adults on board were clearly saddened and subdued. HAPAG officials and Captain Schroeder, however, were doing everything in their powers to make their passengers feel welcome and to allay their fears. The crew politely assisted the passengers with their luggage, graciously ushered them to their cabins, and made them feel at home aboard the ship. This was the first time in years that Alex, Helmut, and the other refugees had been treated with respect by German officialdom. There was a momentary break in the courtesy when Steward Schiendick and his fireman gathered around the piano in the nightclub on B Deck and began singing a boisterous medley of Nazi songs, but Captain Schroeder put a stop to it immediately and sternly warned the miscreants against any further troublemaking.

Down on the pier, under a makeshift tent that had been hastily erected against the rain, a band organized by the Hamburg-America Line played through its repertory of popular tunes to serenade the departing refugees. As the afternoon advanced, the musicians performed such favorites as "Vienna, City of My Dreams," "Muss I Denn"—a traditional German melody that twenty years later became a number-one hit for Elvis Presley as "Wooden Heart"—and several of the Hungarian Dances by Hamburg's most famous musical son, Johannes Brahms.

But as evening descended, the refugees' gloom deepened, and ersatz jollity soon gave way to the finality of farewell. At precisely 7:30 p.m., the ship's horn uttered three mighty blasts, the gangways were hauled up, and the hawsers were loosed from the pilings. Slowly, ever so slowly, the *St. Louis* edged away from the pier into the River Elbe and toward the North Sea.

My father stood on the dock, surrounded by other solemn well-wishers, first waving to Alex and Helmut as they leaned over the railing toward him, and then merely watching as the ship grew smaller, his father and brother sailing away into the fog. As an old man, he wrote down his memories of those moments: "I felt somehow that I would never see them again. Even now, so many years later, there are times when I hear the eerie, moaning sound of the ship's horn, when I see the disappearing boat before my eyes, getting more and more enshrouded by clouds and rain, engulfed by an uncharted future."

TUESDAY, MAY 17, 2011. It is probably high time to come in out of the rain. The low clouds, insistent winds, and steady showers cast a spell reminiscent of that May evening so long ago, but try as I might, I cannot even remotely recreate in my mind what it must have been like for the refugees on board the *St. Louis* as it pulled away from this pier or for those, like my father, left standing on this very spot as they cheerfully waved and silently wished the voyagers well. So with a last long look at the iron waters of the Elbe, we trudge back over the landing bridge to St. Pauli Hafenstrasse, the main boulevard that parallels the river.

It is still only mid-afternoon, and before we return to the *Hauptbahnhof* for our journey back to Oldenburg, we set out on two musical pilgrimages. We first walk north along the Helgoländer Allee for a quarter-mile or so until we reach one of the most notorious avenues in all Germany, the Reeperbahn. For centuries, as long as Hamburg has been a world port, sailors, salesmen, and other roustabouts have stumbled up from the waterfront to join the lascivious parade of lusts and self-indulgence for which this thoroughfare and its side streets are known. Sex shops and honky-tonks, clip joints and night clubs, arcades and saloons and shadowy, nameless interiors promising every pleasure under the sun and moon operate twenty-four hours a day, lit by lurid neon at night and, on this gloomy day, by the gray sky and the eager, furtive desires of the passersby. In the midst of this hormone-fueled atmosphere, the Beatles found their identities and grew into master musicians between 1960 and 1962.

We walk about six blocks west along the Reeperbahn until we come to the corner of a cross street called Grosse Freiheit ("Great Freedom") and a monument known as the Beatles Platz. Metal statues of all five Beatles (their first bassist, Stuart Sutcliffe, played with them in Hamburg) surround a circular plaza made of black concrete to resemble a spinning phonograph record. We pay our solemn, devoted respects and then walk up Grosse Freiheit to the Indra, the night club where the Beatles first performed in Hamburg as teenagers newly liberated from Liverpool.

As I gaze at the Indra's elephant logo and try to imagine walking inside fifty years ago to hear the still-ragged yet already brilliant sound the Beatles developed in this manic laboratory, I reflect on the rightness of paying homage to this music in this place. Like millions of my generation, I was thrilled, moved, and electrified when I first heard the Beatles, on radio station KXOK in my hometown of St. Louis. Like so many of my contemporaries, I think I was initially attracted to the band's youthful, vibrant sound at least in part because they were a joyful antidote to the grief that had descended on America when its vibrant young president was assassinated just seventy-six days before the Beatles made their stunning debut on the *Ed Sullivan Show*.

Then I take the next step and realize another, more personal reason that I'd fallen in love with the Beatles: they made me *happy*. That was no small thing, growing up as I did in a family that lived steeped in sorrow every day, a sadness that could be traced in large measure to the tragic voyage that began right here in Hamburg. What a joyful relief it had been for my eleven- and twelve-year-old self to retreat to my room and listen to those revelatory songs of love and hope. My parents had their unhappy memories and their own music. The Beatles were mine. As we begin to retrace our steps, we walk through the

Beatles Platz and I lay my hand on the statues of John and Paul and whisper, "Thank you."

I was aware of a gulf between my music and my parents' music in my youth, but that gap began to close as I grew older and came to love what Bach and Mozart, Beethoven and Schubert, Tchaikovsky and Mahler and Debussy had left for me to discover. One master I didn't take to right away, however, was Johannes Brahms, who was born here in Hamburg in 1833. I once told my mother that I couldn't figure out why everyone made such a fuss over Brahms. She paused a moment and then said to me, "You will. Wait till you're forty-five or fifty. Then you'll understand."

She was right, more than right. There's an underlying melancholy in nearly every note Brahms wrote that may only speak to us once we comprehend the transitory nature of all things, an understanding and appreciation of life that only a certain number of years on this earth can provide.

The Beatles still thrill me, still please me with their vibrant sounds of youthful exuberance. Brahms reassures me in the manner of a wise and kind companion who is equally comfortable in the presence of fleeting joys and immutable sorrow. I feel deeply fortunate that, as I continue this journey in Alex and Helmut's footsteps, I can turn to all of them.

Brahms was born no more than a mile or so east of here. We retrace our steps along the Reeperbahn, under skies that are still gray but no longer rainy. Leaving the St. Pauli district, we turn right on Budapest Strasse and left along the leafy Holstenwall, walking on for several blocks until we come to the Johannes Brahms Platz, an empty, rather soulless expanse of pavement. Around the corner, we find a monument to Brahms on the approximate site where his birthplace stood until it was destroyed in an Allied bombing campaign in 1943. Amy takes my picture as I pose beside the monument and I hum to myself the solemn opening lines of the "All flesh is grass" movement from his magnificent German Requiem.

A few steps away, on Peterstrasse, we find the Brahms Museum. The docent on duty on this quiet Tuesday afternoon shares her memories of days long gone on the waterfront, when dredgers scooped up sand from the bottom of the Elbe to aid in the river's navigation, making a high-pitched squealing sound as they worked. "How Brahms would have hated that," I observe, and she laughs.

Brahms endured a love-hate relationship with this city all his life. As a young boy, he played the piano in some of the roughest bars in St. Pauli and was subjected to unwanted attention from the prostitutes and their customers, experiences that, he later claimed, scarred him for life and made a loving relationship with a woman impossible. Brahms hoped for years that the Hamburg Philharmonic would hire him to be its music director, but despite his many accomplishments and honored status, the orchestra never did. For that reason, Brahms insisted, he lived the life of a vagabond and never found true happiness. Yet his music touched the hearts of listeners the world over, and when he died in 1897, alone in his cramped apartment in Vienna, the flags on all the ships in Hamburg harbor flew at half mast.

As we head back to the Landungsbrücken U-Bahn station, I catch a final glimpse of that harbor and think again of the departure of the *St. Louis* and how Alex and Helmut must have felt on that dreary day. Despite all they had endured, they must have felt some measure of hope knowing that the voyage that would deliver them and their family to a better world was finally underway.

Forty minutes later, we are sitting comfortably in our seats on the train returning us to Oldenburg. It's warm and dry and, nestled on Amy's shoulder and rocked by the rhythm of the rails, I fall into a peaceful doze. But, despite myself, my thoughts are with the voyagers out on the ocean, and I recall some rueful words from Brahms' beautiful *Schicksalslied*, or Song of Destiny: "It is our lot to find rest nowhere."

5

The Voyage of the *St. Louis*

"THERE IS A SOMEWHAT NERVOUS DISPOSITION among the passengers. Everyone seems convinced they will never see Germany again. Touching departure scenes have taken place. Many seem light of heart, having left their homes. Others take it heavily. But pure sea air, good food, and attentive service will soon provide the usual worry-free atmosphere of a long sea voyage. Painful impressions on land disappear quickly at sea, and soon seem merely like dreams."

Gustav Schroeder, the captain of the *St. Louis*, entered those words into his journal as his ship made its way down the River Elbe toward the North Sea and the Atlantic Ocean. It would be best, he thought, if he and his crew could instill that "worry-free atmosphere" as quickly as possible among his passengers. So he instructed his purser and First Officer to lead a tour of the ship's splendid facilities. Over the next hour, they showed passengers the swimming pool, gymnasium, and sports area, which included regulation shuffleboard courts, on A Deck; the nightclub on B Deck; and the dining hall that featured crisp white linens, leaded crystal glassware, and sterling silverware on C Deck. The first-class social hall had been converted into a synagogue for the duration of the voyage. The purser and First Officer neglected to tell the passengers that, at the express order of Captain Schroeder, a portrait of Adolf Hitler had been taken down from its prominent spot on the forward wall of the social hall.

The *St. Louis* amenities included a hairdresser and barber shop, well-stocked bars on every deck, and a shop that sold binoculars, cameras, books, postcards, and other souvenirs. Purchases had to be made using "shipboard money"—credits purchased from HAPAG up to the value of 230 Reichsmarks—that was good only at sea and could not be reconverted into real currency at the conclusion of the voyage. That shipboard money was necessary, as most of the refugees had been allowed to leave Germany with no more than 10 Reichsmarks in cash, only about four dollars, each.

Thirty-eight hours after departing Hamburg, at 9:30 on Monday morning, May 15, the *St. Louis* arrived in Cherbourg, France, to pick up a few more passengers and to bring aboard several crates of fresh fruits and vegetables for the ship's kitchens. Early that afternoon, the *St. Louis* once again weighed anchor and glided out into the English Channel to begin the transatlantic portion of the voyage. With the newly added passengers, there were now 937 refugees on board. Almost all of them were, like Alex and Helmut, Jews fleeing the Third Reich under great duress. Most had been citizens of Germany, some were from Eastern Europe, a few were Spaniards seeking sanctuary from the Civil War. None of them was traveling for pleasure.

They experienced more rain, fog, and some choppy seas in the channel, but as the ship left the European continent behind, the sun broke through a bank of clouds that lay upon the western horizon. Captain Schroeder ordered the engine room to achieve the maximum speed of sixteen knots. At that moment, only the most pessimistic of the passengers could have felt anything other than hope and relief as the *St. Louis* assumed a steady southwest course.

But they were sailing in blissful ignorance. Members of the Cuban government in Havana, Nazi leaders in Berlin, the U.S. State Department in Washington, and Jewish relief and refugee organizations on two continents were already aware that something was amiss and that the passengers on board the *St. Louis* might encounter difficulties when the vessel entered Cuban waters.

A confluence of economic issues, blatant anti-Semitism, corruption, greed, and political power plays within the Cuban government had begun to shape events. Cuba was still trying to dig itself out from the effects of the worldwide Depression, and unemployment was high. Many Cubans thought that there were already far too many immigrants competing with native-born citizens for scarce jobs. The island's four thousand Jews were an obvious target for the usual charges of international financial manipulations and shady behind-the-scenes string-pulling. An active Cuban Nazi Party encouraged the growth of anti-Semitism by publishing such pamphlets as *Under the Jewish Communist Yoke*.

Three Cuban newspapers, all of which were owned by Jose Ignacio Rivero, an avowed admirer of Adolf Hitler, Spanish Generalissimo Francisco Franco, and Italian dictator Benito Mussolini, also encouraged such sentiments. Rivero had recently been invited to the Italian Embassy in Havana to receive an award for his tireless support of the fascist cause, and he had begun a campaign in his newspapers to restrict Jewish immigration to Cuba. One of his editorials declared, "Against this Jewish invasion we must react with the same energy as have other peoples of the globe. Otherwise we will be absorbed, and the day will come when the blood of our martyrs and heroes shall have served solely to enable the Jews to enjoy a country conquered by our ancestors."

The flashpoint of resistance to the orderly arrival of the *St. Louis*, however, was a dispute among Cuban politicians involving those ancient obsessions, money and power. Manuel Benitez Gonzalez, the immigration officer who had sold his landing certificates to Alex, Helmut, and hundreds of other passengers, was a protégé of Army Chief of Staff Fulgencio Batista, who in a few years would become president of Cuba. But well connected though he was, Benitez was on the outs with the current Cuban president, Federico Laredo Bru. And Benitez had made other enemies within the Cuban government through his shameless profiteering. By selling his landing certificates without checking with other officials, he had managed to amass a personal fortune of nearly a million dollars. Some of those other officials demanded a share of the certificate racket; when Benitez refused, they resolved to kill his golden goose.

So it was that the forces opposed to Jewish immigration on economic or bigoted grounds and those who were determined to halt the lucrative sale of the Benitez certificates found common cause. On the morning of Thursday, May 4, one of Rivero's newspapers reported that a ship would arrive in Havana later that month carrying a thousand Jewish refugees who had obtained permission to land from a rogue officer within the Bru administration. Later that day, a member of the Cuban congress took to the floor to demand that the president issue an ordinance "prohibiting repeated immigrations of Hebrews who have been inundating the Republic and prohibiting permits that are being issued for the entrance of such immigrants to Cuba, until this House can approve a proposed law imposing severe penalties upon fraudulent immigration that makes a joke of the laws of the Republic."

Unfortunately for the refugees on board the *St. Louis*, President Bru chose this moment to demonstrate to his countrymen just who was in charge of Cuban immigration. On the day after the congressional demand, Friday, May 5, eight days before the *St. Louis* steamed out of Hamburg, Bru issued an order—coincidentally, given the number of passengers aboard the ill-fated ship, known as Decree 937—that invalidated all of the Benitez landing certificates. The order stipulated that only with written authorization from the Cuban secretaries of state, labor, and treasury, plus the posting of a $500 bond, could an immigrant gain legal entry into Havana. This announcement was for internal consumption only; though it was transmitted to high HAPAG officials, word never leaked down to the people most affected: the refugees themselves.

Two significant circumstances explain the Hamburg-America Line's decision to keep news of the decree from spreading. To put it another way, HAPAG wanted the voyage of the *St. Louis* to proceed smoothly, but for two different reasons. The first was quite simple: the line needed the money. After months of falling revenue, this excursion that promised 937 customers paying fares ranging from 600 to 800 Reichsmarks each, plus the "contingency" fee, was simply too big a windfall to forgo.

Then there was the more shadowy reason that HAPAG wanted the voyage to proceed: espionage. Otto Schiendick, the second-class steward and Nazi provocateur, was traveling to Cuba as a courier on behalf of German military intelligence, the *Abwehr*. The plan was for Schiendick to meet in Havana with a Nazi spy named Robert Hoffman, who would deliver to him a cache of important documents on top-secret subjects ranging from military installations throughout Central America to the potential vulnerability of the Panama Canal—topics of intense interest to a German military already dreaming of possible adventures in the Western Hemisphere. After securing this information, Schiendick would return to Hamburg with all possible speed on the return journey of the *St. Louis* and make his delivery to his *Abwehr* superiors. The plan was simple and airtight, especially given Hoffman's cover: assistant manager of the Havana offices of the Hamburg-America Line.

When HAPAG director Claus-Gottfried Holthusen learned of the existence of Decree 937, quite naturally he cabled Havana to ask for clarification of the situation. The next day, Luis Clasing, the manager of HAPAG's Havana office, informed Holthusen that he had received the "personal guarantee" of the Cuban immigration director that all would be well when the *St. Louis* reached Havana. Thus reassured, Holthusen kept the news of Decree 937 to himself and informed no one else, least of all Captain Schroeder and his passengers, who left Hamburg with no idea that anything untoward was awaiting them.

The citizens of Cuba soon learned of both Decree 937 and the imminent departure of the *St. Louis*. On Monday, May 8, whipped up by another savage editorial in one of Rivero's papers, forty thousand people attended a boisterous rally in downtown Havana. The organizers warned that this approaching boatload of new immigrants was yet another example of the worldwide Jewish threat. A speaker at the rally called upon his countrymen to "fight the Jews until the last one is driven out."

Such words were sweet music to the ears of Joseph Goebbels. The propaganda minister was eager to show the world that it was not just Germany that had no use for the Jews. He and his colleagues in the German Foreign Office hastily issued a statement. "In all parts of the world," it read, "the influx of Jews arouses the resistance of the native population and thus provides the best propaganda for Germany's Jewish policy. In North America, South America, France, Holland, Scandinavia, and Greece—wherever the Jewish migratory current flows—a marked growth of anti-Semitism is already noticeable. It must be the task of German foreign policy to encourage this anti-Semitic wave."

As the *St. Louis* steamed steadily onward, mounting internal and external pressures on the Cuban government threatened to prevent the ship from disembarking her passengers in a timely fashion. Such organizations as the London-based International Committee on Political Refugees, the American Jewish Joint Distribution Committee of New York, and the Jewish Relief Committee in Havana—all of which were following the progress of the journey—slowly came to the realization that trouble lay dead ahead.

The passengers on board the *St. Louis*, however, knew nothing of those matters and felt only giddy pleasure as they sailed ever closer to the warm waters of the Caribbean. Within a day or two of their departure from Hamburg, most of the adult refugees had cast off their sadness and began taking full advantage of the splendid amenities their vessel offered. A typical day began with a full breakfast that included everything from eggs and fruit to kippers and cheese. The older passengers would then enjoy a few hours reclining in deck chairs under the sun as they sipped from mugs of excellently brewed coffee. After retreating to the dining hall for lunch, they might engage in a game of shuffleboard or deck tennis or swim a few laps in the ship's pool and attend an afternoon tea dance. Younger passengers enjoyed playing a horse-race game in which wooden horses advanced around a track in accordance with the throw of ivory dice. At night, following another sumptuous meal, there were dances, movies, and lectures to enjoy. The amusements must have seemed equal parts marvelous and amazing to those refugees, many of whom had recently spent time in concentration camps and all of whom had spent years as second-class citizens in their own land.

Twelve-year-old Herbert Karliner played the horses, swam in the pool, and also indulged his fascination with long-distance communication by hanging around the telegraph operator, watching him send messages. The operator was very friendly and didn't object to Herbert's presence, but one day the young man came face to face with Captain Schroeder, who told him kindly but firmly that he was not allowed in the telegraph room and would have to leave immediately.

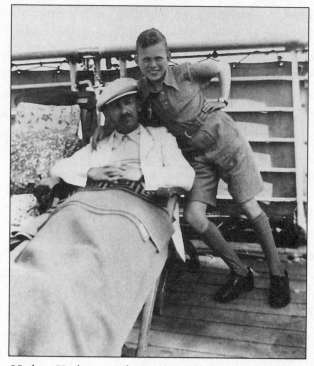

Herbert Karliner, aged 12, poses with his father, Joseph, on the top deck of the St. Louis.
(Courtesy of the United States Holocaust Memorial Museum)

I have no firsthand report on how Alex and Helmut spent their days and nights on board the *St. Louis*. But I imagine that Alex, only five months removed from his ordeal in Sachsenhausen, took full advantage of the opportunity to eat his fill three times a day and simply relax in a deck chair or in his berth. And I can see my uncle, just seventeen years old, checking out a book from the ship's library and reading lazily in the sun, or shyly making the acquaintance of some of the other young people aboard. Perhaps he exchanged a word and a smile or two with Ilse Karliner, Herbert's older sister, who was fifteen.

Ten days out from Hamburg, however, even as the *St. Louis* passengers were growing accustomed to their nice new routines, death intruded into their floating Arcadia. Moritz Weiler had been a professor at the University of Cologne for many years before the Nazis forced him to resign in 1936. The shock of losing his position as a respected academic had taken a toll on his health, and the effort required to flee the country of his birth had weakened him further. As his shipmates enjoyed the many charms of the voyage, Professor Weiler remained bedridden in cabin B-108, visited frequently by the ship's physician, Dr. Walter Glauner. Despite the doctor's best efforts, Weiler died on the morning of Tuesday, May 23. His widow, Recha Weiler, declared her wish that her husband be buried in Cuba, but Captain Schroeder, already gleaning that there might be complications upon their arrival, convinced her of the necessity of a burial at sea.

Shortly after 10:00 that night, after a brief funeral on A Deck attended by Captain Schroeder, First Officer Ostermeyer, and a few refugees, Professor Weiler's body was wrapped in his prayer shawl and then placed into a sailcloth shroud covered by the blue and white HAPAG flag. Then his body slid into the ocean. Remembering Weiler's passing several months later, the captain wrote, "It broke his heart to feel that in his old age he had to leave the land where, all his life long, he had worked on the best of terms with his colleagues. Seeing him in his reduced state, I felt that his will to live had gone." After the funeral, Captain Schroeder presented Recha Weiler with what would become for her a treasured memento: a map marked with the lonely spot in the Atlantic where her husband had been buried. There were now 936 passengers on board the *St. Louis*, most of whom had no idea that their number had been reduced by one.

Two nights later, on Thursday, May 25, the passengers enjoyed a costume ball in the ship's nightclub, a party that traditionally signaled the impending end of a voyage. The band played a series of Glenn Miller tunes and, with everyone assuming that their "shipboard money" would soon be worthless, a great deal of liquor was purchased and consumed, contributing to a most convivial atmosphere. The party finally broke up at three o'clock in the morning. Within twenty-five hours, on Saturday, May 27, the *St. Louis* pulled into Havana Harbor, her horn blasting most of the passengers awake at 4 a.m. The breakfast gong sounded at 4:30, and despite the early hour, the dining rooms were soon full of sleepy, eager people, excited that their two weeks at sea were nearly at an end.

Passengers on board the St. Louis, *some of whom had spent weeks in concentration camps six months earlier, enjoy a dance in the ship's ornate ballroom. Note the Star of David affixed to the central column.*
(Courtesy of the United States Holocaust Memorial Museum)

But as day broke, the passengers gradually became aware that something was wrong. The ship was still out in the harbor and hadn't tied up at the dock. Late on Friday afternoon, Captain Schroeder had received a cable from Luis Clasing, HAPAG's Havana director, instructing him to "not, repeat not, make any attempt to come alongside." Cuban President Bru was standing firm behind Decree 937 and had let the Hamburg authorities know about it in the most unambiguous manner possible. On Friday night, however, Robert Hoffman, who had his own reasons for wanting the *St. Louis* to disembark its passengers, had met with Manuel Benitez Gonzalez, the immigration director, who uttered soothing words of reassurance. "My friend, Bru has to keep up a pretense. Tonight he lets the ship into Cuban waters. Tomorrow he allows it into the harbor. The next day it will be at the pier. Then off they will come, and our worries are over. I am a Cuban. I understand the Cuban mind."

Early on Saturday morning, matters seemed to be moving forward as a white-suited Cuban doctor representing the Havana Port Authority drew up alongside the *St. Louis* and came aboard, to be greeted by Dr. Glauner and escorted to the bridge. There Captain Schroeder presented the Cuban doctor with the ship's manifest, which listed every passenger, and signed a statement in which he swore that none of them was "an idiot, or insane, or suffering from a contagious disease, or convicted of a felony or another crime involving moral turpitude." The Cuban doctor was unsatisfied, however, and insisted on a personal inspection. Every passenger was called to the social hall and filed slowly past the doctor, who made no comments but informed Dr. Glauner of his approval. When he left the ship and his launch sped back to land, everyone on board assumed that, the medical formality having been dispensed with, the *St. Louis* would now make her way to a pier. But she remained at anchor.

Over the next few days confusion reigned, as meetings and negotiations involving President Bru, Manuel Benitez Gonzalez, Captain Schroeder, Luis Clasing, and Milton Goldsmith of Havana's Jewish Relief Committee all failed to arrive at a satisfactory resolution. It was President Bru's unyielding position that the Benitez landing certificates were invalid and thus the vast majority of the *St. Louis* refugees would be entering Cuba illegally should they be allowed to disembark in Havana. Twenty-eight lucky passengers—twenty-two Jews who were able to pay the additional $500 to obtain approved visas, plus four Spaniards and two Cubans—were allowed off the ship. But President Bru stood firm where the rest of the 908 refugees were concerned.

At one point in the discussions, Cuban Secretary of State Juan Remos met with President Bru to argue the moral implications of denying asylum to these victims of Nazism and to remind the president that his stance might cost him the disfavor of the United States. Unbeknownst to the secretary, the plight of the *St. Louis* refugees had indeed become a topic for discussion in official American circles, but so far the direction of those discussions did not, in fact, contradict the Cuban president's position. Assistant U.S. Secretary of State George Messersmith wrote in a memorandum that it was his understanding that the United States would not "intervene in a matter of this kind which was purely outside of our sphere and entirely an internal matter of Cuba."

The abiding strategy of the United States in regard to Latin America for the previous six years had been known as the Good Neighbor Policy (GNP). Formally announced during his inaugural address by President Franklin D. Roosevelt in 1933 and reaffirmed by Secretary of State Cordell Hull later that year, the Good Neighbor Policy held that "no country has the right to intervene in the internal or external affairs of another." Since then, the GNP had led to the withdrawal of U.S. marines from Haiti and Nicaragua in 1934 and, in that same year, ended the lease agreement with Cuba permitting American naval stations on the island, with the exception of the base at Guantanamo Bay. By 1939, the GNP was viewed in Washington as a major foreign policy success story, winning wide support among Latin and South American nations, and a position not to be tampered with lightly. The saga of the *St. Louis*, therefore, would have to be settled by Cuban officials themselves without either overt or covert actions by the United States.

During that weekend, as the ship that was to have ushered them to freedom in the New World lay at anchor and in limbo in Havana Harbor, the 908 refugees passed the time as best they could in the hundred-degree heat and heavy humidity. They took snapshots of the city skyline and purchased bananas, coconuts, pineapples, and other tropical fruits from the enterprising vendors who drew up their little boats alongside the luxury liner. Some relatives of the refugees, who had come to the dock to welcome their families ashore, circled the *St. Louis* in private craft, shouting messages of patience and encouragement. A man paddled his canoe close enough to a second-class porthole to wave to his child, who was being held aloft by his wife. During the long hot nights, the crew of the *St. Louis* trained her searchlights onto the dark oily waters of the harbor to make sure that no one would take matters into his or her own hands and attempt to swim to shore.

On Monday, May 29, Robert Hoffman, the HAPAG assistant manager and *Abwehr* spy, was becoming increasingly nervous that

The St. Louis *at anchor in Havana harbor, as small boats containing relatives of the ship's passengers draw up alongside.*
(Courtesy of the Associated Press)

his mission might be compromised by the inability of his courier to reach dry land. He arranged for a few hours' shore leave for several *St. Louis* crew members, including Otto Schiendick. Shortly after 6 p.m., a launch containing the crewmen made its way from ship to shore, where Schiendick separated himself from the others and walked rapidly to the HAPAG office. There Hoffman handed him a carved walking stick that had been hollowed out and now contained the information eagerly awaited by the military intelligence forces back in Germany. Schiendick then strolled along the Malecón, the grand esplanade that borders the harbor, making full use of his new stick, until his shore leave was over. As the launch brought him and his fellows back to the safety of the *St. Louis*, Hoffman observed him through binoculars. Once Schiendick and his walking stick were back on board, Hoffman cabled his superiors in Berlin that the operation had gone smoothly. From his point of view, what happened to the refugees was now irrelevant; so long as the *St. Louis* returned to Hamburg, as it surely would, his mission would be a complete success.

For the refugees, however, the waiting and particularly the uncertainty were slowly becoming unbearable. By Tuesday morning, May 30, they were beginning their fourth day of not knowing when, or if, they would be allowed to disembark, of seeing increasing numbers of police boats cruising around their floating prison, of being counseled to remain patient. "The first Spanish word I learned was *mañana*," says Herbert Karliner today. "The Cubans kept saying, 'maybe tomorrow,' but tomorrow never came." Tension, exacerbated by the tropical heat and humidity, slowly became fear, and fear evolved steadily into panic, as increasing numbers of passengers began to contemplate the worst-case scenario: the *St. Louis* returning them to Hamburg and the terrors they thought they had escaped.

Dr. Max Loewe, a lawyer from Breslau who had fought for the Kaiser in the Great War and, like Alex Goldschmidt, had been awarded the Iron Cross for his efforts, was one of the passengers who most greatly feared being sent back to Germany. Loewe walked with a limp because the soles of his feet had been beaten by sadistic guards at the Buchenwald concentration camp. As the hours dragged by, with safety in Cuba so agonizingly near and yet still so far away, Loewe grew desperate. At around 3 p.m. on Tuesday, he walked away from the cabin he was sharing with his mother, his wife, and his two children, entered a lavatory on A Deck, and slashed his wrists with a straight razor. Loewe then staggered across the deck of the ship to the very spot where Moritz Weiler's body had been committed to the ocean, climbed the railing, and leaped overboard into the harbor. He thrashed about in the water, shouting, "Murderers! They will never get me!" until a *St. Louis* seaman leaped in after him and managed to get him into one of the police boats that had been hovering nearby. The authorities rushed Loewe to Calixto Garcia Hospital, where he was heavily sedated and admitted to a guarded, private room for treatment. His family was not allowed to leave the ship to visit him.

From that hour onward, the stakes soared. One of the Cuban newspapers not controlled by the Rivero family, the *Havana Post*, sent a reporter down to the docks to file a story about the *St. Louis*. His dispatch concluded, "Witness the care-worn faces of old and young, their once bright eyes grown dull with suffering, and your heart will go out to them. Witness the stark terror in their expressions, and you will realize they cannot be sent back to Germany." Reporters from several international newspapers, who had come to Havana to cover the ship's arrival, sent word home describing the plight of the refugees. In response to the newspaper stories, telegrams began to flood the American consulate in Havana insisting that something be done.

Onboard the *St. Louis*, a committee of passengers was formed, headed by a lawyer, Josef Joseph, who, oddly enough, had been a friend of Joseph Goebbels many years earlier. The committee sent a cable to the wife of President Bru, pleading with her to intercede with her husband on their behalf: "Over 900 passengers, 400 women and children, ask you to use your influence and help us out of this terrible situation. The traditional humanitarianism of your country and your woman's feelings give us hope that you will not refuse our request." Similar telegrams were sent to prominent figures in the United States, but the committee decided to wait for further developments before calling on President Roosevelt.

Meanwhile, negotiations continued. Only yards from the *St. Louis*, a seaplane landed in Havana Harbor bearing two representatives of the American Jewish Joint Distribution Committee, known in familiar parlance as the Joint. One of them, Cecilia Razovsky, had arrived with the hope of caring for the refugees once they were allowed to disembark. The Joint's other emissary was Lawrence Berenson, a Harvard-educated lawyer and the former president of the Cuban-American Chamber of Commerce. He spoke fluent Spanish; had been a personal friend of Fulgencio Batista, chief of staff of the Cuban army; had extensive business experience in Cuba; and had obtained legal visas that had enabled hundreds of German Jews to emigrate to Cuba. Berenson exuded absolute confidence in his ability to work out a deal.

But President Bru would not be budged—not by telegrams, not by a personal request from American ambassador Butler Wright, and most especially not by Lawrence Berenson. Bru actively disliked Berenson, thinking him an arrogant Yankee wheeler-dealer. Furthermore, Berenson's friendship with Batista, which the American thought was one of the most useful arrows in his quiver, was actually a mark in his disfavor as far as President Bru was concerned. Batista, after all, was the mentor of Manuel Benitez Gonzalez, whose landing certificate scheme was at the heart of this whole affair. At a chilly face-to-face meeting on Thursday, June 1, President Bru informed Berenson that he had ordered the *St. Louis* to depart Cuban waters the following day and that no further negotiations would take place until after the ship had sailed. Should any resistance arise, the president added, the Cuban navy would be placed on alert to escort the ship out of the harbor.

On Friday morning, June 2, Milton Goldsmith of the local Jewish Relief Committee came on board the *St. Louis* to tell the frightened passengers that everything possible was being done to ensure their ultimate safety. Captain Schroeder, well aware of the refugees' worst fears, declared, "I give you my word that I will do everything possible to avoid going back to Germany. I know only too well what they would do to you." But shortly after 11 a.m., Goldsmith returned to his office, the captain gave the order "dead slow ahead," and the ship began its journey northward. Max Loewe remained in Calixto Garcia Hospital—without his family—reducing the number of St. Louis refugees to 907. As Havana slowly faded astern, many passengers stood on deck and wept openly. Josef Joseph, the chairman of the passengers' committee, described the scene in his diary: "The sirens signaled the engines and we were moving out of Havana into the sunlit blue Caribbean. Crowds filled every space along the shoreline, waving, weeping, and watching with great sadness. An indescribable drama of human concern and despair played on us as we sailed into the twilight of uncertainty. This is one of the most tragic days on board because we feel cheated of the freedom we had hoped for. What started as a voyage of freedom is now a voyage of doom."

Some press reports indicated that as many as one hundred thousand people watched from the shore to bid *adios* to the departing ship. Many of them were only too pleased, whether for economic or political or anti-Semitic reasons, to witness the exodus. But there were expressions of sympathy as well. On Sunday, June 11, the Cuban magazine *Bohemia* published a long prose poem titled *A La Habana Ha Llegado Un Barco*. It read, in part:

To Havana has come a boat. 907 courageous human beings poised at the rail of the *St. Louis*. Cuba! Like dozing lizards, the luminous advertisements flicker on the buildings. Automobiles glide swiftly by on the Malecon. Hands grasp the rail, eyes bright with the light of hope, skins reddened by the winds of the Atlantic. 907 Jews on the deck of the *St. Louis*. 907 hearts overflowing with hope.

Behind them lies Hamburg with its dirty chimneys and smoke, mixing with the cold gray wind of the North Sea. And the eyes of the men, women, and children shine with a spirit of hope. Each also with tears in his eyes carried with him the memories of barricades, of concentration camps. Some had signs of the chains carried on their wrists. Almost everyone left someone of his own behind, friends, lovers. But now, another turn of life, a marvelous life among sane, just, tolerant people.

We will begin life anew. Cuba is a beautiful land. No longer any fear of nocturnal visits from the police. Now, a new life in the open. Here we will eat fruits we have never eaten before: fragrant pineapples and mangos that look like hearts of gold. It's like a miracle, a delicious miracle . . . Cuba!

The order has come down. No one is permitted to disembark! 907 hearts are filled with anguish. Cuba a stone's throw away! Terra firma before one's eyes! The possibility of a new and free life! Trembling hands clutch the rail of the *St. Louis*. A child is crying as though someone were beating her. In the stern of the ship sits an old woman, small and wizened like a dried chestnut. She wipes tears from her eyes without making a sound. She is crying, without shame, without consolation.

The *St. Louis* departed. The order allowed no exceptions. O dear child, in Cuba you will eat fruits you have never before tasted: fragrant pineapples and mangos that look like hearts of gold.

For the next four days, the ship treaded water through the ninety miles that separated Cuba from Florida, twice sailing so close to the American mainland that passengers could see the lights of downtown Miami. Onboard, the refugees' spirits were raised by a rumor that an anonymous Jewish philanthropist had offered to allow the vessel to land at his private island off the coast of Louisiana—a rumor that turned out to be unfounded. U.S. Coast Guard cutters shadowed the ship to ensure there were no attempts at swimming to shore, and the immigration inspector in Miami, Walter Thomas, made it clear that so long as the Cuban authorities were still debating their final decision on the case, the *St. Louis* would not be permitted to dock at any American port.

Back in Havana, the standoff continued. On Saturday, June 3, President Bru offered to allow the *St. Louis* to land in Cuba if the Joint Distribution Committee would post a bond of $500 per passenger, or a total payment of $453,500, plus guarantees for clothing, food, and housing. In retrospect, it seems that the agony of the refugees could have ended there, had Lawrence Berenson simply accepted those terms. But the lawyer, versed as he thought he was in the ways of Latin America, concluded that President Bru's declaration was nothing more than an opening bid. Berenson cabled his colleagues at the Joint that he was convinced that if they kept out of it and left matters entirely in his hands, he could save them "a considerable amount of money," and made a counteroffer of $443,000.

The difference in those two figures, the considerable savings that Berenson hoped to realize, works out to $11.58 per passenger. It may be a foolish reaction, one utterly detached from reality, but I know that I would be more than happy to pay a fee of $23.16 to purchase the lives of Alex and Helmut.

Berenson had badly miscalculated. President Bru was not interested in bargaining. On the morning of Tuesday, June 6, the Cuban government declared that negotiations over the matter of the *St. Louis* had been "terminated." The president sent a telegram to James Rosenberg, the acting chairman of the Joint, that read in part, "You know, dear Mr. Rosenberg, that Cuba has contributed in relation to its resources and population to a greater extent than any other nation in order to give hospitality to persecuted people. But completely impossible to accede to this immigrant entry into national territory. Subject *St. Louis* is completely closed by the government. Regretfully reiterate the impossibility of their entry into Cuba. Wish to assure you of my sincere friendship."

Rosenberg replied, "Deeply as we regret the decision of your government we wish to assure you that we are mindful and appreciative of the traditional hospitality of Cuba to the refugees who have found a haven in your country. With sincere wishes and expressions of great respect."

The U.S. government and its representatives had been monitoring the *St. Louis* situation for the past ten days, but they maintained that it was solely an internal matter for Cuba to work out with no interference from its Good Neighbor to the north. However, after President Bru had announced his final decision, Coert du Bois, the American consul-general in Havana, did weigh in, curtly telling Berenson that he and his "co-religionists in New York" had botched the case by moving it "off the plane of humanitarianism and onto the plane of horse-trading."

For its part, the Joint issued a press release declaring that it was "bending every effort to find a haven for the 907 unfortunate refugees of the St. Louis, most of them women and children, and continues ready to furnish the necessary funds for their aid." But the sometimes conflicting communiqués released by the committee had begun to torment American relatives of the *St. Louis* passengers. Within days of President Bru's declaration, the Joint received a letter from Eric Godal of Riverside Drive in New York City:

I don't know I am asking too much, if I want to know what the fate of the 900 passengers of the 'St Louis'—between them my mother—will be. I got informations like that: Friday, greater N.Y. Committee: 4:30 PM: 'We are still in conference with

Cuba. Everything is in our hand.' 5 minutes later I called your Committee: 'There are no conferences with Cuba any more and the boat will not be stopped because there is no hope for other negotiations.'

In the last 24 hours no news at all. I even don't know anymore what kind of a message I shall give my mother to console her. Shall I tell her that you are in conference still with Cuba? Or that there are no conferences at all any more? That the boat will go to Europe back now? That they should be prepared for the worst?

I know you will understand the torture of that uncertainty now spread out over weeks even you have no mother or relativs on bord. And if you understand, you will give a statement to the unhappy on bord and their relativs what they are going to exspect now after all those terrible days.

At 11:30 p.m. on Tuesday, June 6, the day President Bru announced the termination of his government's involvement with the refugees, Captain Gustav Schroeder received a terse cable from Claus-Gottfried Holthusen, director of the Hamburg-America Line. It read simply, "Return Hamburg Immediately." At 11:40, from a location about twelve miles off Jacksonville, Florida, Captain Schroeder ordered his helmsman Heinz Kritsch to bring the ship onto a course of east by northeast. The *St. Louis* was headed back to Germany.

The passengers' committee, led by Josef Joseph, decided that the time had finally come to appeal directly to President Roosevelt for permission to land somewhere in the United States. They sent a telegram to the White House pleading, "Help them, Mr. President, the 900 passengers, of which more than 400 are women and children."

The text of the telegram was printed in the June 7 edition of the *New York Times*. That paper and a number of other news outlets had been reporting the tale of the unhappy refugees aboard the *St. Louis* for more than a week, galvanizing American public opinion. There were marches in the streets of New York, Washington, Chicago, and Atlantic City, the demonstrators calling on the Cuban government to allow the

St. Louis passengers to disembark in Havana. Walter Winchell, broad-casting his radio program to "Mr. and Mrs. America and all the ships at sea," insisted that the root of the issue was the root of all evil: not the failure to touch Cuban hearts but the "failure of touching Cuban palms. And we don't mean trees." Another telegram arrived at the White House addressed to President Roosevelt, this one from a number of Hollywood actors, among them Miriam Hopkins and Edward G. Robinson. It read, "In name of humanity urge you bring all possible influence on Cuban authorities to radio return of German liner St. Louis, now at sea return-ing over nine hundred refugees to imprisonment and death in Nazi Germany Urge Cuba give at least temporary shelter until another refuge can be found in democratic country."

Editorials in the *Washington Post*, the *Miami Herald*, the *Philadelphia Record*, and the *St. Louis Post-Dispatch* all decried the treatment of the Wandering Jews of the Caribbean and stated forthrightly variants of the sentiment "something must be done." On June 8, in an editorial titled simply "Refugee Ship," The *New York Times* declared, "The saddest ship afloat today, the Hamburg-American liner St. Louis, with 900 Jewish refugees aboard, is steaming back toward Germany after a tragic week of frustration at Havana and off the coast of Florida. No plague ship ever received a sorrier welcome. At Havana the St. Louis's decks became a stage for human misery. The refugees could see the shimmering towers of Miami rising from the sea, but for them they were only the battle-ments of another forbidden city. Germany, with all the hospitality of its concentration camps, will welcome these unfortunates. The St. Louis will soon be home with its cargo of despair."

On June 9, the *Times* editorialized, "Attempts to trace responsibility for the plight of the refugees on board the Hamburg-American liner St. Louis lead into dark byways of human hard-heartedness. It is difficult to imagine the bitterness of exile when it takes place over a far-away frontier. Helpless families driven from their homes to a barren island in the Danube, thrust over the Polish frontier, escaping in terror of their lives to Switzerland or France, are hard for us in a free country to visualize. But these exiles floated by our own shores. We can only hope that some hearts will soften somewhere and some refuge be

Fred Packer's cartoon from the June 6, 1939, edition of the New York Daily Mirror. *It expressed a sentiment shared by many editorialists and American citizens, though not enough to influence the Roosevelt Administration to offer the ship safe harbor.*

found. The cruise of the St. Louis cries to high heaven of man's inhumanity to man."

One of the most striking images was a political cartoon by Fred Packer, a future Pulitzer Prize winner, that appeared in the *New York Daily Mirror*. Under the headline "Ashamed!," the Statue of Liberty stands with eyes averted as a boat labeled "Jewish Refugee Ship" steams past. Hanging from her upraised right arm, the arm bearing the torch, is a sign that reads, "Keep Out."

But for all those general expressions of support for the *St. Louis* passengers, few people explicitly demanded their admission to the United States. The *Post-Dispatch* editorial made a vague reference to America's "broad expanses of unoccupied or sparsely settled territory" where, presumably, these wretched wanderers could be placed. Other papers declared that once this particular ship was allowed to circumvent the letter of the immigration law, a "dangerous precedent" would be set and other illegal vessels would soon be steaming toward American ports. Even the *Times* never came right out and called for a policy that would allow the *St. Louis* to sail past Miss Liberty and tie up at Ellis Island.

Her "golden door" remained firmly closed to these particular "homeless, tempest-tossed" exiles.

Several interlocked reasons explain why America failed to welcome the refugees to their own shores. The Immigration Act of 1924, still very much on the books, set rigid quotas that limited the number of people who could enter the United States each year. For 1939, the quota from Germany and Austria was 27,370. Adding nearly a thousand more, all at once, would mean that an equal number of German Jews who had already applied for visas would have to be turned away.

Then there was the matter of American public opinion. Newspapers from coast to coast had been documenting the increasing savagery of the Nazis' treatment of the Jews—the events of *Kristallnacht* had been front-page news in dozens of papers—and by and large the American people were sympathetic. But anti-Semitism was by no means restricted to Europe. In 1938, the highly respected Elmo Roper polling agency asked a sampling of the American public, "What kinds of people do you object to?" Fourteen percent of the respondents answered "uncultured, unrefined, dumb people"; 27 percent answered "noisy, cheap, boisterous, loud people"; and 35 percent, the highest number, answered simply, "Jews." The following year, another Roper poll revealed that 53 percent of the Americans queried thought that Jews were "different" from other people and thus should be subject to "restrictions" in their business and social lives. That same poll found that only 39 percent of the respondents believed that Jews should be treated the same as everyone else and that 10 percent of those polled thought that Jews should be deported. Despite their general compassion for the plight of the *St. Louis* refugees, most Americans did not want the United States to become a haven for European Jews. According to a poll taken in the spring of 1939 by *Fortune* magazine, 83 percent of the American people opposed relaxing restrictions on immigration.

Few politicians, including the nation's First Politician, were willing to discount such majority opinion. An attempt to admit twenty thousand Jewish children from Germany, the Wagner-Rogers Bill of 1939, had died in committee. President Roosevelt, already gearing up his campaign for an unprecedented third term and unwilling to become mired in the immigration issue, had spoken not a word on Wagner-Rogers. In response to the telegrams he'd received from the *St. Louis* passengers' committee and elsewhere, President Roosevelt remained silent.

Eleanor Roosevelt, thought by many Americans to be more compassionate than her husband, also received many pleas on behalf of the *St. Louis* voyagers. On June 8, an eleven-year-old girl named Dee Nye wrote to Mrs. Roosevelt, "Mother of our Country, I am so sad the Jewish people have to suffer so. Please let them land in America. It hurts me so that I would give them my little bed if it was the last thing I had because I am an American let us Americans not send them back to that slater house. We have three rooms that we do not use. Mother would be glad to let someone have them. Sure our Country will find a place for them, so they may rest in peace."

Like the passengers' committee and Edward G. Robinson, Dee Nye never received an answer. The United States of America would not permit the SS *St. Louis* to land at any of its ports.

One last possibility in the Western Hemisphere remained. Ships sailing the transatlantic crossing for HAPAG had put in at Halifax, Nova Scotia, for decades. With the *St. Louis* now two days out from Halifax, Captain Schroeder contacted Canadian authorities for permission to enter Halifax Harbor. But perhaps fearing repercussions from its powerful neighbor to the south, the government of Prime Minister William Mackenzie King added Canada to the list of nations that offered no succor to the *St. Louis*.

Joseph Goebbels seized on the news as further proof that the world shared the Nazis' opinion of what they called a "criminal race." "Since no one will accept the shabby Jews on the *St. Louis*," the Propaganda Ministry declared, "we will have to take them back and support them."

It took little imagination to conclude that Nazi "support" more than likely meant sending the passengers to the camps, and fear on board the ship grew to crisis proportions. A band of passengers attempted mutiny, overpowering the crew and temporarily seizing control of the engine room. The uprising was quickly contained, but the refugees had managed to convey their desperation to the outside world, which had begun to take a markedly increased interest in their fate. The *Washington Post* ran a story headlined, "200 Jews Aboard St. Louis Decide on Mass Suicide." It read, in part:

> Driven from every American port, like a pestiferous cargo, the 925 [sic] Jews on the St. Louis are prepared to face a self-inflicted death rather than experience the horrors of German concentration camps, according to wireless dispatches received by friends and relatives of the refugees, as the liner definitely steered a course for Hamburg.
>
> Turned back by Cuba, unwanted by Mexico, the refugees saw their last hope of a new life vanish when they learned that President Roosevelt had refused to consider all appeals made directly to him. With blank despair staring them in the face, 200 of these modern pariahs have now decided to make their supreme protest against the civilization in which their lot has been cast by sacrificing their lives before the St. Louis comes within sight of Germany's shores.
>
> The suicide pact has been made in calm consciousness that the sacrifice might draw world attention to the outrage against humanity committed in their regard. The men and women who have taken it are persons of culture and the high positions they formerly occupied in Germany are a guaranty of their high-mindedness.

The cultured passengers had only been able to communicate with their friends and families on land because they had pawned such items as jewelry, cameras, and clothing with members of the ship's crew in order to obtain the money required to send their unhappy telegrams.

For his part, Herbert Karliner remembers that up to three hundred people on board the *St. Louis* were prepared to jump overboard rather than risk setting foot once more on German soil. He also recalls that the mood of the return voyage to Europe was vastly different from that on the initial crossing; there were no dances, no movies, no games. The menus, which had been individually offered for each meal and included a number of choices, were now presented on a single mimeo-graphed sheet each day, with no options available. Hope had largely been replaced by despair.

Years later, in his memoirs, Captain Schroeder attempted to convey how the trauma of rejection played out among the most innocent of the blameless citizens of the *St. Louis*. He described a game he saw a group of children playing. Two boys guarded a gateway made out of chairs, fierce expressions on their faces, as other children attempted to enter. "Are you a Jew?" the guards would ask, and if the answer was yes, the reply was a sharp, "No Jews allowed!"

The captain, who from the beginning of the crisis had been aware of his passengers' overwhelming desire not to return to Germany, began to devise an audacious plan to save them, should all other means of rescue prove impossible. Schroeder cleared his idea with three of his most trusted officers and with Josef Joseph of the passengers' committee. As a last resort, said the captain, he was prepared to run the *St. Louis* aground off the Sussex coast of England, set her on fire, and evacuate the refugees to shore.

For many on board the ship, Alex and Helmut among them, that plan, ill conceived as it probably was, might ultimately have worked out for the best. But no such dramatics proved necessary, thanks to the efforts of another member of the American Jewish Joint Distribution Committee: its European director, Morris Troper.

Born in New York City in 1892, Morris Carlton Troper attended City College and later New York University, achieving both a master's of commercial science degree and a law degree. He earned his living as a certified public accountant for many years, and indeed that is how he was remembered in the headline of his obituary in the *New York Times* in 1962. But it is for his work with the Joint Distribution Committee that Troper was most greatly honored in his lifetime.

He began his association with the Joint in the immediate aftermath of World War I, when on behalf of the committee, he investigated the conditions of Jewish refugees in Poland, Hungary, and other coun-tries in Eastern Europe. His travels for the Joint took him to the Soviet Union in 1929 and 1936 and to Germany in 1933, where he spent six months observing firsthand the effects of Nazi policies on the Jews. In 1938, Troper was appointed the committee's European chairman, overseeing its operations from the Joint's Paris offices. In early June of the following year, he took on the task of finding a haven for the *St. Louis*.

On June 10, having accepted his assignment from the Joint's American chairman, Paul Baerwald, Troper received two dire telegrams from the Joint's New York office, underscoring the gravity of the situation. One read: "Any immigration this side of water is out of question. This we have not communicated to passengers but wish you to know." And the other advised, "Regard these passengers as doomed once they reach German soil. Time is of essence. Boat has completed more than half of trip."

After first considering and then rejecting Morocco as a possible sanctuary, Troper decided to focus his efforts on European relief agencies that had received financial support from the Joint. His first call went to Max Gottschalk of the Refugee Committee of Belgium, vowing that the Joint would guarantee $500 for each refugee accepted and that the refugees would not become a public burden. The next morning, Gottschalk spoke with the Belgian minister of justice, who consulted with the prime minister, who briefed King Leopold III, who agreed that Belgium would accept 250 of the *St. Louis* refugees. The dilemma that had occupied the Cuban and American governments for weeks was settled in Belgium within twenty-four hours.

With this immensely important breakthrough achieved, Troper turned his attention to three other countries: Holland, France, and England. He called his contact at the Refugee Committee of Amsterdam, who knocked on the door of the Dutch minister of justice, who approached Queen Wilhelmina. On Monday morning, June 12, the justice minister, Carolus Goseling, announced that Holland would accept 194 of the refugees. Within two years, Justice Goseling would be murdered in the German concentration camp Buchenwald.

With these two destinations in hand and with negotiations proceeding smoothly in France and England, Troper sent a telegram to Captain Schroeder: "Wish inform you making every effort land your passengers with several possible prospects enroute which we hope will become definite next thirty-six hours."

Troper's hope soon became a reality. In London, the Joint's Chairman Baerwald met with the American ambassador to England, Joseph P. Kennedy, the father of the future president. Kennedy then delivered to authorities in the British government a letter from Baerwald spelling out the same terms—$500 per passenger and a guarantee that the refugees would not become public burdens—that had been accepted by Belgium and Holland. Meanwhile, Troper met with Louise Weiss, the director of the Central Refugee Committee in Paris. Weiss then spoke with Alexis Leger, the French foreign minister, and Albert Sarrault, the interior minister. By the evening of June 12, the governments of France and England had agreed to accept about two hundred fifty refugees each.

On the night of Tuesday, June 13, a week after the *St. Louis* had headed back to Europe and exactly a month since her departure from Hamburg, Troper cabled the ship from Paris with the happy news of his successful negotiations: "Final arrangements for disembarkation all passengers complete. Governments of Belgium, Holland, France, and England cooperated magnificently with American Joint Distribution Committee to effect this possibility."

The passengers' committee wired back, "The 907 passengers of St. Louis dangling for last thirteen days between hope and despair received today your liberating message of 13th June that final arrangements for all passengers have at last been reached. Our gratitude is as immense as the ocean on which we have been floating since May 13, first full of hope for a good future and afterwards in the deepest despair. Accept Mr. Chairman for you and for the American Joint Distribution Committee and last but not least for the governments of Belgium, Holland, France and England the deepest and eternal thanks of men women and children united by the same fate on board the St. Louis."

After breakfast the next morning, in the presence of Captain Schroeder, the committee read Troper's telegram to the assembled passengers. The news was met with unrestrained cheering and sobs of joy. They were Wandering Jews no more.

Captain Schroeder now set a course for Antwerp, Belgium, where the *St. Louis* would finally make landfall and where the other three countries of asylum would make arrangements to accept their respective refugees. Meanwhile, there were hastily arranged gatherings in all four countries, as both public and private organizations met to hammer out the details of this immense humanitarian undertaking.

One such meeting occurred in Paris on the morning of Thursday, June 15, in the office of Amédeé Bussières, the chief of the French national police. Troper attended, as did Louise Weiss of the Parisian refugee committee and Raymond-Raoul Lambert, representing the most visible national Jewish relief organization, the *Comité d'Assistance aux Réfugiés*. Everyone agreed at the outset that, generous as this offer from the French government had been, no one should assume that a precedent had been set; this was strictly a onetime gesture made under extraordinary circumstances. Weiss suggested that the French ministry of foreign affairs should work with the other three countries to issue an official communiqué making that position explicitly clear.

Bussières, with a meaningful glance at Troper, declared his regret that "our American friends" had not accepted the *St. Louis* refugees when they were on their doorstep but rather sent them back to Europe. But Bussières then went on to say that the French government would not accept the Joint's generous offer of $500 per passenger. Rather, he said, the various French refugee organizations, working in tandem with their American counterparts, should share the costs of providing for the refugees until such time—and surely that time would come soon—that the unfortunate displaced persons would find a permanent home. Lambert gave his agreement and, after a decision that the French refugees would be transported to Boulogne-sur-Mer once they'd landed in Antwerp, the meeting adjourned. Everything seemed to be under control.

Troper and his wife, Ethel, spent the night of Friday, June 16, in a comfortable room of the Century Hotel in Antwerp, where the *St. Louis* was due to arrive the next day. At 4 a.m. on Saturday, the Tropers met in the lobby of their hotel with a contingent of sixteen people representing the four welcoming countries. They traveled in three cars to the Dutch city of Vlissingen, known in English as Flushing, a port town located at the head of the estuary leading to Antwerp. The journey was delayed when one of the cars suffered a flat tire, but the traveling party managed to meet for a quick cup of coffee in a restaurant in downtown

Vlissingen before going to the police station. There Troper signed the necessary papers to obtain a permit to board a tugboat that would take everyone out to the site where the *St. Louis* had dropped anchor.

It was a misty, foggy morning. Shortly after 9 a.m., the tugboat left the dock at Vlissingen and made its way through rough seas out to the ship. The scene was recorded by a representative of the Joint:

> No words can describe the feelings of everyone on the tug when sighting the *St. Louis* with its human cargo, all standing as one man along the rails of the port side of the steamer. Although those strained moments seemed to be long hours, yet it took only a few seconds for the tug to find itself alongside the *St. Louis*, with all passengers waving and yelling in unison. Mr. Troper was met on board the steamer in the hallway, lined on each side by the children of the passengers, one hundred on each side. From every corner of the boat, the grown-up passengers called to Mr. Troper, "God bless you!" A little girl, Liesl Joseph [the daughter of Josef Joseph], eleven years old this very day, stepped forward, greeted Mr. Troper and, in German, welcomed him with these words: "We, the children of the *St. Louis*, wish to express to you our deep thanks from the bottom of our hearts for having saved us from a great misery. We pray that God's blessing be upon you. We regret exceedingly that flowers do not grow on ships; otherwise we would have presented to you the largest and most beautiful bouquet."

Visibly moved, Troper bent to kiss Liesl, then straightened to shake the hand of her father, the head of the passenger committee. But there was business to attend to and a deadline to reckon with; the 907 refugees had to be divided into the groups bound for the four countries, and everything had to be worked out in the short time it would take Captain Schroeder to steer the *St. Louis* down the estuary to Antwerp. At 7:00 p.m., a train was scheduled to leave for Brussels with the Belgian contingent of refugees aboard, so there was precious little time for idle pleasures.

The ship's first-class social hall became the site where each refugee would be assigned to one of the four countries. Troper and an assistant from the Joint, Emanuel Rosen, sat at a large table, flanked on one side by the representatives of Belgium and Holland, and on the other by those from France and England. The refugees were so delighted and relieved that they were finally on the verge of disembarking (and not doing so in Germany), that for the most part their destination was of secondary concern. Troper announced that he and his colleagues would do all they could to ensure that families were not broken up and to accede to special requests if a refugee insisted on being placed in a particular country. But for the most part, the selection was performed in a somewhat random manner, and thus, though Troper and his fellows had no way of knowing it, they casually if conscientiously made decisions that were to have profound implications for the lives of everyone on board.

Alex and Helmut would have had a legitimate reason for requesting an assignment to England, as Bertha had made arrangements to immigrate to Leeds as a gardener. Either they made such a request and were turned down or they reasoned that it didn't much matter where they disembarked, as the Nazis would no longer be a threat to them in any case. Had they been assigned to the English group, the odds are great that they would have survived to a natural old age. It's highly possible that my parents would then have chosen to flee to England to join their family when they escaped Germany two years later. Thus I could very well have been born and raised in that green and pleasant land.

But fate, or Morris Troper, determined that my grandfather and uncle would disembark in France.

By the time the *St. Louis* tied up at Pier 18 in Antwerp Harbor, the selection committee had determined that 214 refugees would be assigned to stay in Belgium. By 9 p.m., after consuming great quantities of sandwiches, beer, and coffee provided by the ship's kitchen, the selection committee had made its final determinations: 181 refugees would travel to Holland, 288 would go to England, and Alex, Helmut, and the six Karliners would be among 224 refugees bound for France.

Before the Belgian contingent left the ship, passengers' committee chairman Josef Joseph presented Troper with a Declaration of Thanks and Gratitude. It read, in part:

> Dear Mr. Troper, at this moment when the 907 passengers of the *St. Louis* are to be distributed to the hospitable countries of England, Holland, France, and Belgium, after a fantastic trip to the tropics and back, we have this to say to you:
>
> After we had to leave the harbor of Havana by order of the President, your intervention gave us the courage to believe that we had not been forgotten and left to our fate. Your act will be engraved forever in our hearts and in the hearts of our children and grandchildren. We shall never forget it. May God Almighty reward you and your colleagues in the JDC for what you have done. May it please God to bless your future work. And if in closing we ask you, dear Mr. Troper, not to forget the passengers of the *St. Louis*, we do this because we have all learned to love you and hope that you will think well of us.
>
> With our deepest respect and sincerest thanks, The Passengers of the *St. Louis*.

Every one of the 907 passengers signed the declaration.

That afternoon Belgian police scuffled with a Nazi-inspired group called the National Youth Organization, an ugly echo of the conditions that had forced the refugees to leave their homeland in the first place. The NYO was protesting the arrival of the *St. Louis*, distributing handbills on which was printed the cheery message: "We, too, want to help the Jews. If they call on our offices each one will receive free of charge a length of rope and a long nail." After a few minutes of pushing, shoving, and shouting, the police confiscated the handbills and dispersed the crowd.

Later that afternoon, the 214 passengers who were bound for Belgium were served a last meal on board the *St. Louis*, and then shortly after 5 p.m., they began to file slowly off the ship. After more than a month at sea, it was difficult for some of them to believe that they were

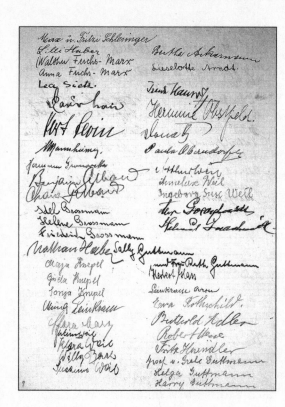

A portion of the list of St. Louis *passenger signatures on the Declaration of Thanks and Gratitude presented to Morris Troper on June 17, 1939. Alex and Helmut's signatures appear in the middle of the right-hand column.* (Courtesy of the United States Holocaust Memorial Museum)

actually disembarking, and several turned around frequently to wave to those still on board. A woman who was among the most enthusiastic wavers stumbled, fell heavily, and broke her leg. She was picked up by an ambulance and spent her first night on Belgian soil in a hospital. Troper slept that night at Antwerp's Century Hotel. Before retiring, he sent a telegram back to the Joint in New York. "Work distribution 907 passengers completed believe everything OK 300 tons baggage and 5,000 pieces hand luggage going sleep after seventeen consecutive hours most trying ordeal I ever experienced regards Troper."

At 5:00 a.m., Sunday, June 18, the 181 refugees who were headed for Holland were awakened and served a last breakfast. A riverboat, the *Jan van Arckel*, pulled alongside the *St. Louis*, and the Dutch contingent, carrying boxes of sandwiches and sweets from the purser, filed off the luxury liner and onto the little steamer. Accompanied by hearty cheers from the remaining *St. Louis* passengers, the *Jan van Arckel* slowly pulled away at 9:30 to begin her journey through the complex waterway system to Rotterdam. Along the way, she was followed by an escort of police boats—not unlike her escort out of Havana—and saluted by hundreds of well-wishers who lined the canals, waving, whistling, and welcoming the wanderers.

That afternoon, Morris Troper, his "trying ordeal" of the previous day ameliorated by a good night's sleep, returned to the *St. Louis* to oversee the final transfer of refugees. The 288 passengers bound for England and the 224, among them Alex and Helmut, accepted by France, would take another HAPAG ship, the *Rhakotis*. A 6,700-ton freighter christened the *San Francisco* when she was built in 1927, she'd been renamed *Rhakotis* in 1935. Outfitted to carry no more than fifty passengers, she was about to be boarded by ten times that many people. Representatives from HAPAG had hastily made preparations; the plan was to sleep men and women separately in double-decker steel bunks both fore and aft, with meals to be served at long tables amidships.

Boarding began mid-afternoon on Sunday, and shortly before 4:00 the *Rhakotis*, now filled with its new human cargo, was towed upstream. The Antwerp port authority had ruled that she could not spend the night in the vicinity of the *St. Louis*. Captain Schroeder penned a personal note to Troper, thanking him for "organizing so efficiently the distribution of my passengers." That evening, as scheduled, the *St. Louis* began another transatlantic voyage, destination New York City. Making her way up the estuary toward open water, she overtook the *Rhakotis* where the smaller ship lay at anchor. The refugees lined the rails as their former floating home passed slowly by, watching, in the words of one of them, "with one dry eye and one wet eye." For their part, the crew of the *St. Louis* called out encouragingly, "Good luck to the Jews!"

Nearly all of the 231 crew members had signed on for the return voyage to New York. One who hadn't was the second-class steward Otto Schiendick, who left the ship in Antwerp carrying his hollowed-out walking stick, eager to be reunited with his *Abwehr* contacts in Hamburg.

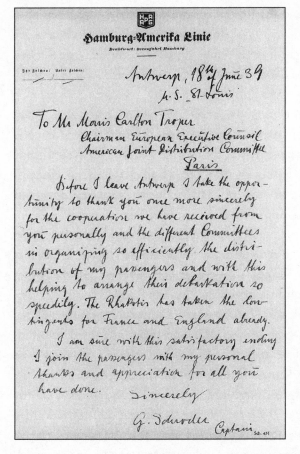

Captain Schroeder's letter of appreciation to Morris Troper, dated June 18, 1939. (Courtesy of the United States Holocaust Memorial Museum)

Alex and Helmut, the six members of the Karliner family, and their 216 fellow passengers on the *Rhakotis* steamed back into Antwerp harbor the following morning and were served a hearty breakfast. There was some largely good-natured grumbling about the close proximity of the bunks and dining tables, with one refugee noting sardonically, "We practically had breakfast in bed." But the food received rave reviews, as it included the first fresh eggs the passengers had enjoyed for weeks.

At two o'clock that afternoon, Morris Troper returned for a final farewell to the refugees, who applauded and whistled wildly as he drove away from the dock to return to his office in Paris. An hour later, the *Rhakotis* weighed anchor and began its journey, first to

Boulogne-sur-Mer and then on to Southampton. A heavy rain began to fall, dampening the spirits of the passengers, who surely must have felt that they'd been sufficiently tempest-tossed for one voyage. One of them confided to his diary, "I fear it is still possible for a cable to recall us to Germany."

The odyssey of the unhappy people who had boarded the *St. Louis* in Hamburg, those unwanted former citizens of Germany and Austria who had desired so desperately to gain security in the New World, only to find themselves—most of them—forced back to the uncertainties of the Old World, was nearly over. But the controversy surrounding their voyage has continued, unresolved, to the present day.

The debate was originally joined in the American Jewish press. On June 13, as the *St. Louis* was steaming back toward Europe but before the deal brokered by Troper had been announced, Samuel Margoshes published an editorial in a newspaper known in Yiddish as *Der Tog*, but which called itself the *National Jewish Daily*. Margoshes headlined his editorial "The Doom of the 907," and harshly blamed the Joint Distribution Committee and other Jewish organizations for the failure of the *St. Louis* to find a welcome port in the United States.

The editorial began by quoting a frantic cablegram sent by the passengers' committee: "It reads: 'We are floating to our death. Where is your promise to save us?' In my ears these words sound not so much as an appeal but rather as a terrible indictment of our entire Jewish leadership in America."

Margoshes then leveled his own indictment against the Joint, referring to the "horse-trading" of Lawrence Berenson: "Admittedly, the Joint Distribution Committee was in no easy financial position. On the other hand, can there be any doubt that had the Joint ransomed the prisoners on the St. Louis, that there would have been such an outpouring of gratitude and generosity on the part of American Jewry as to more than offset the sacrifice made by the JDC? Had the Joint rushed to the rescue, instead of counting its pennies and then haggling about the price of 907 Jewish lives, it would have today been the master not only of the heart but also of the pocket of American Jewry. Alas, it was not to be. 'Cuba was lost for us by haggling,' a committee of the refugees wired me the other day. It is not the first time in Jewish history that counting costs lost a Jewish battle."

In his conclusion, Margoshes denounced the lack of effort he perceived among the leading Jewish organizations—including the General Jewish Council, the American Jewish Committee, the B'Nai B'rith, and the American Jewish Congress—on behalf of the *St. Louis* refugees: "It is a bitter thing to say, and I say it not without pain, but the fact remains that as far as preventing or alleviating the tragedy of the 907, Jewish leadership in America might have just as well never existed or been away on a long vacation. Whatever *was* done for the rescue of the Jewish refugees was done in the dark and was shrouded in mystery. No wonder it failed. Its failure spells not only the doom of the 907 but also the bankruptcy of Jewish leadership in America."

Three days later, with Troper's deal now public knowledge, the *Jewish Daily Forward* fired back with a front-page editorial of its own:

> Jews throughout the world have lived in a nightmare during the last two weeks, with the sufferings of the unfortunate refugees aboard the SS *St. Louis* constantly in mind. We lived with these refugees all the time that the boat was floating in American waters. When the refugees left the shores of Cuba to go back to Europe, our deepest sympathy went with them. And together with them, the JDC [the Joint], our most important Jewish relief organization, turned its entire attention to Europe, in order to rescue the refugees. "Five days and five nights," as it was stated in the cable from Paris, "the European Director of the JDC, Morris C. Troper, was chained to his desk. He appealed to all democratic governments in Europe, and made every possible effort to rescue the refugees." At last the JDC succeeded in rescuing the unfortunate victims of Hitlerism. For that we must be grateful. The rescue work of the JDC is an important chapter in Jewish history. The JDC spared no effort, ignoring the attacks that some Jewish newspapers directed against it. Evidently the JDC was bent upon rescuing the refugees and had no time to enter into discussions with irresponsible newspapers and writers.

The *Forward* then called out *The National Jewish Daily*, the *Jewish Morning Journal*, and the *Freiheit* for what it called "shameless attacks" upon the Joint "at a time when the most complicated and delicate negotiations about the refugees were going on!" The editorial concluded, "The important work of the JDC deserves our gratitude and it deserves also a better and more sympathetic attitude on the part of the press."

But the debate about who was to blame for the fate of the *St. Louis* passengers extended beyond dueling Jewish periodicals. The failure of the United States to respond adequately to the crisis had serious implications for the moral standing of the U.S. as a civilized country in an increasingly dangerous world. One of the first to indict the United States for failing an ethical test in the choppy waves off the coast of Florida was a spokesman for another religious perspective. Bishop James Cannon Jr. of the Southern Methodist Church wrote a long letter to the editor of the *Richmond Times-Dispatch* headlined "Shame of the St. Louis." It read, in part:

During the days when this horrible tragedy was being enacted right at our doors, our Government at Washington made no effort to relieve the desperate situation of these people, but on the contrary gave orders that they be kept out of the country. Why did not the President, secretary of state, secretary of the treasury, secretary of labor and other officials confer together and arrange for the landing of these refugees who had been caught in this maelstrom of distress and agony through no fault of their own? Why did not our Congress take action in accordance with the free and humane spirit which has characterized our people and our Government in the past?

The failure to take any steps whatever to assist these distressed, persecuted Jews in their hour of extremity was one of the most disgraceful things which has happened to American history, and leaves a stain and brand of shame upon the record of our nation. The fact that the Dutch, the Belgians, the French and the British are reported to have arranged to admit these trapped refugees simply adds to the shame upon our own

Government that we have known and seen their misery and have played the part of the priest and of the Levite rather than of the Good Samaritan, and that we have passed by on the other side and left these Jews to whatever fate might befall them on their return to Europe.

Thus the larger argument was joined. On one side was the administration of President Franklin D. Roosevelt, which insisted that its hands were legally tied by the Immigration Act of 1924 and which was unwilling to establish what it considered an untenable precedent by admitting this particular ship when the world's oceans were filling up with vessels carrying refugees from the four corners of an ever-more perilous world. On the other side were the advocates of those refugees, who looked to America to embrace its creed and provide a sanctuary for the homeless, hopeless, and desperate, to open the gates to its storied shining city on a hill and welcome these wanderers in their time of trouble.

What should Mr. Roosevelt have done, given both the legal and political realities of 1939 and the danger posed to the 907 by a forced return to Europe?

Among the most recent voices to join the debate are those belonging to American University professors Richard Breitman and Allan Lichtman in their 2013 book *FDR and the Jews*. They argue first of all that much of the responsibility for the failure of the *St. Louis* to find safe anchor in the Western Hemisphere lies with the government of Cuba and with Lawrence Berenson. In the matter of the president, Breitman and Lichtman find Roosevelt innocent of the charge of "indifference to Jewish refugees."

Rooted in a rich soil of isolationism, the U.S. Congress had passed three Neutrality Acts during the 1930s, essentially declaring that America should not and would not intervene in foreign affairs. The acts of 1935, 1936, and 1937 imposed an embargo on the sale of arms to any belligerent in any war anywhere. By the spring of 1939, as a large-scale war in Europe appeared ever more likely, President Roosevelt decided it was vital to repeal or revise the Neutrality Acts to give him greater flexibility in opposing Nazi Germany. The Democratic Party controlled both houses of Congress, but President Roosevelt knew that neutrality would be a hard sell to Democratic senators from southern states and he needed their support.

Professors Breitman and Lichtman conclude that political calculations, neither idealistic nor craven but based on simple vote-counting arithmetic, are responsible for the president's silence on the matter of the *St. Louis*. They argue that "Roosevelt could have admitted the St. Louis passengers to the United States only by exceeding the immigration quotas," and thus alienating a certain segment of the Congress. "A quarrel with Congress over the *St. Louis* had the potential to doom his efforts to revise the Neutrality Acts and aid the nations resisting Hitler's aggression. Had such events come to pass, posterity would have judged FDR far more harshly than it has in our time."

I understand the book's argument about the political realities of the time, but another of the authors' assertions has been sharply rebuked by passengers who made that fateful voyage aboard the *St. Louis*. Breitman and Lichtman assert that " [T]here is no truth to the notion, found in some literature, that American officials ordered the coast guard to prevent any passengers from reaching American shores." A group of *St. Louis* survivors, including Herbert Karliner, have insisted otherwise in a statement issued shortly after *FDR and the Jews* was published: "We saw the Coast Guard planes that flew around the ship to follow its movements," they declared. "We saw the Coast Guard cutter that trailed us and made sure the *St. Louis* did not come close to the Florida coast. We heard the cutter blaring its warning to stay away. It was President Franklin Roosevelt who decided our fate, who denied us and our family's permission to land, forcing us to return to Europe, where many of the passengers were murdered by the Nazis. We categorically reject any and all attempts to distort these indisputable historical facts."

I am hardly an uninterested party in the debate over the meaning of the *St. Louis* and the Roosevelt administration's handling of the complex diplomatic and political implications of its voyage. But neither am I blinded by my personal stake in the events of May and June 1939. I'm aware that, in most cases, policies are dictated by laws, and that the

Immigration Act of 1924 was the unyielding given circumstance of the drama enacted fifteen years later. I understand and accept that, as is the case with most presidents, Franklin Roosevelt could not afford to get too far in front of public opinion, and that the American public of 1939 was in no hurry to concern itself with a boatload of Jewish refugees. And, of course, no one, neither everyday citizen nor administration official, could have anticipated the depth of the horror that awaited so many of the passengers of this singularly unhappy vessel.

Nevertheless, fully cognizant that more than seven decades after the fact I am in possession of knowledge unavailable to the principal actors of that drama, I cannot help wondering why President Roosevelt did not make an exception for those 907 wanderers and sign an executive order allowing the *St. Louis* to pull into safe harbor in Miami or Baltimore or in the tender welcoming shadow of Miss Liberty's life-affirming torch. I remain ever grateful that my mother and father were allowed to come to America in 1941. Would that my grandfather and uncle had been granted a similar welcome two years earlier.

In the spring of 2009, the U.S. Senate came as close as the American government ever has to conceding that, just perhaps, something more might have been done on behalf of the 907 refugees. The Senate passed Resolution 111, which "acknowledges the suffering of those refugees caused by the refusal of the United States, Cuban, and Canadian governments to provide them political asylum." In his remarks introducing the resolution, Wisconsin Senator Herb Kohl pointed out that "the United States failed to provide refuge" to the passengers and concluded by declaring, "The *St. Louis* is only one tragedy out of millions from that time, but seventy years later it still haunts us as a nation."

A final word about the ship that carried Alex and Helmut so far from their homeland and so close to freedom. The *St. Louis* was bombed by the Royal Air Force in 1944 as she lay at anchor in Hamburg. After the war, the ship was partly renovated and for a time served as a floating hotel. In 1950, with their profits plummeting, the new owners sold the *St. Louis* for scrap and she was broken up.

For his role in finding refuge for the passengers of the *St. Louis*, Morris Carlton Troper was awarded the Legion of Honor by the French and presented with both the Legion of Merit and the State Conspicuous Service Cross by the United States.

Captain Schroeder survived the war and died in 1959. Two years before his death, he was awarded the Order of Merit by the West German government "for services to the people and the land in the rescue of refugees." There is currently a street in Hamburg named for him. For his efforts to find a safe haven for his passengers during the voyage of May and June 1939, Captain Gustav Schroeder was honored posthumously by Yad Vashem in Israel as one of the "Righteous Among the Nations."

To the Nazi leadership in Germany, the meaning of the voyage of the *St. Louis* was simple, unambiguous, and reassuring: for all its demonstrations of concern for the Jews, the rest of the world was apparently unprepared to do much on their behalf. The Nazi monthly *Der Weltkampf* published an editorial that stated, "We are saying openly that we do not want the Jews while the democracies keep on claiming that they are willing to receive them—and then leave the guests out in the cold! Aren't we savages better men after all?"

And Adolf Hitler himself declared mockingly, "I can only hope and expect that the other world, which has such deep sympathy for these Jewish criminals, will at least be generous enough to convert their sympathy into practical aid. We, on our part, are ready to place these criminals at the disposal of other countries; even, for all I care, on luxury ships."

6

Boulogne-sur-Mer

THURSDAY, MAY 19, 2011. Too late, I think. I'm too late. In the glare of a brilliantly sunny late afternoon, I stand on the concrete pier that surrounds the horseshoe-shaped harbor of Boulogne-sur-Mer on the north coast of France, gazing with finely mixed emotions into the murky green water. Fifty yards away, six young men kick around a soccer ball, their collective skill apparently blocking from their minds the fear that an errant pass might send the ball plunging down an irretrievable thirty feet into the drink. On the harbor's far side, an immense Greek cargo ship is being unloaded with the assistance of two cranes and at least a dozen strapping dockworkers. Far offshore, three industrious cormorants are scanning the waves for an early dinner, floating in seemingly aimless patterns until they drop bodily as if shot, plunging into the sea and then rising again with a gleaming, wriggling fish in their jaws. The bustling life of a seaside town is all around me.

I am more than a little awed to be standing here. And I feel as if I've missed the boat, literally. Alex and Helmut have come and gone.

Yesterday morning, Amy and I bade farewell to Hilu and Roland, climbed into our little Meriva, and drove west along the autobahn, leaving Germany and entering Holland. We set aside the Goldschmidt family saga for a while and explored the lives of Amy's ancestors, whose roots for more than a century were planted in the rich soil of the Dutch province of Friesland. We visited the tiny village of Arum, where her great-great-grandfather Pieter Pieters Menage and great-great-grandmother Tjitse Blanksma were born in 1840, and walked wonderingly along Arum's main street and through its tidy cemetery, looking for family. Back on the road, driving through the flat Frisian countryside, I often thought I was looking at a seventeenth-century Dutch landscape painting, a Ruisdael or Hobbema, with deep green fields; a few lonely trees; a canal or two; grazing cows, horses, or sheep; and a couple of distant church spires breaking up the horizon.

We spent the night in the historic city of Harlingen, on the North Sea coast, in a cozy old hotel with slightly slanted wooden floors, our window looking out onto a canal that flowed into the sea. This morning, our travels took us south along the coast to the beautiful town of Hindeloopen, where Amy's great-great-great-grandfather Pieter Thomas Menage was born in 1802. Hindeloopen is a magical little village of flowers and tiny old houses nestled in the protective embrace of an earthen dike. Amy and I were enchanted and vowed to return someday soon.

By then the day had started to slip away from us, so we regretfully left Hindeloopen behind to spend several hours on heavily traveled motorways that took us through and around a maze of smoggy cities from Amsterdam and Utrecht to Breda, and from there across the Belgian border to Antwerp, Ghent, and Brugge. Rain fell intermittently and the traffic was intense, so we were much relieved when the traffic thinned somewhat at the French frontier and the sun emerged from a bank of heavy clouds. There are actual hills in northern France, which were a welcome sight after the unending flatness of Holland and Belgium.

We had printed out Google Maps directions to the hotel we'd booked in Boulogne, and when we got off the motorway at the edge of town, we thought we were only minutes away from stretching out on our bed and resting our eyes. No such luck. At the end of the motorway's exit ramp, we encountered a detour, which threw us off our directions to such an extent that we wandered through side streets and battled one-ways for a good twenty minutes before we were able to find our lodging. As I was cursing this minor turn of fate, it occurred to me that since Alex and Helmut had to endure so much uncertainty and unpleasantness on their journey to Boulogne, perhaps it was only right that I experience 1/1000th of 1 percent of their tribulations.

Now, as I stand where they stood when their ocean-going odyssey finally ended, I am haunted by an admittedly irrational feeling of failure and the thought that we've come racing across the Low Countries to greet my grandfather and uncle as they stepped off the boat . . . only to have missed them. It's all part of my equally irrational desire to save Alex and Helmut from the fate that befell them a decade before I was born, the fruitless fantasy that brought me here in the first place. But I manage to shake off those sad and useless thoughts by recalling that there is work to be accomplished in the morning: the task of learning more about my relatives' brief encounter with this city.

There has been a settlement on this site for at least two thousand years. In 43 AD, the Roman emperor Claudius launched his invasion of the British Isles from here, when the town was known as Bononia and served as an important fortress city in the northernmost regions of the empire. The walls of the fort were renovated in the early fourth century and survive to this day, though parts of the battlements that remain—looking out over the English Channel from the hills that rise above the port—date from yet another repair job undertaken during the thirteenth century. Boulogne fell to the English in 1544, but was then brought back into French possession when King Henri II purchased it six years later. In 1805, the French emperor Napoleon, perhaps inspired by the example of Emperor Claudius, amassed a grand army in Boulogne and planned an invasion of England, but events on other fronts forced him to abandon the project.

Within the walled sections of this ancient city stands the magnificent Cathedral of Notre Dame, renovated in the nineteenth century to replace the original medieval cathedral, which was torched by revolutionaries in the early 1790s. The old earl's castle is also sheltered by the Roman wall, as is the city hall and the Bibliothèque Municipale. On Friday morning, under a deep blue sky, we walk up the hill from our hotel and pass through one of the four gates in the wall. For the first time since my long-ago eighth-grade French class, I actually find a use for the phrase *"Où est la bibliothèque?"* and we locate the library. With the assistance of two friendly librarians, one of whom speaks enough recognizable English to make up for our primitive French, we find several tall leather-bound editions of Boulogne newspapers from the spring of 1939.

"ALL OF THE FRENCH AND FOREIGN PRESS have been talking for some time now about the lamentable odyssey of Jews who fled Germany and who, on board steamships, have traveled from port to port, never finding the haven that they sought. But now France, perhaps the most hospitable nation in the world, is going to offer them the welcome that so many others have refused. More than two hundred Jewish refugees from the *SS St. Louis* will arrive early tomorrow morning in Boulogne-sur-Mer."

So read an article in the June 19, 1939, edition of *La Voix du Nord*—the *Voice of the North*—a regional newspaper serving several cities in northern France. Over the next few days, dispatches from the *Voice* reporter kept readers abreast of what was happening to these weary visitors to their hospitable shores.

At a few minutes past 4:00 a.m. on Tuesday, June 20, in calm seas, the *Rhakotis* pulled into Boulogne's outer harbor at the end of its relatively brief journey from Antwerp. It was a very warm morning and, due in part to the heat, a thick fog arose and blanketed the coast for miles in both directions. Foghorns sounded their booming calls, waking the passengers on board the *Rhakotis*, who were undoubtedly eager to finally set foot on dry land.

Toward 9 a.m., the fog began to lift, the skies cleared, the sun broke through the remaining wisps of mist, and the foghorns ceased their moaning. On board the *Rhakotis*, which was carrying both the French and English contingents of *St. Louis* refugees, small buckets of water were set out to facilitate a morning washing-up for the 224 arriving passengers. At about 10:00, a small shuttle boat, the *France*, left the inner harbor and steamed out to the *Rhakotis*. It was time for those disembarking in France to say farewell to the refugees bound for Southampton. Tears were shed by passengers who had become fast friends while in exile for more than a month and who now questioned whether they would ever see one another again.

Though outfitted for no more than fifty passengers, the *France* managed to accommodate all 224 refugees. They were greeted by Raymond-Raoul Lambert, the secretary general of the *Comité d'Assistance aux Réfugiés*, who had attended the planning meeting with Morris Troper in Paris five days earlier. Lambert declared grandly, "I welcome you on Free French soil." The *France* then made its way carefully past the breakwater and into the safety of the Boulogne harbor.

At 10:55 a.m., the *France* tied up at the dock. It was low tide and the boat rode the waves well below the level of the pier, where upward of two hundred people awaited the arrival of their visitors, a crowd made up of journalists, members of the Boulogne Jewish community, curious townspeople, and a few indigents drawn into the unexpected hubbub. As a gangway was attached to the side of the little boat, leading up to the pier, the exiles on board began to cheer and wave hats and handkerchiefs, many of them shouting, "*Vive la France!*" with tears visibly streaking their cheeks.

Three elderly women in their seventies were the first to disembark. They were quickly followed by a stream of young people and their parents, some pushing prams, and a crowd of older men, who formed the majority. Most of the adult passengers wore light-colored raincoats, and all carried a boxed breakfast that the CAR representatives had prepared for them. Each of the sixty children was presented with a bag full of fruits and sweets. "Some of the faces were sad," reported the press, "but nonetheless the refugees appeared to be in good health and seemed to be in good spirits."

On the pier, the journalists took photos and exchanged a few words with the newcomers, who were then ushered onto a fleet of waiting buses and driven about a mile to an establishment called the Hotel des Emigrants, at 41 Rue de Liane, where they would rest for several days before moving on to a less temporary address in France. Their luggage would follow, taken off the boat by the longshoremen of Boulogne, who refused payment for their labors. By 11:30, after having been the scene of so much unusual animation, the docks had resumed their normal pace.

A headline from the June 21, 1939, edition of the Voice of the North: "224 Jewish Refugees From the 'St. Louis' Disembarked Yesterday Morning in Boulogne." The subheadline reads, "The oldest of the group was 80 years old and the youngest only two months."

At the Hotel des Emigrants, the refugees were greeted by M. Sagnier, a member of the Boulogne Chamber of Commerce, and served a meal of hot coffee, croissants, local cheese, and soup. Everyone began to relax a little, and the reporters from *La Voix* were able to spend some time talking with the weary but happy travelers:

We were introduced to the most senior member of the contingent, an 80-year-old lady who has a son in Cuba. She got a glimpse of him from the deck of the *St. Louis* but was not permitted to go embrace him on land. The youngest refugee was a darling child, barely two months old.

One woman, whose husband already lives in Cuba, wanted to give us her impressions. "Our suffering during this voyage was more emotional than physical. Think of the pain that I suffered when I learned that I was not permitted to join my husband. The saddest moment of our long crossing was when they refused to let us disembark in Cuba. An epidemic of despair spread rapidly among us and we had to organize a suicide watch and formed an orchestra to cheer up those who were most desperate. I must say that we were well taken care of on board, but you can imagine our joy when we heard that we would be authorized to land at last." When our conversation ended, we were introduced by the CAR's Gaston Kahn to a charming three-year-old toddler who was in his grandmother's arms and who was unaware that his father, a physician in Berlin, had just died in a German concentration camp.

A reporter from *La Voix* interviewed a young woman from the *St. Louis*, who provided her impressions of the increasingly dangerous quality of daily life within Nazi Germany:

You are unaware of what is going on in my country. Espionage is everywhere. One day I telephoned one of my friends and someone was listening in on our conversation. "Wait," they said to me, "What is that last sentence you just uttered supposed to mean? This is the Gestapo . . . stay right where you are. We'll be there in fifteen minutes." In much less than fifteen minutes the agents were in my home. One of them said to me, "You called a certain person. In the future you are forbidden to call her." The Gestapo is everywhere; you run into their agents in all the streets, you see them in all the buildings. One of my friends' little boy was stopped in the street by a man who asked him, "What did your father say at lunchtime about Mr. Adolf Hitler? What did he say about the regime?" You in free France are unaware of what could happen in your country.

By mid-afternoon, the meal ended, the reporters packed up their notebooks and cameras, and the refugees settled into their rooms at the Hotel des Emigrants. They were permitted to stroll through the hotel's courtyard to get some fresh air and to use all the establishment's somewhat threadbare facilities, but for forty-eight hours they were not allowed to leave. On Thursday afternoon, however, the doors of the hotel were thrown open and the refugees were given the freedom to stroll wherever they wished through the streets of Boulogne. How wide those boulevards must have seemed to them after their long weeks at sea.

Their liberty lasted through the weekend. On Sunday morning, about thirty children, including the three youngest offspring of Joseph Karliner, left on a bus bound for the Villa Helvitia, a home managed by the *Oeuvre de Secours aux Enfants* (Agency for the Rescue of Children), known as the OSE. Then on Monday morning, June 26, the dispersal of the rest of the French contingent of *St. Louis* passengers took place. The journey began at 7 a.m., when forty-nine people, including Mr. and Mrs. Karliner and their older daughter, Ilse, left for Portiers. Then sixty-five departed for Le Mans, thirty-three for Laval, thirty for Paris, and eighteen, all of them men without spouses, including Alex and Helmut Goldschmidt, for the Professional Re-Education Center in the little village of Martigny-les-Bains in the French district known as the Vosges.

Before they rode away, the refugees expressed their thanks for the hospitality of the authorities, charitable organizations, and the citizens of Boulogne. They also sent telegrams of thanks to French Prime Minister Edouard Daladier and Minister of the Interior Albert Sarraut. Then the motors of the transport buses and autos roared to life and the two hundred souls who had been granted asylum in France, they who had so recently been among the more than nine hundred and had now been further divided, drove up the hill from the harbor and went their separate ways. They had been on French soil for seven days and now they were Wandering Jews once more.

FRIDAY, MAY 20, 2011. In the midst of uncovering these latest events in my grandfather and uncle's odyssey, we are inexplicably interrupted. At noon, we are politely informed that the Bibliothèque Municipale closes for lunch . . . until two o'clock. Eager to continue our research,

I mutter curses under my breath at this Gallic self-indulgence. A two-hour lunch break? On a weekday? As it happens, however, we spend those hours enjoying a delicious *petit déjeuner* of crepes and mineral water at a cozy café across the Place de la Résistance from the library, rambling the ramparts of the old city under a clear blue sky, and finally enjoying a doze, lying in each other's arms in a sunny, sheltered corner of the ancient walls. Not for the last time, I reflect that this continental manner of taking time away from work—by enjoying a long lunch or spending the entire month of August on vacation—is ultimately so much healthier and more civilized than our breathless American pursuit of getting and spending.

We are back in the library promptly at 2:00 and spend the next two hours gathering information from the *Voice of the North*. I emerge with eyes swimming from the effort of focusing on small newsprint and with a heart made heavy by my unresolved sense of failure, my irrational yet very real wish that I'd been here seventy-two springs ago to meet my relatives at the pier and usher them to safety. My mood grows no lighter as we walk back across the square and enter the magnificent Cathedral of Notre Dame just in time to witness the closing moments of a funeral. Six solemn pallbearers hoist the casket to their shoulders and, as they slowly carry the departed to his final resting place, the cathedral is filled with the sound of an organist playing a particularly ornate version of "Auld Lang Syne." My eyes fill to overflowing.

For the next couple of hours, Amy and I part company. Heading out for a run in Oldenburg a few days ago, she had sustained a foot injury. Armed with a phrase book, she walks off gingerly to buy a new pair of running shoes. I go to search for a trace of the Hotel des Emigrants.

Nine days after D-Day, on June 15, 1944, nearly three hundred planes of the Royal Air Force bombed the inner harbor of Boulogne-sur-Mer to prevent the German navy from using it as a base. The harbor and the segment of the Liane River that flows into the English Channel were completely destroyed. The boulevard running parallel to the river, the Rue de Liane, and the Hotel des Emigrants, at 41 Rue de Liane, were obliterated. Nevertheless, I am determined to stand where Alex and Helmut did when their long oceanic ordeal had ended and they enjoyed that first meal of hot soup. So, map in hand, I walk south of the harbor along a rebuilt Rue de Liane, looking for number 41.

The *Voice of the North* had mentioned that the hotel was "on the banks of the Liane," but today there are no buildings on the river side of the rue. On the opposite side of the street, I find a rather soulless apartment building with the number 42. This will have to do, I tell myself, and I take a couple of pictures with my little digital camera to commemorate my visit. But it's a deeply unsatisfying moment. No traces of the hotel remain, nothing for me to touch, to grasp, to embrace. I feel cheated.

Walking with eyes cast down as I cross the Rue de Liane, I incur the wrath of a motorist who has to slam on his brakes to avoid me. I sprawl onto the grass at the river's edge and gaze disconsolately at the current. I am chasing phantoms, I think, and nothing solid remains. Hell, I rage to myself, I don't even have any memories of these people I'm following. I recall our days in Friesland earlier in the week and envy Amy's memories of her grandfather Pete, who told her stories about his childhood journey to Friesland with his father Ysbrand, saying with a straight face that the captain had let him "drive the boat home." She spent summers with Pete in Iowa, where he raised pigs and chickens on his farm and refurbished feedbags in a workshop overrun with wild rabbits. He fed hobos during the Depression, earning the honor of their mark on his gate identifying him as a generous man. She remembers her grandfather's Zen-like last words to her in his eighty-ninth year: "You like rabbits. You run fast. You'll do OK."

I have none of that, I mourn. I never saw Alex or Helmut, never heard them speak or sing or laugh, never witnessed them perform any act, profound or quotidian. I wasn't there to help them hang a picture, mow the lawn, buy the weekly groceries, or hold their hands when, at the end of a long life well lived, death came to claim them, gently and peacefully, without violence or hate.

Fighting an inexorable wave of self-pity, I lie back on the grass and gaze upward into the unsullied blue bowl of the universe. I close my eyes and within minutes I am asleep, letting my subconscious do battle with my sense of loss. I awake in better spirits and walk briskly back to our hotel. Amy has conquered the language barrier and bought new sneakers, and I admire them happily. Life has gone on, as it does.

Later that evening, our last in Boulogne, we walk to the end of the pier and the entrance to the harbor. Because of the air raid of 1944, much has changed since Alex and Helmut's ship pulled in on June 20, 1939. This evening, accentuating the contrast, four paragliders have raced off the green cliffs extending away from the harbor to the east, and their colorful sails are soaring gracefully in the shifting air currents high above the sand.

But the entrance to the inner harbor is largely unchanged, with a narrow passageway of pilings leading from the open channel to the safety of the docks. The cliffs are still here, the long sandy beach is still here, the gulls with their melancholy calls are still here, and the sunshine and the endless waves are still here—just as they were on that solstice eve seventy-two years ago when my grandfather and uncle made their slow approach past the winking harbor lights to what must have seemed a genuinely safe mooring. I gaze out across the broad English Channel toward the beach in Dover where Matthew Arnold heard "the eternal note of sadness" in the unceasing tides and saw his "ignorant armies clash by night," and then look back to the harbor, trying my utmost to imagine what Alex and Helmut felt as they glided to their landing here in France. As I think of them passing slowly by on that June morning long ago, I am moved to lift my right hand in greeting; anyone watching would see me waving extravagantly at nothing at all.

They had experienced such terror in Germany and then the uncertainty of their long ocean voyage and now—*voila!*—it seemed that someone had use for them after all. Germany had kicked them out; Cuba, the United States, and Canada had turned their backs; and now here was France, against whom Alex had fought twenty-five years earlier, welcoming them into this sheltered harbor with its green cliffs, peaceful sands, and the noble dome of Our Lady looming protectively over them from the ancient walled city on the hill.

Toward dusk on a quiet evening in the year 636, according to local legend, worshippers emerging from a thatched chapel on these cliffs noticed a wooden ship without sails, oars, or a rudder enter the harbor and slowly approach land. When the people hurried down to the water's edge to investigate, they discovered that the ship was empty save for a three-foot-high carved statue of the Virgin Mary holding the child Jesus in her left arm. Over the gentle lapping of the surf, they heard a voice proclaim, "I choose your city as a sanctuary and a dwelling of grace." Awed, the people of Boulogne-sur-Mer built a shrine to Mary that, over the coming centuries, attracted pilgrims from all over Europe, among them Geoffrey Chaucer's Wife of Bath. It became one of the most important destinations in all Christendom, the site of many miracles.

On this golden evening by the sea, I wish I could have journeyed here in time to witness another one.

7

Martigny-les-Bains

SATURDAY, MAY 21, 2011. We awake to a thick fog blanketing the harbor, as nature replicates for us the conditions experienced by Alex and Helmut on their arrival. But the sun soon burns the mist away, presiding over a splendid spring day. Our route takes us up through hills wreathed with deep green forests and garlanded with vines and poppies and down through a valley that witnessed two of humankind's bloodiest battles. It is a day of feeling the freedom and exaltation of traveling through beautiful, unfamiliar countryside and of unhappy reminders of the reasons behind the journey. When we return home and, fumbling for a word to best describe for friends the overall mood of the trip, I settle on "schizophrenic," I think of this day as the one when I first truly began to recognize the delicate balance we're maintaining between limitless joy and inconsolable sorrow.

We drive our hardy little Meriva southeast from Boulogne past the ancient town of St. Quentin, founded by the Romans to replace an even older Celtic settlement that the Italian invaders had burned to the ground, and the holy city of Reims, the site of the coronation of the kings of France from the twelfth through the nineteenth centuries. We leave the expressway at Châlons-en-Champagne and immediately find ourselves driving through vineyards of Chardonnay, Pinot Noir, and Pinot Meunier grapes that will in time, through the sweet sorcery of the local *vignerons*, be transformed into the sparkling wine that has made

Through a rear-view mirror darkly . . . a picture of me taking a picture of our two constant companions, Helmut and Alex.

this region of France renowned throughout the world. Punctuating the rolling acres of grape-bearing vines are breathtaking fields of blood-red poppies that conjure up both Claude Monet's blooming painted hillside and the melancholy memorial flower of remembrance. Indeed, as if to make sure we do not forget, our route crosses the River Marne. In two battles fought along its banks during World War I, more than 750,000 soldiers from France, England, Germany, Italy, and the United States were either killed or grievously wounded. Today the river flows peacefully through the quiet valley, its gentle current a tranquil blue ribbon that binds together the vines and poppies, row on row.

We stop in the town of Bar-le-Duc and purchase two fresh baguettes and a hearty portion of goat cheese at a friendly *fromagerie*. A few miles down the road, we stop at a dusty little village, its few buildings all made of stone, and enjoy our lunch in a quiet churchyard. As we eat, my thoughts turn once again to Alex and Helmut. Did they, too, partake of crusty bread and flavorful cheese, perhaps washed down with a local vintage, on their June journey from Boulogne? Were they as transfixed by the countryside as we have been on this sunny May afternoon? Were they happy on that day so long ago? Dear God, I whisper, I hope so.

Shortly after 5 p.m., we pull into the town of Contrexéville and check into our hotel, the charming Inn of the Twelve Apostles. We are in the French *departement*, or state, known as the Vosges, which for many years has been the home of spas and health resorts, due in large measure to the region's naturally occurring thermal springs. Since 1774, when King Louis XV's doctor built the first spa here, Contrexéville water has been valued for its restorative powers. First bottled and sold in 1908, it's been owned and distributed by the international Nestlé company since 1992.

The Twelve Apostles has been here for more than a century, and its rooms reflect the fashions of a bygone era, though it does offer free Wi-Fi as an accommodation to modern desires to stay in touch. It also has a small swimming pool containing the town's warm healing waters, and Amy decides to shed the stiffness brought on by a day in the car with a vigorous swim. I, however, am anxious to see my grandfather and uncle's destination and decide to drive the eight or ten miles to Martigny-les-Bains alone.

The road to Martigny is a small country highway that meanders its pleasant, unhurried way through fields of wheat and stands of beech trees, over two bridges that cross a stream and a railway, and past the occasional farm, everything sharply illuminated by the still-brilliant sun slowly sinking toward the horizon. As I near the village, I pass a scene of utter pastoral peace and charm, a field of sheep whose newborn lambs leap and play in blissful abandon. I laugh out loud, which helps somewhat to ease the tension in my tightly held jaw and the hands that clench the steering wheel. I know that my relatives spent time in a formerly posh establishment known as the Hotel International, and as I enter the town limits of Martigny-les-Bains, I am anxious to see it and equally anxious to learn what my reaction will be.

I drive slowly down the main street, peering expectantly all around me. Then I see the outlines of the grand hotel to my left . . . and in sheer

What remains today of the luxurious Hotel International in Martigny-les-Bains. "O let not Time deceive you, you cannot conquer Time."

shock slam on the brakes. Luckily, no one is behind me, or I would doubtless have been rear-ended. The engine has stalled, but I manage to coax it to life again and steer the Meriva into a parking space at the edge of what was once an expanse of green lawn leading up to the splendors of the Hotel International. My heart thumping in my chest, I manage to climb out of the car, where I stand staring up at what is now a glorious ruin.

My legs have been rendered weak and my mouth hangs open stupidly as I begin a slow stumble forward, my eyes staring fixedly at broken towers, crumbling walls, and shattered windows. As I draw closer to the rictus of a doorway, the nearby village church bells begin to peal the arrival of seven o'clock. The unrelenting toll of hours sounds across the clear evening air and I think of W. H. Auden: "All the clocks in the city began to whirr and chime: 'O let not time deceive you, you cannot conquer Time.'" From a grove of trees to my left comes a loud cawing from a murder of crows, their calls a mocking accompaniment to the pitiless verdict of time and history.

For the next thirty minutes, I walk slowly and sadly through what remains of the Hotel International. Everywhere is peeling wallpaper, buckling floors, and the iron skeletons of wooden banisters. Doors have fallen into what were exquisite suites, threadbare carpets flap from once-regal stairways, the dust of decades lies thickly throughout. Retreating once more to the comfort of literature, I remember Charles Ryder and his shock upon returning to Brideshead and seeing the stately mansion fallen into decay.

I gather up a torn corner of brown wallpaper and a shard of broken glass as souvenirs and make my way slowly back to the car. I remain in a state of emotional paralysis, not quite able to comprehend the reality of what stands, all too real, right there before me. Perhaps the abandoned building echoes my own long-held fears of abandonment. But as I turn again to face the ruins of the Hotel International, I realize that this sight is a harsh reminder of what was to come for Alex and Helmut. The contrast between the smiling countryside and the unhappy story I am following keeps surprising me. Yet their time in Martigny-les-Bains could very well have been the high point of their ordeal.

"MARTIGNY, THE PRETTIEST of the Spas of the Vosges, is 218 miles from Paris and five hours via the Eastern Railway, situated on a plateau of 1,257 feet; it is the highest of the watering places in the basin of the Vosges. Known as the Thermal Versailles, Martigny has no equal in the Vosges and is supplied with every modern comfort. Everywhere there is an abundance of air, light, and space, essential factors in hygiene that make Martigny-les-Bains an especially salubrious resort. At no place better than Martigny can children benefit from such a healthful cure, and take their amusements or exercise in such safety, without need of the least supervision. Moreover, the healthiness of the country children excites the admiration of our visitors; the inhabitants are robust, and the longevity of the population is well known all around."

Those proudly forthright words appeared toward the end of the first decade of the twentieth century in a flier heralding the virtues of Martigny-les-Bains. And they weren't translated from the original

A promotional flier promoting the Hotel International in 1909. "Electricity in all the Rooms!"

French. Martigny was such a popular destination for citizens of London, Manchester, and Liverpool that a vigorous marketing campaign was conducted in English. Within this particular flier was a full-page advertisement for the Hotel International; among its offerings, proclaimed the ad, was a formal Five O'Clock Tea served on "the fine terrace with its magnificent view" and "Electricity in all the Rooms!"

The Hotel International was only one of many attractions of which the town could boast. There was also a casino, a fine park, an orchestra that performed nightly at the park's bandstand, a golf links that had been recently designed by a Mr. Cowington of Nice, and several healing springs, including the "Source des Dames," or Ladies' Spring, which "is somewhat lighter in composition and includes a small quantity of iron to aid in the cure of Dyspepsia and Anemia."

Martigny-les-Bains had been a thriving spa town since the 1860s, and by 1912 it had reached its zenith as a healing destination. In that year, the Hotel International's register included visitors from Paris and

London as well as from such faraway cities as Budapest, Monaco, Berlin, St. Petersburg, Nairobi, and Istanbul.

But the hotel's—and the town's—fortunes changed two years later, in 1914, at the outbreak of the Great War. The hotel shut down for the duration, and for more than four years, the cavalcade of the well-heeled unwell stopped coming to take the healing waters. Business resumed during the early twenties, but the Crash of 1929 was a severe blow to the area's fortunes. By 1933, the grand Hotel International had closed its doors for the last time as a place of revelry and the pursuit of good health.

That same year, Adolf Hitler assumed power in neighboring Germany. Within months of the establishment of National Socialist rule on January 30, thousands of German Jewish refugees streamed across the border to find a haven in France. Unlike the United States, with its quota-driven Immigration Act of 1924, France had never passed legislation that limited immigration. In fact, due largely to the devastation of its labor force in the Great War, France was actively encouraging foreigners to cross its borders to take up the plow or the wrench or to assume a place in an assembly line to help revive its moribund economy. And with both political and personal conditions in Germany deteriorating steadily for the Jews, more and more of them chose to settle their affairs in the land of their birth and begin life anew in the land of liberty, equality, and fraternity. Upon their arrival, these new immigrants found themselves taking part in the latest act of the long-running and sometimes uneasy saga that has been the history of the Jews in France.

The year 1492 is famous in American history for the first voyage of Christopher Columbus and infamous in the history of the Jews as the year they were expelled from Spain. But a century earlier, in 1394, the Jews were forced to leave the kingdom of France. Over the next four hundred years, about forty thousand Jews managed to make their way back into France, with most of them toiling in rural regions and only about five hundred allowed to make a life in the thriving capital of Paris. But then came the French Revolution, and to the astonishment, perhaps, of the Jews themselves, they learned that the Declaration of the Rights of Man and of the Citizen extended to them as well. France became, along with the United States, the first country on earth to bestow upon the Jews full political, legal, economic, and social equality.

A few niggling exceptions remained on the books, such as the *More Judaico*, a special oath that Jews had been required to utter in court since the Middle Ages ("If I am not telling the truth, may I be stricken with plagues such as those visited upon Egypt when we escaped"), which was not abolished until 1846. Until 1831, synagogues received no public funding, unlike Christian churches. In that year, however, a special vote in the Chamber of Deputies established that the two religions would receive equal grants from the Ministry of Cults.

During the middle decades of the nineteenth century, Jewish participation in French social, financial, political, and cultural life indicated the degree to which their emancipation had taken hold. Established in Paris in 1812, the Rothschild bank soon took its place among the most important financial institutions in Europe. Achille Fould was appointed finance minister in 1848 and then four years later served as Napoleon III's minister of state. And the dazzling opera and theater stages of Paris were nightly illuminated by the contributions of composers Jacques Offenbach and Giacomo Meyerbeer, playwright Ludovic Halevy, and actress Sarah Bernhardt.

Then came humiliating defeat in the Franco-Prussian War of 1870–1871, an economic recession, and the rise of a persistent and, at times, virulent anti-Semitism. French pride was deeply wounded by their military defeat as well as the political aftermath, the ceding of the provinces of Alsace and Lorraine to the victorious Germans. In the inevitable search for scapegoats, the fact that many Jews spoke French with German accents placed them under suspicion in the eyes of the easily manipulated. Some blamed the recession of the early 1880s on the pernicious influence of the Rothschilds and other Jewish bankers. Then in 1886, a man named Edouard Drumont published a twelve-hundred-page, two-volume book called *La France juive* in which he named the Jews as the source of all the ills, social and economic, that plagued modern France. By the end of the year, Drumont's book had sold more than a hundred thousand copies. Six years later, encouraged by the continuing hearty sales of the book, Drumont founded a daily newspaper, *La Libre parole*, to extend the reach of his anti-Semitic views. Two years after that, the Dreyfus Affair ignited France, calling into question the acceptance by their country's majority that so many French Jews had assumed was theirs.

On November 1, 1894, a front-page article in *La Libre parole* announced the arrest of "the Jewish officer A. Dreyfus" on charges of treason. The paper declared that there was "absolute proof that he had sold our secrets to Germany." Based on entirely trumped-up evidence, a thirty-five-year-old officer named Alfred Dreyfus was arrested and accused of being a spy for Germany. Dreyfus was from a wealthy family in the Alsace region, which had been annexed by Germany in the aftermath of the war in 1871, and was thus suspected of harboring German sympathies. More suspicious yet, Dreyfus was a Jew whose primary allegiance—the newspaper charged—was to his "race" rather than to his country.

After a four-day trial, Captain Dreyfus was unanimously convicted and sentenced to life imprisonment on Devil's Island, a military garrison off the northern coast of South America. Two years later, evidence emerged that another French army officer, Major Ferdinand Walsin Esterhazy, was the real culprit, but high-ranking figures in the army, determined to protect the institution's reputation, initiated a cover-up. Major Esterhazy was indeed brought to trial, but further forgeries were presented in court as evidence against Captain Dreyfus, and Esterhazy was acquitted.

But slowly, the arc of the affair began to bend toward justice. On January 13, 1898, on the front page of the newspaper *L'Aurore*, the celebrated writer Emile Zola published his electrifying open letter to the president of France titled "J'Accuse . . ." Zola pointed to numerous judicial errors in the handling of the trial and the lack of credible evidence, and he concluded his impassioned letter by accusing the government of engaging in anti-Semitism, which he ringingly called "the scourge of our time." Largely as the result of "J'Accuse . . . ," Captain Dreyfus was brought back to France from Devil's Island in 1899 for a retrial. He was convicted yet again, but, said the court, owing to "extenuating circumstances" his sentence was reduced from life imprisonment to ten years.

The Dreyfus Affair both caused and exposed major rifts in French society. Families and friendships were torn asunder by conflicting views of the captain's guilt or innocence. There were the Dreyfusards, who supported the view that he was innocent and had been the victim of, in Zola's phrase, "a miscarriage of justice," and there were the anti-Dreyfusards, who believed that death, not Devil's Island, would have been the proper sentence. Egged on by editorials in *La Libre parole* and other organs of the popular press, thousands of anti-Dreyfusards marched through the streets of scores of French cities, calling for the arrest of Jewish citizens, smashing the windows of Jewish-owned stores, and occasionally breaking into and looting synagogues. The plague of anti-Semitism even infected such great artists as the painters Edgar Degas, Paul Cezanne, and Pierre-Auguste Renoir, who began to speak dismissively of "Jewish art."

The Hungarian writer Theodore Herzl, assigned by a Viennese newspaper to cover the initial Dreyfus trial, came away from his weeks in Paris convinced that, even in France, the cradle of revolutionary equality, Jews could never hope for full acceptance and fair treatment. Thus, he reasoned, Jews required their own homeland. In 1896, Herzl published a book called *Der Judenstaat* and founded the World Zionist Organization, which called for the founding of a Jewish state in Palestine.

The Dreyfus Affair also gave rise to an international sporting event. The most widely read sports daily in France, *Le Velo*, was proudly Dreyfusard in its views. Anti-Drefusards, anxious to have their own sporting news to consume every day, founded a rival rag called *L'Auto* in 1900. But by 1903, *L'Auto's* circulation had declined to the point that its wealthy backers feared that it might go out of business. So to boost interest in the paper, *L'Auto* announced the launch of a new long-distance bicycle race with an itinerary and cash prizes that would vastly exceed those of any race currently in existence. Thus was born the Tour de France.

Finally, in 1906, twelve years after his arrest and conviction, Dreyfus was acquitted of all charges by the High Court of Appeal. He was reinstated into the ranks of the French army with the rank of major and was awarded the Cross of the Legion of Honor. In 1914, he volunteered for service in the Great War, rising to the rank of lieutenant colonel. Alfred Dreyfus died two days before Bastille Day in 1935, aged seventy-five.

In 2006, French President Jacques Chirac presided over a ceremony marking the one hundredth anniversary of Dreyfus's acquittal. In the presence of the living heirs of both Dreyfus and Zola, Chirac declared that "the combat against the dark forces of intolerance and hate is never definitively won."

The dark forces of anti-Semitism retreated in France in the aftermath of the Dreyfus Affair, but it was a tactical retreat only, not a surrender; conditions more favorable to their advancement would return soon enough. In the meantime, the atmosphere brightened.

Although the affair had exposed anti-Semitic elements in the French army, it didn't dampen Jewish enthusiasm to take part in the military affairs of their homeland. The Jewish population of France in 1914 was roughly 120,000. An impressive 38 percent of that number, or 46,000 Jews, fought for France during the War to End All Wars, with about 6,500 dying in combat. When peace returned to the land, Jewish artists, from Amadeo Modigliani and Marc Chagall to Darius Milhaud and Tristan Tzara, were major reasons that Paris took its place as the most celebrated cultural city in the world during the 1920s.

But it was not only artists who were made to feel welcome in France in the years following the Great War. France had suffered a greater percentage of national loss during the war than that of any of the other major combatants. Nearly 1.7 million French soldiers and civilians perished in the war, or nearly 4.3 percent of the entire population. (By way of comparison, Germany lost 3.8 percent, the United Kingdom lost 2.2 percent, and the United States lost 0.13 percent of its population.) During the decade that followed the war, many voices in France expressed the fear that the country's stagnant population—in 1925, for instance, France grew by only sixty thousand citizens, while Germany's population increased by half a million—would inevitably lead to another war with its Prussian neighbor and a likely defeat. To rebuild its population, including its vastly reduced labor force, France embarked on an ambitious and aggressive campaign to attract foreigners to cross its borders and establish a new homeland for themselves.

Encouraged by the national government, factories recruited workers from across Europe in an attempt to get their production lines humming again. In August 1927, the National Assembly passed a new and significantly liberalized naturalization law. Whereas before a person had to be at least twenty-one years old and had to have been a resident of France for ten years to be considered for citizenship, the new law required only three years' residency and a minimum age of eighteen. By the end of 1927, with the new law in effect for only four months, the number of newly naturalized French citizens was triple that of the previous year. With the United States having enacted its much more restrictive immigration law three years earlier, in 1924, France was now seen as a new haven for refugees, and the numbers kept growing over the next several years. In 1933, the year Adolf Hitler came to power, between twenty-five thousand and forty thousand German citizens crossed the border seeking refuge in France, about 85 percent of them Jews.

If both native-born and newly arrived Jewish citizens questioned the degree to which their new homeland welcomed their presence, a wildly affirmative answer seemed to arrive in 1936, when France became the first country to elect a Jewish prime minister. True, four months before the election he had been dragged from his car and beaten by an anti-Semitic mob, but on June 4, Leon Blum assumed the prime minister's office as leader of the government known as the Popular Front. Although Blum was denounced as a "cunning talmudist" by a right-wing member of the National Assembly, the country certainly had come a long way from the railroading of Captain Alfred Dreyfus.

But the worldwide economic depression of the early thirties, which by no means spared France, caused something of a backlash against more liberal immigration statutes, as economic security grew more precarious and foreign-born workers were viewed with greater suspicion and hostility. By the mid-thirties some of the welcoming provisions of the previous decade had been rolled back and thousands of refugees—their citizenship no longer so easily obtained—had been thrown into prison. As the decade approached its end, hundreds of thousands of Republican sympathizers poured over the border from Spain, refugees from the bloody Spanish Civil War. The immigration issue became a topic for heated debate in the National Assembly and elsewhere in France as the country weighed its egalitarian ideals against the social and economic realities of the uncertain present. This was the atmosphere that gave rise to a new conception of how to honor the creed of fairness for all, an idea rooted in the French soil.

Beginning in 1933, a proposal was made to settle refugees in rural areas of France to assist the country's farmers with their dawn-to-dusk endeavors. No less than their urban brethren who oversaw factories, French agricultural workers were still feeling the effects of the devastation wrought on the national population by the Great War. So it seemed a natural fit to pair newly arrived men and women who were eager to work with farmers who needed capable laborers to tend the vineyards in the sparsely settled hinterlands of France.

Two of the voices who spoke out in favor of this idea belonged to leaders we've already met. Raymond-Raoul Lambert, who as secretary general of the *Comité d'Assistance aux Réfugiés* (CAR) greeted the *St. Louis* passengers when they landed at Boulogne-sur-Mer, wrote approvingly of the proposal in a widely read Jewish journal in the summer of 1933. And Louise Weiss of the Central Refugee Committee of Paris, who helped broker the French agreement to accept the *St. Louis* passengers, lobbied for the idea later in the decade. The popularity of the proposal ebbed and flowed through the thirties, closely tracking the country's economy, but after the widely reported atrocities of *Kristallnacht* on November 9, 1938, which resulted in a new flood of Jewish refugees from Germany, French authorities were spurred to act.

In the immediate aftermath of *Kristallnacht*, the government agreed to a recommendation from an international Jewish relief organization to accept 250 children under the age of fifteen and added that it would accept a thousand more children if homes could be found for them in the provinces. Over the next few months, CAR and other refugee organizations, sensing a shift in public opinion, increased their efforts. In early 1939, CAR purchased property in the Burgundy region on which to build an agricultural center for refugees. The master plan was for a series of such "agricultural retraining centers," where refugees would learn farming techniques and receive instruction in such professions as the wood and iron trades. Whereas Jewish relief groups saw the plan as an opportunity for refugees to escape the dangers of Nazi Germany and learn a new skill in the bargain, the French government was more interested in the plan as a means of providing the immigrants with tools that would more quickly enable them to find a new home away from France. But the two sides reconciled their differences for the most part and worked together for the venture's success. A CAR representative wrote in a Paris newspaper that the new Jewish agricultural settlements would "put an end to the anguish of these unfortunates who have been searching the world over for a hospitable land" and would also "give new life to deserted villages, to houses in ruin, to uncultivated land."

In the late winter and early spring of 1939, five of these agricultural centers were organized, with funds provided by three groups: CAR; the American Jewish Joint Distribution Committee; and the Jewish Group for Coordination, Aid, and Protection, an organization sponsored chiefly by Robert de Rothschild of the famous French banking family. One of the centers took shape in Argenteuil, the charming village on the River Seine that was once the summer home of the great painters Claude Monet, Auguste Renoir, and Georges Braque. Agricultural centers also sprang up near Nice at Sainte Radegonde and the Villa Pessicarl, and in the south central French *departement* of Corrèze, the birthplace of film director Eric Rohmer.

The agricultural settlement that would see the largest influx of refugees was organized in Martigny-les-Bains, a destination spot that had boasted an internationally regarded luxury hotel thirty years earlier and was now fully living up to CAR's description of it as a "deserted village" with "houses in ruin." On March 31, 1939, the Jewish newspaper *La Tribune Juive* reported:

> Our German Jewish refugees who were not legally in France were until now not able to get a residence permit and were subject to imprisonment for breaking the residence laws. To ameliorate this lamentable state of affairs, a number of refugee assistance groups have come up with the idea of creating "welcome centers" to house persons whose legal status is irregular, centers where they

would be authorized to stay by the Ministry of the Interior. The aid groups have just created such a center in Martigny-les-Bains, an abandoned summer resort a few kilometers from Vittel. The refugees take professional re-education classes, taught by French professors, with the goal of preparing them for other occupations while they await emigration to their final destination.

About a week later, an article appeared in *L'Univers Israélite*, a Jewish weekly published in Paris:

The Jewish Group for Coordination, Aid, and Protection is setting up a center in Martigny-les-Bains for German and central European Jews to provide professional re-education to facilitate their emigration. The Group has arranged access to a large hotel and the center will be operational as of next week. The importance of this undertaking will not be lost on our readers, and we are issuing an urgent appeal for help in providing the refugees at Martigny-les-Bains with games and activities to occupy their leisure time. We would be particularly grateful for the generosity of those who could provide one or more radios, dominos, checkers, chess sets, etc., even if they are used. Simply contact the Group (4 Rue du Cirque, Paris), and they will arrange to pick up the goods and ensure their transport to the Center. We would also be grateful to our readers if they could send directly to the Center for Refugees in Martigny-les-Bains, Vosges, any magazines, periodicals, books, or newspapers, in French or German, that they have finished reading.

All the objects donated to the center, from books to dominos, arrived at the Hotel International, the once imposing retreat for the beautiful people of Europe who came to take the local restorative waters, a building that would now provide both dorm rooms and classrooms for Jewish refugees. The hotel had fallen on hard times since its heyday and had most recently been called upon to shelter a few refugees from the fighting in Spain. Peter Hart, a volunteer for the center and author of the memoir *Journey Into Freedom*, wrote of his reaction upon arriving at Martigny as part of an advance party in late February of 1939: "Nobody had prepared us for what we would find inside the Hotel International. Wallpaper was hanging from the walls in strips and everything from the floor upwards was black with dirt; cobwebs hung everywhere. There were no washbasins in any of the bedrooms and no running water on any of the floors. It was icy cold and no stove in sight. There was no time to waste if we wanted to sleep that night and get some rooms ready for the first arrivals in two days' time. We worked until we collapsed late that evening and for twenty hours the next day. In the large dining room a vast amount of equipment was stored. It had just arrived from Paris and consisted of beds, mattresses, blankets, kitchen and office supplies, machines, workbenches, tools, and various canned goods. Everything was brand new and still wrapped up."

On March 23, 1939, at the Joint offices in Paris, Raymond-Raoul Lambert reported on the early stages of the agricultural center at Martigny-les-Bains, where "we have land and farms and, under the supervision of monitors supplied by the French ministry, the work is being carried out. We intend to place on the land a certain number of young people whom we hope will be able to emigrate or find a home in the French countryside eventually. Martigny-les-Bains currently has fifty people working the land and we hope to place a further five hundred refugees there."

The Martigny center's farm consisted of about seventy acres of land not far from the Hotel International and included at first five cows, two horses, a dozen sheep, forty chickens, and several roosters. A blond ex-gym teacher from Vienna, a man named Schindler, was in charge of the farm and taught most of the agricultural courses to an initial group of thirty students, none of whom had ever turned the soil but who, Peter Hart whimsically observed, "took to the work like ducks to water." In no time, Herr Schindler assumed the sunburned persona of a French farmer.

With the coming of spring, the student refugees planted a vegetable garden. The garden's initial harvest, supplemented by the eggs from the chickens, the milk from the cows and sheep, plus the resulting butter and cheese, brought a certain level of self-sufficiency to the center. Within a very short time, the center began to sell some of its products to the villagers of Martigny-les-Bains and the surrounding countryside.

Within the formerly splendid walls of the Hotel International, the refugees slept and washed upstairs in the guest rooms, while down below in the meeting rooms the center conducted classes in a number of trades, all designed to make emigration more likely for these newly trained workers. Described by Hart as "looking like a University for all ages," the center offered classes in metalworking, welding, woodworking, shoe repair, automobile repair, electrical work, dressmaking, and the millinery trade, all supervised by professors from the National Professional School in nearby Épinal. Meals were served in the hotel's still spacious dining rooms, with most of the food provided by the center's farm. Medical care was easily obtained in the center's infirmary, also housed within the Hotel International, which employed a nursing staff operating under the direction of the doctor of Martigny. The refugees' leisure time was also well provided for; in addition to the donated chess sets and other games, the refugees had access to a piano, several radios, a Ping-Pong table, and a soccer field. Plans were announced for a clay tennis court.

The Hotel International also had a small synagogue in one of the meeting rooms. A rabbi was hired to lead prayers and services and to preside over the ritual slaughtering of farm animals so that kosher meals could be served.

The retraining classes offered a challenge to some of the refugees who had enjoyed professional status in their former lives. The organizers of the center had deliberately decided not to provide courses in academics or the law, lest well-connected members of those professions, fearing competition, raise public objections to the program. A center that turned out agricultural workers and other manual laborers maintained a much lower and safer profile. Thus, many a pair of hands that had never hefted anything heavier than a dictionary sported shiny calluses from wielding an awl or a hammer, or from carrying gas cylinders to the welding shop.

Some refugee centers in France accepted children, but the agricultural center at Martigny was purposefully organized as a mature undertaking; only single adults and couples without children were assigned there. The refugees elected representatives to meet regularly with the center's management to resolve disputes and ease occasional tensions. The refugees were officially confined to the hotel, its grounds, and the center's farm. In order to venture out into the village, a refugee needed an authorized affidavit signed by one of the center's deputies granting permission. But as time went by and the refugees and villagers mingled more and more on market days and other occasions, barriers both physical and social began to disappear. Spring and summer bring beautiful days to the French countryside and, in contrast to the hate and danger most of the refugees had so recently escaped, the village of Martigny-les-Bains lived up to its reputation as a place of healing for its grateful new residents.

Into this peaceful, pastoral atmosphere Grandfather Alex and Uncle Helmut arrived on Tuesday, June 27, 1939. Along with their sixteen fellow passengers on the *St. Louis*, Alex and Helmut were checked into the center, assigned a room in the Hotel International, and informed that they would be expected—in addition to their daily class work—to volunteer for duty in the kitchen, the laundry, or the garden. The center's representative, who was fluent in both French and German, told them that a well-run kitchen and laundry and a well-kept garden were all vital to a flourishing community and that no one at the center viewed those daily tasks as mere drudgery, but rather as important contributions to the center's high morale.

After dinner in the hotel dining room and a good night's sleep, followed by a hearty breakfast, Alex and Helmut were interviewed by another of the center's representatives to determine which classes would suit them. Perhaps Alex was influenced by the fact that he came from a long line of rural horse dealers, or maybe he recalled the pleasure his older son took in maintaining the chicken run at the elegant Goldschmidt house in Oldenburg. Whatever his reasons, my grandfather chose to learn the craft of raising chickens on the Martigny farm. Helmut also chose to spend his days on the farm, where he assisted in tending the sheep and in planting and nurturing sturdy crops of potatoes, beans, oats, and wheat.

For the next two months, father and son rose at dawn five days a week to attend to their duties on the farm. Helmut, summoning his organizational skills, assisted in the neat arrangement of tools, seeds, rope, and other supplies in the farm's barn and stable. At noon, the two of them would unwrap sandwiches of cheese and sausage, made for them that morning in the hotel kitchen, and join their fellow farmers for lunch either in the fields or, if the sun was particularly fierce that day, in the shade of a shed of planks that had been fashioned in the woodworkers' shop. Three evenings a week, they washed dishes after dinner in the hotel kitchen before retiring to the game room, where Alex enjoyed an ongoing skirmish on a chess board with a man from Stuttgart who had spent his day learning how to cobble shoes. Helmut read quietly in a corner. After quaffing a schnapps or a glass of hot tea, they would retire by ten.

Those two months must truly have seemed idyllic for my grand-father and uncle, following their harrowing six weeks at sea and six years of ever-increasing terror and humiliation. The work was hard and the hours were long, but their labors were directed toward the success and well-being of this unique community. If they were not wholly free men, if their options did not include taking the train to Paris and from there making a second attempt to reach the New World, they surely must have thought that their rural redoubt was a beautiful, if temporary, shelter from the perils of their homeland. As Alex scattered feed for his chickens and Helmut tended his crops, they must have dreamed of a happy harvest of ripe vegetables and plump poultry in the coming autumn and of their own liberation by the time spring returned to the surrounding hills.

On July 14, Bastille Day, Alex and Helmut joined their fellow refugees in laying a wreath at the war memorial in Martigny's public square. Then the townspeople and the refugees took part in a ceremony on the front lawn of the Hotel International, where one of the refugee gardeners had planted flowers of red, white, and blue to spell out *Vive la France*. That night, the Bastille Day fireworks were set off within the boundaries of the agricultural center, and again refugees and citizens of Martigny mingled happily in the warm, festive summer night.

In early August, the French periodical *L'Univers Israélite* published a feature about the center at Martigny, complete with photographs of the hotel and some of the workshops. Titled "A Fine Communal Accomplishment," the article described the center's activities and its "extremely cordial" relations with the people of Martigny-les-Bains. Its concluding paragraph reads, "One cannot over-emphasize the importance of this achievement. Condemned to idleness and dependent on public assistance which was always insufficient, these refugees would be doomed to a life of poverty in an urban setting. As active members of a community where they are introduced to new activities, despite the difficulties of re-adapting, they realize that with a bit of energy and thanks to the solidarity of the Jewish community, they can once again aspire to be the architects of their own destiny."

Four weeks later, German troops overwhelmed Poland, France declared war on Germany, and my grandfather and uncle's destinies were once again subject to the architects of uncertainty.

SUNDAY, MAY 22, 2011. The peaceful sounds of chiming church bells and cooing doves awaken us to a cool, cloudy morning in Contrexéville. Downstairs in the dining room of the Inn of the Twelve Apostles, we linger over croissants, locally harvested honey, tasty locally made strawberry preserves, and pots of aromatic tea. After breakfast, we stroll through the municipal park, admiring the graceful fountains and carefully cultivated flower beds and doing our best to decipher the rules of a game of bocce that seems to be an essential Sunday morning ritual for the elderly men of Contrexéville. As noon approaches, we climb into the Meriva and make the pleasant drive down to Martigny-les-Bains. I eagerly point out to Amy the green field where the lambs had frolicked yesterday afternoon, but today the expanse of grass and clover stands empty. I wonder for a moment if I imagined the sheep, and as we enter the village, I half expect to see a thriving Hotel International, guests on the wide veranda enjoying a formal luncheon amid tuxedoed waiters. But no . . . the ruined facade of the old hotel is as bleak and unrelenting as it was the evening before.

Today, though, we have an appointment with the living. I have made contact with Madame Gerard Liliane, a woman in her eighties who remembers the glory days when her little village was a destination spot for travelers throughout the continent. I am eager to learn what she recalls of the summer of 1939 when—who knows?—she may have mingled with Alex or Helmut and gasped in delight as the fireworks illuminated the night sky over Martigny on that long-ago Fourteenth of July. As we pull into her driveway off the Rue de Dompierre, the sun emerges from behind its cloud cover and the stone walls of her snug little house seem to gleam. Leaning on a cane, Madame greets us extravagantly and ushers us into her parlor where she offers us slices of a strawberry cake she baked that morning. We are joined by her granddaughter Manon, who will be our translator; Madame's English is as nonexistent as our French.

Over the next hour and a half, we learn that we have just missed the annual Escargot Festival, which culminates in the naming of Miss Shell, an honor won last year by Manon's sister; that the Hotel International was the finest establishment of its kind in all of the Vosges; and that Martigny's city hall recently sold the hotel to a real estate company that plans to convert the building into a medical center for the treatment of stress, anemia, anorexia, and bulimia. Madame Liliane produces another newly baked wonder, a chocolate cake this time, Manon puts on an Edith Piaf CD, and everyone sings along lustily to the Little Sparrow's defiant anthem "Non, Je Ne Regrette Rien." It is a jolly gathering and *tres Francais*. When we depart several hours later, we exchange warm two-cheek kisses in the debonair French manner.

But the long afternoon has ended on a note of frustration. Though she was nine or ten years old in that summer of 1939, Madame Liliane claims no memories of encountering refugees at the agricultural center headquartered at her beloved Hotel International. I pull out a copy of the article in the *L'Univers Israélite* that I've brought with me—the article that emphasizes the friendly relations between refugees and townspeople—and Madame scans it eagerly but says that she had no idea that the people staying at the hotel that summer were refugees, most of them from Nazi Germany. I suppose that it's certainly possible that a little girl would have been protected from the details of where the hotel's residents had come from and why they had left their homes, but today Madame Liliane thinks of herself as a historian of the hotel. It is from her that I received the flier touting the many healthy virtues of Martigny-les-Bains in general and of the Hotel International in particular, details that I quoted earlier in this chapter. How could she have remained ignorant of this crucial period in the chronicles of her village, a place she has called home for more than eighty years?

Neither of us knows for sure, of course, but as I show Amy around the hotel's sad remains, we discuss Madame Liliane's memory. We recall the not-quite-believable claims of people who lived in close proximity to Dachau or Treblinka and never noticed anything amiss, even as sinister smoke curled up from the chimneys of the crematoria. Was this self-styled historian sweeping a somewhat damning segment of history under the rug? Or—a more benign explanation—was she simply more engaged by stories of well-to-do guests sipping champagne and sharing a tureen of lobster bisque on a golden afternoon in 1912 than she was in a tale of refugees raising sheep as the shadows of war lengthened in the late summer of 1939?

As we gaze a final time at the place that was Alex and Helmut's shelter for those halcyon months, we acknowledge that in one crucial respect, it doesn't matter whether or not Madame Liliane was aware of the truth. We had traveled to Martigny to learn a few precious details about how my grandfather and uncle had passed their time here and had discovered this particular oracle to be mute. In the absence of hard facts, we are left with the metaphor of the crumbling grand hotel and its image of ruthless time, a *memento mori* of steel and stone and warped wood that reminds me yet again of the futility of my desire to save my doomed relatives. There is nothing to do but drive pensively back to our comfortable Inn of the Twelve Apostles.

Yet, thwarted as I feel by Madame Liliane's failure of memory, saddened as I am by the hotel's stark reminder that all things must pass,

I continue to experience a certain exhilaration brought about by the realization that I am seeing the same countryside and breathing the same air as Alex and Helmut did while living in Martigny seventy-two years ago. I am witnessing the very place where they greeted each new morning and where they rested each night after their toil in the fields. I am bearing witness.

As we once more pass the green field on the edge of town, I see that the sheep have returned and the lambs are as frisky and joyous as on the previous afternoon. Tossed between emotions, the sorrow of my loss and the satisfaction of my quest, I find myself wondering if any of these lambs could possibly be the descendants of the sheep that Helmut tended during those tranquil summer days so long ago. The fanciful idea enchants me. I stop the car, and Amy and I spend a good ten minutes watching the woolly revelry.

And because my mind works in the way it does, I recall lines from Wordsworth's immortal Ode: "Let the young Lambs bound as to the tabor's sound! We in thought will join your throng, ye that feel the gladness of the May! We will grieve not, rather find strength in what remains behind; in the soothing thoughts that spring out of human suffering; thoughts that do often lie too deep for tears."

APRIL 2012. Despite my best detective efforts and those of the dedicated researchers I've met through the United States Holocaust Memorial Museum, there has always remained a small but vexing break in the thread of Alex and Helmut's journey through France. I know that they spent those summer months of 1939 at the agricultural center in Martigny-les-Bains and that they arrived in Montauban in October 1940. But where were they during those roughly thirteen months from September 1939 to October 1940? In the first quarter of 2012, even as I have begun setting down their story, some answers to that question emerge from an unexpected but most welcome source.

In early February, quite out of the blue, I receive a letter from Cheshire, England, written by a Steven Behrens, who had come across my earlier book, *The Inextinguishable Symphony*, and determined that we are related. We share a common great-great-grandfather, Elkan Simon Behrens, the father of the Bremen coffee importer Ludwig Behrens, who was the father of Toni Behrens, who married my grandfather Alex Goldschmidt. Steven's great-grandfather was Ludwig's cousin. My family is so small that any news of a direct relative is good news indeed. Steven and I begin an enthusiastic e-mail and telephone exchange and plan to meet, either in Cheshire or in our ancestral homeland of Germany, as soon as possible.

Meanwhile, Steven's tireless genealogical research turns up a clue to Alex and Helmut's whereabouts during those missing thirteen months. Max Markreich, who married Toni's sister Johanna and managed to emigrate safely to the Western Hemisphere in 1939, left behind a fascinating trove of letters at the time of his death in 1962. One of them was a letter my grandfather sent to Mr. and Mrs. Markreich in their internment camp in Trinidad. The letter is dated January 27, 1940 . . . precisely in the midst of those mysterious months. The return address is listed as Camp du Martinet, Sionne, Vosges.

In his letter, Alex declares,

When we began our departure almost ¾ of a year ago on the *St. Louis* we could not imagine how things would turn out for us. Now our journey has taken us even further and our family is totally torn apart. I hear from Toni, Eva, Günther, and Rosemarie, though I have been without news from them for a while. I have also not had any news from Helmut for two weeks. We are temporarily separated as I came to this hospital in Contrexéville about three weeks ago because of constant eczema on my head and neck, but it is healing now. Our address is still the same as the one at the beginning of this letter. Helmut is big and strong, but it is very regrettable that he cannot get a professional education. I am very much looking forward to seeing him again, although I am *very well off* here.

In September, when we came to this camp, I never thought that the war would last so long, but expected a rapid fall of Hitler's regime. I am still today of the opinion that everything will end suddenly, that Hitler's chances are getting worse from week to week, and that he is in a blind alley from which he cannot turn back. So we are not giving up hope, my dears, that we will be reunited again in the not too distant future. No one knows where or when.

So that's where they were, for at least part of that time. I seize a map of France and find that Sionne is a village about thirty-five miles north of Martigny-les-Bains and only about five miles away from the larger town of Neufchâteau, which I remember from a road sign as we drove away from Contrexéville. I check the Internet for the tourist office of Neufchâteau and e-mail them requesting information about the establishment of refugee or internment camps in that region of France immediately following the outbreak of war in September 1939. After a few exchanges, I receive a very kind, informative dispatch from Monsieur Julien Duvaux of Neufchâteau. He essentially clears up the mystery of most of those thirteen months and confirms the accuracy of the return address on Alex's letter of January 1940.

On September 1, 1939, as Helmut's spring lambs were being readied for market, the German army smashed into Poland. Two days later, France and England declared war on Germany and the Second World War began. Preparations for fighting had been going on for some time, as had plans for the large numbers of foreigners, particularly Germans, who were living in France. On September 14, a national radio announcement ordered all male German citizens in France who were between the ages of fifty and sixty-five to prepare for internment. There followed a flurry of weddings, as an addendum to the decree promised freedom for all foreigners who had married a French woman.

In the Vosges region, soldiers from France's 208th Regiment were dispatched to see that the national internment plans were carried out. The citizenry was simultaneously being primed to accept both the importance and the legitimacy of the action. An editorial in a local newspaper posited that people who held German passports were now threats to French national security and concluded by stating flatly,

"The German citizens should not be allowed to remain at liberty." A week later, all Germans found themselves under house arrest and their papers given over to the police.

The agricultural center at Martigny-les-Bains, conceived so carefully as a place of hope and renewal for hundreds of refugees, most of them victims of the very German regime now at war with France, was summarily shut down following the proclamation of September 14. Alex and Helmut were loaded onto a bus and taken up the road to Neufchâteau, where an internment camp had been hastily set up within the walls of a factory. Two satellite camps, Camp du Martinet, in the village of Sionne, and Camp du Châtelet, in Harchéchamp, were established when it became clear that the Neufchâteau factory was far too small. During the autumn of 1939, the three camps of greater Neufchâteau held about twenty-two hundred German citizens, all guarded by the Second Battalion of the 208th Regiment. Alex and Helmut were transferred from the main camp at Neufchâteau to Camp du Martinet in Sionne, which was under the command of Lieutenant Francois Laurens. There they stayed for months, having suddenly metamorphosed in the eyes of their captors from displaced persons in need of a new and useful occupation to enemy aliens.

The history of these camps in and around Neufchâteau has not been told, not even by the rigorous and dogged archivists of the United States Holocaust Memorial Museum. The reason is fairly simple: the records have been destroyed. In June 1940, as the recognized government of France relocated from Paris to the city of Vichy, about 220 miles to the south, the camp commandants were given secret orders to burn their files. In the words of M. Duvaux, "It was then impossible to find the archives of the camps of Neufchâteau."

As I ponder what became of what was once referred to as the "Welcome Center" at Martigny-les-Bains, as I think of the ruined hopes of those who planned what *L'Univers Israélite* called "this fine communal accomplishment," those who organized the classes and straightened the furrows in the farm's vegetable garden, and as I contemplate the fate of those refugees who spent that one fruitful summer there, I more completely understand my initial visceral reaction to my first sight

of the now decayed Hotel International. In his ninety-fourth sonnet,
Shakespeare writes:

> The summer's flower is to the summer sweet,
> Though to itself it only live and die,
> But if that flower with base infection meet,
> The basest weed outbraves his dignity:
> For sweetest things turn sourest by their deeds;
> Lilies that fester smell far worse than weeds.

8

Montauban

MONDAY, MAY 23, 2011. After the deep emotions of the past week, today we need do nothing more strenuous, either physically or emotionally, than being tourists in the sunny French countryside. Our hosts in Montauban are wrapping up a holiday in the Pyrenees today and will welcome us to their home tomorrow. So until tomorrow afternoon, we are free to follow the call of the open road.

We wish a warm farewell to the staff of The Inn of the Twelve Apostles and are on that inviting road by 8 a.m. Had I known then what I would later learn, I would have taken the country road to Neufchâteau and Sionne, but instead we choose to spend a few hours on the limited-access A31 speeding south. The highway takes us around Dijon, birthplace of the great eighteenth-century composer Jean Philippe Rameau and the city that lends its name to a famous condiment (though we are surprised to learn that nearly all of the mustard seed used for Dijon mustard is imported from Canada). We leave the expressway a few miles north of Lyon, preferring to see the land up close from a series of D roads as we travel west and south. We cross the Loire, the longest river in France, and pass vineyards, orchards of apple and cherry trees, and fields of artichokes and asparagus. The land becomes hilly and we frequently notice the remains of ruined castles from antiquity and restored tenth-century châteaux commanding the surrounding landscape from the tops of hills.

As lunchtime approaches, we drive into the ninth-century hill town of Montbrison, birthplace of the conductor and composer Pierre Boulez. Maestro Boulez was my mother's boss for several seasons, when he conducted the Cleveland Orchestra in the early 1970s. As we search the narrow streets of Montbrison for a *fromagerie*, I regale Amy with Boulez stories: of how the orchestra members made fun of his devotion to contemporary music and his disdain for Romantic composers by calling him "The 20th Century Limited"; of his brilliant recording of Stravinsky's "Rite of Spring," a performance so enthralling that it was chosen by the Soviet government to represent Russian art at the 1970 World's Fair in Osaka; and of how M. Boulez once chatted very amiably and without a hint of condescension with my brother and me at an after-concert party when we were both still in our teens.

Our hunt for *fromage* is successful and we leave the town with an aromatic cylindrical block of its signature blue cheese, Fourme de Montbrison, a cheese that has been manufactured in the region for centuries and has earned the coveted certification known as *Appellation d'origine contrôlée*, or AOC. Signifying that a cheese or wine possesses certain distinct qualities, has been produced for many years in a traditional manner, or enjoys an uncommon reputation because of its geographical origin, the mark of the AOC is highly prized, particularly in this land of so many arrogant *affineurs*. General Charles de Gaulle once famously alluded to the fractious nature of France by asking, "How can one possibly govern a country that has 246 varieties of cheese?"

But if balky governance is the price to pay for such a luscious repast, we tell ourselves, it may well be worth it. We lunch in a lush green field spotted with bright yellow daisies, surrounded by cloud-topped hills. We are in the Auvergne, a sparsely populated region of forests, streams, and extinct volcanoes, where the ancient language of Occitan is still spoken and was brought to music lovers worldwide by Joseph Cantaloube in his hauntingly beautiful "Songs of the Auvergne." The sun is bright and warm, the bread and cheese delectable, and once more it is hard to remember the pain that has brought us to this splendid setting.

In late afternoon, we reach the charming village of Saint-Nectaire, named after St. Nectarius, who came from Rome in the fourth century to bring Christianity to ancient Gaul. Nectarius discovered a temple dedicated to the god Apollo and forcibly reorganized it into a Christian church that still stands guard over the village as the Basilica of Notre Dame. For his trouble, Nectarius was surprised in his sleep and run through by a devout Apollinian, which hastened Nectarius's elevation to sainthood. Today, St. Nectaire is renowned for yet another local artisan cheese, which also proudly bears the stamp of the AOC. It is my favorite cheese of the entire journey, and we purchase several wedges, some for tomorrow's lunch and the remainder as gifts for our hosts in Montauban.

In the lengthening shadows of the oncoming evening, we follow the winding road higher and higher into the range of mountains known as Les Puys until the road straightens, the trees fall back, and we find ourselves on the banks of a glittering lake that reflects the image of the mountains beyond. We have reached our destination for the night, a village called Chambon-sur-Lac, with a population of about 350 souls. At the aptly named (for once) Hotel Bellevue, we are given a small room with an immense breathtaking view over the lake. We dine on local fowl, vegetables, and salad, a meal concluded with the flourish of yet another example of delicious fermented curd, which sends us up to bed repeating the wisdom of Monty Python: "Blessed are the Cheesemakers!"

In the clear, crisp air of morning, we continue on our way as the road rises above the timberline to an altitude over eight thousand feet. The shaggy coats of the cattle and sheep that graze here are designed for cold temperatures. For the first time on our journey, we are obliged to engage the Meriva's heater. At the top of the pass, we climb out of the car and shiver both from the cold and in exaltation at the glorious view of craggy volcanic rocks and alpine fields and, in the shimmering distance, what seems to be the whole of southern France stretching invitingly before us. But even as I revel in the natural beauty all around me, I once more consider what has brought me here and how much our happy jaunt differs from Alex and Helmut's journey to the south of France in 1940.

For a minute or two, I am seized by a mad impulse to stay up here with the sheep and the bracing mountain air and to forsake this nonsense of following in my relatives' footsteps. I could remain above the trees and live on cheese, I tell myself, until it's time to fly back home. Enjoy myself on high and leave the sadness down below. But even as I tempt myself, I realize it's all for naught; my journey may indeed be folly, but I have come here with a job to do. So with a last look at the indistinct panorama stretching away to the horizon, we climb back into the car and begin winding our switchback way to sea level, out of the pure incorruptible atmosphere of the mountains and down to the scene of the crime.

Once we return to the flatlands, we again follow express highways, which speed us west and south. We continue to see the sweet green highlands of the Auvergne on our left for miles, but by mid-afternoon we notice a profound change in the landscape. The basic color of the countryside is no longer green but a tan-to-russet shade of brown. The broad trees of farther north have given way to scrubby growth reminiscent of the American Southwest. The sun flares down relentlessly as we leave the expressway at the outskirts of Montauban and follow detailed directions to the home of our hosts, Jean-Claude and Monique Drouilhet. Their two-story house is topped with terra-cotta tiles, giving it a distinctive Mediterranean appearance. Their garden contains a number of subtropical flowers and cactus plants that thrive in hot, dry conditions. With a start, we realize that we have arrived in that storied part of the world known as the South of France.

Jean-Claude and Monique come out to greet us and we embrace warmly. He is a man of middle height, with a full head of gray hair and a ready smile under sparkling eyes. She has an exotic dark complexion and seems just a bit restrained next to her buoyantly enthusiastic husband.

Jean-Claude was born in 1934. At seventeen, he entered the teachers' training college in Montauban with the intention of becoming an elementary and middle school teacher. He graduated four years later and then spent the next two years teaching middle school and studying agronomy at the University of Toulouse, about thirty miles to the south. In January 1958, he was drafted and sent to fight in Algeria as part of France's nearly eight-year war to deny Algerians their independence. Jean-Claude served more than two years in the war, attaining the rank of sergeant, before returning to Montauban, where he taught middle school biology and geology and established a school radio station that was entirely staffed by students.

In the midst of his tour of duty in Algeria, Jean-Claude had obtained a leave to marry Monique. She was born in 1937, the daughter of a French army officer who spent much of World War II fighting General Rommel's army in North Africa, leaving his wife and Monique and her three siblings alone for the duration. After the war, Monique stayed with a godmother in Normandy, where food was more plentiful, before returning to Montauban to take and pass the civil service exam. She joined the city's Administration for Public Finances and served as the chief controller of taxes.

When Amy and I enter their comfortable home, we immediately notice the many examples of Native American art and crafts that Jean-Claude and Monique have collected: paintings, sculptures, blankets, and dreamcatchers are everywhere. When we are all seated in the bright living room with glasses of wine, the windows thrown open to welcome the late afternoon breeze, Amy, who grew up in the West, asks Jean-Claude about his obvious interest in Indian heritage. He smiles and says, "I believe it is an article of faith for many Native Americans that everything is connected. And I think my love of American Indian art and your presence in our house today are both undeniably connected to what happened here in Montauban 181 years ago." He leans forward in his chair and weaves for us an amazing tale.

When the earliest French settlers journeyed to the New World in search of furs and fish, they established alliances with many Native American tribes. Among their closest allies and trading partners were the Osage, whose territory included parts of present-day Missouri, Kansas, Arkansas, and Oklahoma. The painter George Catlin, who captured the likenesses of many Native Americans, described the Osage as "the tallest race of men in North America, either red or white; there being indeed few of the men at their full growth being less than six feet in stature, and very many of them six-and-a-half, and others seven feet."

By the early eighteenth century, so deep a measure of trust had been established between the French and the People of the Middle Waters, as the Osage referred to themselves, that a French explorer named Étienne de Veniard invited a delegation of chiefs to Paris. There they were presented at court, took in the splendors of Versailles, went hunting with King Louis XV in the royal forest preserve of Fontainebleau, and attended an opera conducted by André Campra. Upon their return to their homeland, the Osage chiefs regaled their people with the splendors they had seen. The grandson of one of the chiefs, a young man named Kishagashugah, was so dazzled by what he had heard that he vowed, "I also will visit France, if the Master of Life permits me to become a man."

Many years later, in 1827, having indeed grown to sturdy manhood, Kishagashugah decided to fulfill his vow. He gathered eleven of his fellow People of the Middle Waters and many furs, which he knew were highly prized in Europe, to present as gifts to the current king of France. The twelve outfitted a raft to take them down the Mississippi River to New Orleans, where they would board an oceangoing vessel for the Atlantic crossing. All went well until they ran into a thunderstorm just north of St. Louis. Their raft capsized, their rich store of furs sank to the bottom of the river, and they only just managed to escape to shore with their lives.

Bedraggled and dispirited, their well laid plans thwarted, Kishagashugah and his followers fell into the clutches of a sharper and charlatan named David DeLaunay, a French-born resident of St. Louis who ran a sawmill and a boardinghouse but now saw an opportunity to make some real money as an impresario. He convinced the Osage that he was the right man, with all the right connections, to introduce them to the crowned heads of France. Six of the tribe smelled a rat and decided to return to the Middle Waters, but Kishagashugah and five of his companions joined DeLaunay aboard the steamship *Commerce* and made their way down the Mississippi to New Orleans. From there, they sailed upon the good ship *New England* and landed at Le Havre, France, on July 27, 1827.

Pandemonium greeted their arrival. DeLaunay had sent word ahead that he was bringing with him real-life savages from the New World, and by the time the *New England* dropped anchor in the harbor, a large percentage of Le Havre's population was swarming over the docks, hoping to catch a glimpse of them. Protected from the curious cheering crowd by a phalanx of soldiers, the Osage rode by carriage to the city's finest hotel, where they were wined and dined for ten days. The Indians attended the theater and made a few other well-choreographed appearances, spectacles open to anyone willing to pay DeLaunay a handsome fee for the privilege of gawking at them. Though all the money went to DeLaunay, the Osage profited in other respects. One young warrior reported later that while in France, he had been "married many times." On August 7, they embarked via steamboat for Rouen, where the crowds, once more primed by DeLaunay's publicity apparatus, had been waiting for four days.

On August 13, the caravan reached Paris. On August 21, at 11:00 a.m., Kishagashugah and his colleagues were afforded the honor of an audience with King Charles X at the beautiful royal palace of Saint Cloud, which overlooked the Seine a few miles west of Paris. His Majesty declared that he was very pleased to welcome his visitors, reminding them that the Osage had always been faithful allies of the French in the New World. The queen proudly introduced the royal children. There was music and food in abundance. Then Kishagashugah, his face painted the Osage tribal colors, red and blue, holding before him a ceremonial staff ornamented with feathers and ribbons, said to the king, "My great Father, in my youth I heard my grandfather speak of the French nation, and I formed then the purpose of visiting this nation when I should become grown. I have become a man, and I have accomplished my desire. I am today with my companions among the French people whom we love so much, and I have the great happiness to be in the presence of the King. We salute France!"

The encounter between these two separate worlds made news in both France and the United States, as newspapers documented the Indians' every move. The correspondent for the *Missouri Republican* wrote, "The six Osage Indians, who lately arrived in France, make a considerable figure in Paris. They have been introduced at Court, caressed at diplomatic dinners, admired at the grand opera, and in short distinguished as the social lions of the day. *Messieurs les Sauvages* eclipse *Milords Anglais*."

His great ambition realized, Kishagashugah was now amply ready to return to the Land of the Middle Waters. But he had not fully understood the terms of his agreement with David DeLaunay, who now informed him that he had arranged many more engagements throughout France, opportunities for ticket-buying citizens to gaze at the exotic visitors from across the ocean, all the while further lining DeLaunay's pockets. So instead of going home, the Osage began wandering across France, displaying themselves to crowds that, as the novelty wore off, became smaller and smaller. After many months of this itinerant life, DeLaunay was arrested and thrown into prison on charges of fraud. Their protector and translator now taken from them, the Indians found themselves on their own, strangers in a very strange land.

They tried for a while to continue their pocket Wild West Show and managed to book themselves appearances in Italy and Switzerland, in addition to their remaining dates in France. When the tour ended, three years after their arrival in France, they found themselves destitute and alone more than five thousand miles from Osage Country, with no means to get home. Fortunately, word of their situation reached the sympathetic ears of Louis William Valentine Dubourg, the bishop of Montauban. Bishop Dubourg had done missionary work among the Osage years earlier and had lived near their ancestral homeland when he was the first bishop of St. Louis, Missouri, and the founder of what later became St. Louis University. Now hearing of the sad plight of these Osage, the bishop sent for Kishagashugah and his fellows.

So it was that in the spring of 1830, those six Native Americans, who had arrived in France with such fanfare and were now nearly starving, slowly crossed the fourteenth-century bridge over the River Tarn and presented themselves at the gates of the Montauban Cathedral. A curious crowd gathered as the bishop called for food and drink for the Indians and solicited funds to finance their return to America. In late April, the necessary money raised, the six Osage sailed for home. Two of them died during the crossing, but Kishagashugah survived to complete his long-dreamed-of pilgrimage.

That is not the end of the story, however. In the late 1980s, while still teaching natural sciences at the middle school, Jean-Claude came across a reference to Montauban's Osage connection. Intrigued, he researched the descendents of Kishagashugah and discovered that the tribal government of the modern Osage Nation is headquartered in Pawhuska, Oklahoma, the county seat of Osage County. He wrote to the mayor of Pawhuska, suggesting that after all these years, the People of the Middle Waters and the citizens of Montauban should renew their acquaintance. Thus was born the sister-city relationship between Montauban and Pawhuska—the relationship that led me to Jean-Claude and his kind assistance and hospitality.

"So you see," says Jean-Claude with a smile, "because Kishagashugah came to Montauban to honor his vow to follow in the footsteps of his grandfather, you have come to Montauban . . . to follow in the footsteps of your grandfather." I look away, my eyes suddenly full of tears.

"I think the native peoples of your country are quite right," continues Jean-Claude, his voice a bit huskier than before. "Everything is connected."

ONCE UPON A TIME, many years ago, there was a colorful country of wide plains and towering peaks, inhabited by noble swordsmen and gentle damsels, husbandmen and troubadours, shepherds and poets, a land that went by the name of Occitania. Its borders encompassed most of what is now southern France, as well as parts of Italy and Spain and the principality of Monaco. It had its own flag, which featured a distinctive twelve-pointed star, and its own unique language, known as Occitan, which appeared for the first time in written form in the tenth century but had existed as a spoken language for at least two hundred years before that. During the early Middle Ages, in the time of Charlemagne and the Visigoths, Occitania was politically united, but eventually the country came under attack by the kings of France and gradually lost its independence. One of the turning points in Occitania's attempt to remain a self-governing entity came in 1621, when a poorly armed but determined gang of Occitan fighters barricaded themselves in the church of St. Jacques and held off a regiment of King Louis XIII's army for three months before surrendering. Over the next three centuries, the language and some of the customs of Occitania began to fade from the world's awareness. But in the past hundred years or so, its distinctive voice has been heard again, as Occitan is now taught in public schools. In no other place has that revival been more vibrant than the site of that three-month siege of 1621: the city of Montauban.

Not everyone in Montauban shares a gauzy, fairy-tale view of Occitania. In most respects, the city's sensibilities are firmly rooted in the present day. It is the capital of the *departement* of Tarn-et-Garonne, with all the administrative concerns that accompany such a designation. The metropolitan area of Montauban is home to more than a hundred thousand people; two of the principle industries are agriculture and the manufacture of cloth and straw hats. The city is an important hub in the extensive railway system of France, with high-speed trains departing for Paris, Nice, and Bordeaux several times a day from its grand nineteenth-century station, the Gare de Montauban-Ville-Bourbon. On weekend afternoons, enthusiastic fans jam the Stade Sapiac to cheer on US Montauban, a rugby football club. Montauban is also home to a university; a theater; a daily newspaper, *Le Petit Journal*; and an orchestra, *Les Passions*, devoted primarily to baroque music.

But the city is well aware of its past, and many citizens are quick to remind visitors that their city's name is spelled Montalban in the Occitan language. The city's chief architectural wonder is the bridge spanning the river Tarn. Construction of the bridge began in 1303 on orders from King Philip the Fair and was completed more than thirty years later. Nearly eight hundred years old now, it handles heavy automobile and truck traffic as nimbly as it did carriages and oxcarts during centuries past. The seventeenth-century Place Nationale, the striking town marketplace, is surrounded by pink brick houses above double rows of arcades. During the Terror of the French Revolution, those unfortunates who were about to meet their deaths at the guillotine were first brought to the Place Nationale so a bloodthirsty mob could jeer and throw vegetables at them.

Olympe de Gouges, a playwright, journalist, and early feminist, born in Montauban in 1748, was guillotined in Paris, partly because of her uncompromising stand on behalf of women's rights. Also born in Montauban, in 1749, was André Jeanbon Saint-André, the man who suggested blue, white, and red as the colors of the French flag. Thirty-one years later, the city witnessed the birth of its most celebrated resident, the great painter Jean Auguste Dominique Ingres. Montauban's fine art museum, located at the eastern end of the old bridge, is named for Ingres. In 1944, Leonardo da Vinci's *Mona Lisa* was transported from the Louvre in Paris and hidden in a vault beneath the Musée Ingres to prevent the Nazis from carrying it off.

Montauban also houses the Musée de la Résistance et de la Déportation. Its holdings include a painting by G. R. Cousi depicting the infamous event of July 24, 1944, when four members of the Resistance were hanged from two graceful plane trees in a public square in Montauban. The square is known today as the *Place des Martyrs*. Although no major battles were fought there, Montauban certainly contributed its share of martyrs and other victims to the sorrowful history of France during the Second World War.

After France's formal declaration of war on Germany on September 3, 1939, and the decrees relating to the internment of German citizens in France on September 14, there followed an eight-month period largely devoid of military activity, a time that came to be known as the "phony war." That phrase, attributed to William Borah, a U.S. senator from Idaho, abruptly disappeared from common usage on May 10, 1940, when Germany launched its lightning assault upon Belgium, Luxembourg, and the Netherlands. It defeated those countries within weeks, and in less than a month, German tanks had swiftly circumvented the supposedly invulnerable Maginot Line and swept into France.

When the German army stormed into Paris in the early morning hours of June 14, the troops marching exultantly down the Champs Elysées and under the Arc de Triomphe encountered a nearly deserted city. Along with thousands of its citizens, the French government had fled Paris and headed south, first to Tours and then to Bordeaux. Paul Reynaud, the prime minister of what was known as the Third Republic, turned for assistance to Marshal Henri-Philippe Pétain. The general had made his reputation as the architect of the French strategic victory at the battle of Verdun during the First World War. But Verdun later became a symbol of the folly of that "war to end all wars." Over the course of eleven months in 1916, nearly seven hundred thousand French and German soldiers died in the effort to move the battle lines a few thousand yards in either direction. Twenty-four years later, as the Germans approached Paris, Renaud asked Pétain to serve as his vice prime minister. Then on the evening of June 16, two days after German troops had entered Paris, Renaud resigned and recommended that a new French government be created with Marshal Pétain as its prime minister. The general was eighty-four years old.

A debate ensued over how to respond to the overwhelming might of the German forces. Renaud argued for continuating French defensive efforts, moving the government to French colonies in North Africa, and relying on the French navy rather than its ravaged army. But with the countryside still in chaos, Pétain and others opted simply to surrender. Shortly after noon on June 17, Pétain took to the national airwaves and declared, "France is a wounded child. I hold her in my arms. The time has come to stop fighting." Listening to the radio broadcast while at lunch at a bistro in the southern port city of Marseille, the French composer Darius Milhaud felt his heart break and witnessed other patrons of the restaurant weeping in despair. He wrote later, "I realized clearly that this capitulation would prepare the soil for fascism and its abominable train of monstrous persecutions."

Five days later, on June 22, the world witnessed one of the most elaborately staged surrender dramas in its anguished annals of humiliation. Adolf Hitler himself insisted that the armistice be signed in the very same railroad car and on the very spot where, twenty-two years earlier, the Germans had surrendered at the end of World War I. Hitler had the train car removed from a museum and brought to a little clearing in the forest of Compiègne, about forty miles north of Paris. French officials signed the armistice, believing it to be a temporary document. A real and lasting peace treaty would emerge after the expected German defeat of Great Britain, which was assumed to be only a few months if not weeks away, now that nearly all of Western Europe had fallen before the might of Germany's *Blitzkrieg*. But at the beginning of June, as France was falling, British forces staged a miraculous retreat from the French coastal city of Dunkirk, escaping across the English Channel to fight another day. Britain did not fall, so the provisional armistice remained on the books until the Liberation.

Under the terms of the armistice, France was divided into two main parts. The Occupied Zone—about 60 percent of the country, including its most economically robust regions, beginning north of the river Loire and then extending south to the Spanish border to include the entire Atlantic coastline—was administered by a German military governor operating from Paris. The Unoccupied Zone—south and southeastern France, about forty *departements* in all—was ruled by Marshal Pétain and his government, newly removed to the French city of Vichy. Ostensibly the French government administered the entire country, although the armistice acknowledged and respected "the rights of the occupying power." Everyone was fully aware that all real power flowed from Berlin and not Vichy. Pétain was a puppet.

France was required to deliver to the German police any refugees from the Third Reich whom the government in Berlin might demand. The French negotiators objected to this provision at first, declaring it a betrayal of those who had entered their country seeking asylum from Germany. But when the Germans made it clear that they would not yield on this demand, the French surrendered once again. In the next few months, a band of Gestapo agents visited a number of internment camps in the Unoccupied Zone and made a list of about eight hundred refugees; the Vichy government duly delivered them. Among those sent back to Germany was Herschel Grynszpan, the man who Nazi officials blamed for the pogrom known as *Kristallnacht*, since Grynszpan's assassination of a German diplomat in Paris in early November 1938 ostensibly triggered the campaign of violence. Once returned to Germany, Grynszpan was never seen again.

On July 1, 1940, the French government, including the members of Parliament, gathered in the town of Vichy, located in the Auvergne region of south-central France. Like Martigny-les-Bains and Contrexéville, Vichy long enjoyed a reputation as a spa town because of its thermal waters. In the 1860s, Emperor Napoleon III took the cure five times.

He built lavish homes in Vichy for his mistresses and glittering casinos for his courtiers. Vichy was chosen to be the seat of the new government in part because of its relative proximity to Paris (about four hours by train) and partly, thanks to its Napoleonic legacy, because it was the city with the second-largest hotel capacity in all of France.

Within days, the world would learn of the shocking new direction in which the Vichy government would lead France. On July 10, the senators and deputies who remained from the Leon Blum–led Popular Front National Assembly of 1936 voted overwhelmingly to revoke the constitution of the Third Republic and to grant Pétain full powers to declare a new one. The vote, taken in the ornate Vichy opera house, was 569 to 80; those who voted in the negative were later lauded for their courage and celebrated as the Vichy 80.

Pétain wasted no time putting his new authority to use. Within forty-eight hours, he issued three constitutional edicts. The first one bestowed upon him the title of *Chef de l'État Français*, or head of the French state. The second declared that the head of state possessed a "totality of government power"—legislative, executive, judicial, diplomatic, and administrative—and was thus responsible for creating and executing all of the country's laws. The third edict, dissolving the Senate and Chamber of Deputies indefinitely, condemned France to the authoritarian rule of one man: Marshal Pétain.

On July 12, Pétain addressed the country and declared, "A new order is commencing." The French national motto—Liberty, Equality, Fraternity—forged in the revolutionary fires of 1789, was replaced with a slogan long espoused by right-wing groups: Fatherland, Family, Work. Democratic liberties and guarantees were immediately suspended in favor of a paternalistic, top-down system that emphasized government control of the individual and unfettered corporate power. Pétainists condemned what they called the indecency and depravity of the previous regime, with its tolerance for jazz, short skirts, and birth control, and called for the reintroduction of traditional family values to daily life. The crime of *délit d'opinion*, or felony of thought, became illegal, and citizens were frequently arrested for publishing, or even uttering, criticism of the regime. Former Prime Minister Paul Reynaud, who had essentially turned over control of the government to Marshal Pétain, was arrested in September 1940 and sentenced to life imprisonment.

Almost immediately, the Vichy government began a dual campaign promoting the emergence of this new "true France" and affixing blame for the country's quick and humiliating defeat on the battlefield in the spring. At the heart of both efforts was the desire to weed out "undesirables," those whose treachery, Pétain believed, had undermined what otherwise would have been a decisive victory against the German invader. These undesirables, long termed the Anti-France by the right wing, included Protestants, Freemasons, foreigners, Communists, and Jews.

Although additional undesirable elements of the French population, including Gypsies, left-wingers, and homosexuals, were targets of official discrimination, the campaign of anti-Semitism that began almost immediately after the establishment of the Vichy government was nothing short of an all-out assault. The French undoubtedly studied the Nazis' Nuremburg Laws for guidance, but the flood of edicts and ordinances that began in July 1940 was not prompted by orders from Berlin. Henri du Moulin de Labarthète, who served as Marshal Pétain's chief of staff, declared unambiguously, "Germany was not at the origin of the anti-Jewish legislation of Vichy. This legislation was, if I dare say it, spontaneous, native." In 1947, Helmut Knochen, a German storm trooper and the director of the security police in France, recalled that "we found no difficulties with the Vichy government in implementing Jewish policy."

The objective of the new government's initial laws was the restriction of the rights of foreigners living in France, measures that, while affecting foreign Jews, weren't specifically anti-Semitic. On July 13, Pétain issued an edict stating that "only men of French parentage" would be allowed to belong to the civil service. On July 22, another decree was announced, this one allowing the government to revoke the citizenship of all French men and women who had acquired their status since the passage of the liberal naturalization law of 1927. The next day saw the passage of a law that called for the annulment of citizenship and the confiscation of the property of all French nationals who had fled

France after May 10, the start of the German offensive, without an officially recognized reason. This was the first measure that seemed specifically aimed at Jews, and among those singled out was Baron Robert de Rothschild, who had helped to fund the agricultural center at Martigny-les-Bains. The Vichy officials justified this new law by charging that Rothschild and his co-religionists had revealed themselves to be "Jews before they were French" by abandoning their country at the very moment it needed them most; thus, they declared, these people no longer deserved the honor of French citizenship.

Over the next ten weeks, more laws were issued in the Vichy regime's by now undisguised attempt to solve its "Jewish problem." On August 27, the Daladier-Marchandeau ordinance of 1939, prohibiting anti-Semitism in the press, was repealed, and several notorious Jew-baiting publishers were permitted to renew their activities in print. On August 16, the government announced that, henceforth, only members of the newly created *Ordre des Médecins* would be allowed to practice medicine, whether as doctors, dentists, or pharmacists. The catch was that membership in the *Ordre* was restricted to persons born in France of French fathers, and by now the designation "French" was in the process of being radically redefined. On September 10, a similar decree was announced that affected the practice of law. The Vichy minister of the interior, Marcel Peyrouton, declared that doctors and lawyers were under an obligation to exclude from their ranks those "elements" who by certain "acts or attitudes" had shown themselves "unworthy to exercise their profession in the manner the present situation demands."

The definition of what constituted a "French" person and what constituted a Jew was spelled out in a decree issued on September 27. Taking its cue from the notorious 1935 Nuremberg Laws, the measure stated that anyone who had more than two grandparents "of the Jewish race" was a Jew. The law went on to declare that any Jew who had fled to the Unoccupied Zone was henceforth banned from returning to the Occupied Zone. It also called for a census of Jews in the Occupied Zone to be conducted within the coming month, required that the word *Juif* now be stamped on identity cards belonging to Jews, and called for yellow signs to be placed in the windows of stores owned by Jews.

The signs were to carry the words, in both French and German, "Jewish Business." Other stores, of their own volition, soon began sporting signs that read "This business is 100 percent French."

The culmination of this legal attack on the rights and position of Jews living in France was the *Statut des Juifs*, or Statute on Jews, enacted by the Vichy government on October 3, 1940. The law began by reiterating that anyone with more than two Jewish grandparents would be considered a member of the Jewish "race"; from now on spouses of Jews would also be designated Jewish. But the main intent of the statute was to affirm the second-class standing of the Jews of France by specifically banning them from many positions in public life. Henceforth no Jew could be a member of the officer corps in the military or a civil servant, such as a judge, a teacher, or an administrator; no Jew could work as a journalist, a publisher, a radio broadcaster, or an actor on stage or in films; no Jew could work as a banker, a realtor, or a member of the stock exchange.

Other anti-Semitic statutes would follow in the coming months, laws that called for the confiscation of radios and telephones from Jewish homes in France, established curfews that allowed Jews to be on the public streets for only certain hours every day, and confined Jews to using only the last car in the trains of the Paris Métro.

Though the drumbeat of official anti-Semitism had been growing ever louder since the establishment of the Vichy regime in July, the cymbal crash of October 3 was a stunning blow to the Jews of France, who had certainly heard tales of Nazi atrocities from across the German border but who had never expected such measures would be enacted in their homeland. Raymond-Raoul Lambert, the CAR director who had met the *St. Louis* passengers at Boulogne-sur-Mer, wrote in his diary after the announcement of the *Statut des Juifs*, "I wept last night like a man who has been suddenly abandoned by the woman who has been the only love of his life, the only guide of his thoughts, the only inspiration of his action." It would not be long, however, before feelings of betrayal would give way to fears of a far greater danger than a broken heart.

But where the Jews saw peril in the *Statut*, others saw opportunity. If one of the stated goals of the still-new government was the segregation of Jews from mainstream French society, then exceptional vigor in the pursuit of that goal could only win favor in the eyes of Vichy officials. On October 4, an addendum to the previous day's law authorized officials throughout France to place under confinement or into conditions of forced labor any foreign-born Jews who might be living in their jurisdictions. Thus a young man from Montauban whose meteoric rise through the French bureaucracy had been propelled by tragedy saw his opening.

René Bousquet was born in Montauban in 1909, the son of a radical socialist notary. As a boy, he became fast friends with Adolphe Poult, whose father, Emile Poult, was the chief executive of a successful French confectioner. The firm, Biscuits Poult, was founded in 1883. It manufactured cakes, biscuits, wafers, tarts, and cookies of all shapes and sizes, which were consumed with relish in Montauban, site of its main factory, and throughout France. Emile Poult was thus a wealthy man, and his son Adolphe and René Bousquet spent many happy hours together at the Poult family estate.

The River Tarn, which flows through Montauban, has long been the source of the worst flooding in all Europe, with the possible exception of the Danube. In March 1930, following a winter of high snows near the river's source in the Cevennes Mountains and exceptionally heavy spring rains at lower altitudes, the Tarn flowed deep and fast through Montauban, rising more than fifty-six feet above its normal level in just twenty-four hours. In what was subsequently termed a millennial flood, about a third of the surrounding *departement* was under water, thousands of houses were swept away, much of the low-lying regions of Montauban were destroyed, and more than three hundred people drowned.

Many of the town's inhabitants helped to save the victims of the flood, including Adolphe Poult and René Bousquet, each almost twenty-one years old. The two friends saved dozens of lives in nearly thirty-two hours of continuous exertion. Then, his judgment probably compromised by exhaustion, Adolphe misstepped, fell into the raging river, and was swept away. His body was never recovered.

For what were termed his *"belles actions,"* Bousquet became something of a national hero, awarded both a gold medal and the Legion of Honor. He also won the undying affection and loyalty of his friend's father, Emile, who was devastated by the loss of his son and embraced young René as his surrogate heir.

Over the next ten years, Bousquet quickly rose from one high-profile position to the next, initially boosted by his celebrity and then well served by his unerring ability to cultivate mentors. Bousquet began as the protégé of Maurice Sarraut, a socialist senator and the publisher of an influential newspaper in nearby Toulouse. In April 1938, Sarraut became minister of the interior in the government of the Popular Front and appointed his protégé to the position of *sous-préfet*, or ministerial representative, for a city in northern France. In 1940, shortly after the armistice, Bousquet, at age thirty-one, was serving as prefect. But Sarraut had been swept out of power with the rest of the Third Republic. In order to remain in favor with his new superiors in Vichy, Bousquet knew that he would have to do something to catch their attention.

He saw his chance in the edict of October 4, which gave prefects the authority to intern or place under house arrest any foreign-born Jews within their jurisdiction. Bousquet did some research and found that in the nearby *departement* of Vosges, there were sixty German Jews living in a camp in Sionne. He quickly called his counterpart in Vosges and offered to take these "undesirables" off his hands. The other man agreed, leaving Bousquet with a nice cache of refugees but with no place to house them. Bousquet asked Émile Poult, now a powerful figure in the largely right-wing French business world, if he knew of a space sufficiently commodious to house sixty Jews for a few weeks. The older man offered his dear young friend the use of his factory in Montauban. The area within the factory gates where trucks were loaded with their daily shipments of cookies and cakes was large enough for sixty cots, with extra space for exercise. The high walls that surrounded the factory would make escape unlikely and its location was highly convenient: just a few hundred yards down the street from the Montauban railway station.

Thus, on October 13, 1940, Grandfather Alex and Uncle Helmut arrived at the Gare de Montauban-Ville-Bourbon on a train from the north. They and their fifty-eight fellow undesirables were quickly marched about two blocks down the Avenue de Mayenne, turned right, and walked through the open gate of Biscuits Poult, which would serve as their address for the next four weeks.

I really have no idea how Alex and Helmut spent that month within the walls of the cookie factory. I like to think that they were allowed to walk around the lot several times a day, that they were fed generously, and that M. Poult begrudged them at least one wafer or tartelette from his vast inventory at each meal. I cannot imagine how they came to terms with being prisoners held behind secure walls after the comfort of their initial warm welcome in France. I know that on November 6, Marshal Pétain, on a tour of the Unoccupied Zone, made a stop in Montauban, where he gave a speech in the Place Nationale before a wildly cheering crowd. Perhaps Alex and Helmut could hear bits of the celebration from the open-air Poult courtyard. I know that two days later, on November 8, the prefect of the *departement* of Tarn-et-Garonne sent a memorandum to the chief of police of Montauban that stated, "Per our telephone conversation, I have the honor of requesting from you a patrol to accompany sixty foreign Jewish refugees to Camp Agde. Those individuals will assemble at noon in the custody of the municipal police at the Poult building. The train is due to depart for Agde at 3:30 p.m." Indeed on the following day, November 9, 1940, two years to the day after *Kristallnacht*, under the watchful eyes of the police, Alex and Helmut walked back up the Avenue de Mayenne to the station and boarded a train heading south to the shores of the Mediterranean Sea, as their forced odyssey through France continued.

René Bousquet, whose friendship with Emile Poult brought my relatives to Montauban, continued his rapid rise through the ranks of the Vichy regime. Less than two years later, he was made secretary-general of the national police. In that capacity, he planned and carried out the infamous roundup of more than thirteen thousand Jews on July 16 and 17, 1942. His victims were first held for five days at an enclosed bicycle track in Paris—the *Vélodrome d'Hiver*, or Winter Velodrome—and then shipped to various extermination camps. After the war, Bousquet was tried on charges of "compromising the interests of the national defense" and received a sentence of five years of *dégradation nationale*, or a ceremonial loss of rank. But that judgment was immediately lifted because Bousquet made a convincing case that, while appearing to collaborate with the Nazis, he had been secretly assisting the Resistance all along. After lying low for a while, Bousquet returned to politics and helped finance François Mitterrand's successful campaign for president in 1981. Then, in the late 1980s, the Romanian-born Nazi hunter Serge Klarsfeld filed a complaint against Bousquet for crimes against humanity. After many delays a trial date was set, but before Bousquet ever saw the inside of a courtroom, he was assassinated in his own home on June 8, 1993. The gunman was reportedly a right-wing sympathizer who did not want the full story of René Bousquet to be revealed.

Bousquet's imprisonment of the Jews at the Velodrome in Paris in July 1942 was one of the shameful preludes to the mass deportations that began the following month when the Vichy government approved transports that delivered the Jews of France to the killing centers of Germany and Poland. In late August 1942, the spiritual descendant of the bishop of Montauban, the gentle man who welcomed the Osage and helped them return to their homeland in 1830, raised his voice in protest. Pierre-Marie Théas, bishop of Montauban since 1940, wrote a pastoral letter condemning the deportations, declaring, "I give voice to the outraged protest of Christian conscience and I proclaim that all men and women, whatever their race or religion, have the right to be respected. Hence, the recent antisemitic measures are an affront to human dignity and a violation of the most sacred rights of the individual and the family." He planned to mail his letter to his fellow priests in the surrounding parishes so that they could help amplify his protest.

But his secretary, Marie-Rose Gineste, warned the bishop that if he put his remarks in the mail, agents of the Vichy government would no doubt intercept the envelopes and destroy their contents. So she made multiple copies of his letter, which also implored parishioners to save Jews from deportation, mounted her bicycle, and over the next four days pedaled more than sixty-five miles over hilly roads through towns, villages, and hamlets to each parish in the surrounding region. On the following Sunday, August 30, Bishop Théas's letter was read from every pulpit to packed congregations, the only exception being a church with a Vichy sympathizer as its priest. In response to the call, many French families began to shelter Jews in their homes.

Bishop Théas was arrested by the Gestapo in 1944, and sent to the concentration camp known as Stalag 122, which was located near the forest of Compiègne, the site of the French surrender. He survived the ordeal and died of natural causes in 1977 at the age of eighty-two. Marie-Rose Gineste took an active role in the Resistance, hiding Jews, forging identity cards, and leading many Jews to safe houses in the surrounding countryside. She remained in Montauban and continued to ride her sturdy little bicycle until she was eighty-nine years old. Then, in December 2000, she donated the bicycle to the Holocaust memorial at Yad Vashem in Israel. She died in the summer of 2010, aged ninety-nine.

For their efforts on behalf of humanity, Bishop Pierre-Marie Théas and Marie-Rose Gineste were both named by Yad Vashem as "Righteous Among the Nations."

THURSDAY, MAY 26, 2011. I learn all this during two rich, full days under the hot southern sun of Montauban, in the bracing company of Jean-Claude and Monique. Wednesday begins with a tour of the town. Jean-Claude points out local landmarks. We see the bullet holes that remain in the stone walls of the church of St. Jacques, where the outnumbered Occitan irregulars were defeated in 1621. There are the slightly raised cobblestones in the Place Nationale where tumbrels paused so that townspeople might jeer and hurl vegetables at the condemned victims of the Revolution on their way to the guillotine. Next is a little stone plaque on Rue Adolphe Poult, almost invisible on an embankment by the River Tarn, heralding the bravery of the young man during the great flood of 1930. Jean-Claude also takes us to the *Place des Martyrs*, where the four members of the Resistance were hanged in 1944. The public square still contains the withered stump of one of the four trees.

We visit the Musée de la Résistance et de la Déportation, which displays posters from the Pétain era illustrating the dangers of the international Jewish conspiracy that the National Revolution was determined to defeat. In one poster, taken from an exhibition called *Le Juif et la*

France, a bearded man with an enormous nose, his eyes popping and beads of lascivious sweat breaking out on his forehead, fondles with clawlike fingers a globe of the world. In another, a righteous French policeman holds two wriggling, shifty-eyed men by the scruffs of their necks. They, too, sport oversized noses and are both clutching bags that are presumably filled with ill-gotten money. The poster is captioned with a single word: *Assez!* or Enough! When I ask Jean-Claude if he recalls seeing this sort of ugly propaganda in his youth, he sighs and says, "Everywhere."

Our next stop is the Montauban city archives. There, in the police files from 1940, we find the index cards that helped me trace the movements of Grandfather Alex and Uncle Helmut. Both cards feature a red letter *J* in the upper-left corner, along with the assurance that the local prefect examined the cards on October 25. The cards note their arrival in Montauban on October 13 and their departure for Agde on November 9. They list Helmut's profession as student and Alex's as salesman and poultry farmer, revealing that my grandfather must have retained pleasant memories from his brief months in Martigny-les-Bains. Both cards indicate that Alex and Helmut's address while in Montauban was the "Cantonnement Poult," or the temporary quarters provided by the proprietor of the cookie factory.

Again, I experience that curious mix of excitement and sorrow that always seems to accompany any tactile evidence of my relatives' existence. I cherish them because I possess so few items that speak to their once having lived, breathed, and walked this earth. Yet virtually everything I discover along this journey is another strand of the net that slowly but inexorably closed around them during their time in France. I hold the cards close and, when no one is looking, kiss them quickly, one after the other.

Our final destination for the day is another public square in Montauban, this one dedicated to the memory of the French soldiers who fought in the wars of the twentieth century. There are separate monuments for each of the world wars, for Algeria, and for Vietnam. The square is dominated by a twenty-two-foot statue called *Hope Chained*, a monument dedicated to the thousands of people deported to their

From the files of the central police station of Montauban in 1940, the identity cards of Alex and Helmut. The father is listed as a salesman and a poultry farmer, the son as a student. Probably more important to the authorities, though, was the defining "J."

deaths in Eastern Europe during the 1940s. I am humbled and honored to learn that Jean-Claude has organized a small memorial service in memory of Alex and Helmut.

About two dozen people, alerted by a notice Jean-Claude placed in the local newspaper earlier in the week, have gathered in the square as the shadows of early evening begin to lower the temperature of a blazing afternoon. Jean-Claude has asked a local florist to deliver a basket of red, yellow, and white daisies, over which is a small red banner that reads, "For my grandfather Alex and my uncle Klaus-Helmut." He has also brought along two flags on aluminum poles. He plants them in the grass on either side of the concrete path leading to the base of the *Hope* monument, the site of our little ceremony. Both flags are red, white, and blue: the French *Tricolour* and the American Stars and Stripes. The American flag was presented to Jean-Claude by his Osage friends in Oklahoma, and it incorporates an image of *End of the Trail*, the doleful sculpture by James Earle Fraser, into its design. While it seems odd in this context, I reflect that it's not so inappropriate to recall the extermination of the Native American population when mourning the evil that humans have wrought.

Shortly after 6 p.m., Jean-Claude says a few words in French, explaining what has brought Amy and me from America to join them this evening. He introduces Eugène Daumas, a member of the Tsigane, or Gypsy, population, who speaks briefly about the six thousand men, women, and children of his kind who were deported from France between 1940 and 1946. Then I hand the basket of flowers to Amy and, in halting English, tell the assembled of my conflicted feelings, of my anger at those Montaubanians of seventy-one years ago, of my bottomless gratitude to those gathered today, and of my particular gratitude to Jean-Claude and Monique for the honor and kindness they have shown my family on this memorable day. Amy and I walk to the base of *Hope Chained*, where we place the flowers and I whisper a few words to Alex and Helmut. The crowd slowly disperses into the warm evening. With no further words passing between us, Jean-Claude and I embrace.

On Thursday morning, we four take a drive north and east of Montauban to the village of Septfonds. Locally, the town is renowned for the seven springs for which it is named and for its production of colorful straw hats. But beyond the immediate horizon, the name Septfonds has a far more malevolent meaning, one that Jean-Claude wants to be sure we learn. About two miles outside the town limits, we come upon an immaculately kept cemetery, the final resting place for eighty-one Spanish men and boys who crossed the border into France as refugees from the bloody Spanish Civil War. At a camp set up in Septfonds more than fifteen thousand men, women, and children lived in cramped, highly unsanitary conditions from early 1939 until the beginning of 1941, when the camp became a prison for Jews and other undesirables subject to the racial laws of the Vichy regime. The peaceful Spanish cemetery is its own memorial to the ordeal of the Spanish refugees. To find any mention of what happened to the Jews of Septfonds, we must get back into the car and drive several more miles over the rolling countryside.

Fortunately, Jean-Claude knows the way, as there are no road signs. We soon come to a small, enclosed patch of field set off from the surrounding farmland by a low fence. Within is an empty replica of a barracks, modeled after the inadequate shelters provided to the thousands of Jews who survived here for months until they were shipped East. There is also a granite monument in the shape of a headstone, erected in memory of those interned and deported from here between 1939 and 1944.

It's a cloudy day with a cool breeze, a welcome relief after yesterday's unrelenting sun. An almost complete silence prevails, broken only by the occasional bird song or the sound of the black-and-white cows mooing in an adjacent pasture. The four of us keep the silence, my thoughts a jumble of sadness for the long-dead victims and deep appreciation for the pastoral peace of the landscape.

Next, we drive a few miles to the stunning medieval village of Saint-Antonin-Noble-Val, founded by the ancient Celts in the ninth century. We walk the narrow, winding streets, admiring old wooden doorways and stone gargoyles, the eleventh-century abbey, and a shop selling eighteenth-century clocks. In the market square, Jean-Claude shows us a centuries-old chopping block, complete with an iron sluice for the quick disposal of blood, where many generations of chickens met a sharp, quick end. Also in the square is a stone monument to the local partisans who contributed to the Resistance. I point it out to Jean-Claude who rolls his eyes, grimaces, and says emphatically, "Oh, yes . . . every village and town in France has erected a monument to their heroic Resistance fighters. With such brave people in every corner of France, how on earth did Philippe Pétain ever come to power?" It is a question for which he seems to know the answer, so I do not press him but vow to bring it up again later.

By the time we return to Montauban in the late afternoon, the warm southern sun has reappeared. At Jean-Claude's suggestion, we cross to the western side of the Tarn and drive through thinning traffic to the Avenue de Mayenne, a bedraggled little boulevard of shuttered shops and posters advertising athletic shoes and an upcoming outdoor concert by an Algerian rapper. We leave the car at an unused market square, walk half a block, and suddenly I am staring at the walls of what served for four weeks as my grandfather and uncle's forced domicile seven

The abandoned Poult cookie factory on the Avenue de Mayenne in Montauban that served as Alex and Helmut's forced domicile for a month in 1940.

decades ago. Above graffiti-covered sheet metal gates are red lacquered panels bearing the words "Émile Poult" and "Biscuits." Above that are arched windows of green glass bordered by red and white bricks. A block and a half up the avenue is the railroad station. Again, I call upon my imagination to help me visualize an image from the past, to recreate the scene of Alex and Helmut trudging in a line of their fellow prisoners down the street from the station in October and then retracing those steps in November. But my eyes only reveal to me the soiled pavement, empty save for a discarded water bottle and an underfed terrier trotting along the gutter, sniffing the ground as he goes. Once again, I tell myself ruefully, I am too late.

We walk around the corner, along the Rue Ferdinard Buisson, to an alleyway that leads to the rear of the abandoned Poult factory. Once again, we are blocked by a high metal gate, but it is possible to push a section aside and glimpse the courtyard where, presumably, the prisoners slept and took what little exercise was allowed them. The concrete floor of the enclosure has been pierced by weeds; everywhere are unmistakable signs of neglect and ruin. My relatives have moved on. There is nothing to do but go home.

This evening, our last in Montauban, Jean-Claude pours us drinks on the patio of the Drouilhet home, accompanied by the family cat whom Jean-Claude insists has no name, although Monique cuddles the cat and calls it Chou-Chou, a term of endearment that literally means "cabbage cabbage." After a dinner of chicken, pasta, and a local vintage, Jean-Claude recalls his pleasure at visiting his Osage friends in Pawhuska and breaks into a vigorous solo performance of *Oklahoma*, "when ze wind comes right behind ze rain!" We all join in and then warble "Tonight" from *West Side Story*, "Fugue for Tinhorns" from *Guys and Dolls*, Elvis's "Heartbreak Hotel," and a few more show tunes and rock ballads, leaving me to reflect, not for the first time, how successful our musical exports have been in burnishing America's reputation around the world.

After the laughter dies down and the sun has long set, I remind Jean-Claude of his remark regarding the Resistance memorial in Saint-Antoine-Noble-Val. I observe that he'd sounded a bit cynical and wonder what he thinks of contemporary attempts to honor those who fought both the Nazi invaders and the French collaborators.

Grinning a bit sheepishly, he replies, "I hope I never sound cynical where the Resistance is concerned. I do get a little impatient when officials today pretend no one collaborated and everyone resisted. That is simply not true and no amount of whitewashing will make it true . . . any more than trying to whitewash away your history of annihilating your native people will make that truth go away."

Jean-Claude pours himself a bit more wine and continues. "My father fought in a local Resistance group called Prosper, and so did my uncle. The Nazis captured my uncle and sent him to Buchenwald, and he never returned." He looks at Monique and then back at me. "This is why I have been so eager to help you in your search for your relatives. Doing this research is a way for me to pay tribute to my father and my uncle and all Resistance fighters." He pauses, takes another drink. "This is my heritage, you see. And it is my duty, as a Resistance man today, to help you and to show the respect which is due to the members of your family who suffered so much."

I hold Amy's hand tightly, smile at Jean-Claude, and whisper, "*Merci!*"

After a moment, Jean-Claude grins at Monique and says, "There is, after all, a history of Resistance here in Occitania. We still look fondly at those bullet holes from 1621 . . . for us, 390 years is not so long ago. And 1940 and 1942, that is only yesterday. We continue to resist today. Only last year an international seed and chemical company came here and tried to get our farmers to grow genetically altered corn. We resisted . . . and we won! We kicked the bastards out!"

Jean-Claude jumps to his feet, walks rapidly inside, and returns a minute later with a well-thumbed book in his hand: an English edition of *The Plague* by Albert Camus. "Camus was born in Algeria, where I fought to stay alive for more than two years," he says passionately. "He knew that the fight against fascism and racism and corporatism is never solely in the past, and never really over. That is what *la peste*, the plague, is . . . an enemy of humankind that may retreat from time to time but never is truly defeated." He opens the book to the last page and reads aloud.

"The plague bacillus never dies or disappears for good; . . . it can lie dormant for years and years in furniture and linen-chests . . . it bides its time in bedrooms, cellars, trunks, and bookshelves; and perhaps the day would come when, for the bane and the enlightening of men, it would rouse up its rats again and send them forth to die in a happy city."

Jean-Claude closes the book, sits down, drains his glass. After a minute, we all stand, reluctantly acknowledging the late hour and the end of this long, intense day. We wish one another goodnight. As Jean-Claude and I clasp hands, he says to me with a rueful smile, "Tomorrow as you drive south, and for the rest of your time in Europe, and when you get back to America . . . watch out for rats!"

I will, I assure him. I will.

9

Agde

FRIDAY, MAY 27, 2011. Once more this morning the southern sun is shining with all its might. We enjoy a final breakfast with Jean-Claude and Monique and after several embraces, deep expressions of thanks, and invitations for them to visit us in Maryland the next time their travels take them to Oklahoma, we point our little Meriva south and resume our pursuit of Alex and Helmut. As I do whenever I get into the driver's seat, I gently touch the photos of my relatives that remain affixed just above the rearview mirror; today I say aloud, "OK, guys . . . meet you on the shores of the Mediterranean!"

Today we eschew the more scenic and colorful back roads in favor of speed and simplicity, sticking mainly to the limited-access autoroute system of expressways. From Montauban, we continue south and circumvent Toulouse, the onetime capital of old Occitania and now the fourth-largest city in France. Our route then takes us southeast. One of the glories of medieval architecture, the beautiful walled city of Carcassonne—a settlement with more than twenty-five hundred years of history spanning Romans, Visigoths, Saracens, Crusaders, the kingdoms of Aragon and France—lies before us on a hill in the arid plains of Languedoc. But we content ourselves with gazing at the storied fifty-two towers of the ancient battlements from a rest stop off the autoroute. Somehow, echoes of the romantic ballads of the troubadours who lived and loved in Carcassonne waft their way to us above the roar of a six-lane turnpike.

At Narbonne, we have the choice of heading due south again, for Perpignan and Barcelona, or swinging northeast toward Montpellier and Avignon. I have always loved road signs, and seeing these lyrical names on the familiar green overhead indicators fills me with an excitement I cannot name. Continuing straight ahead is not an option, as we have reached the shores of the magical wine-dark Mediterranean Sea. Saving the southern direction for another day, we bear left on the A9, and after another twenty miles or so we leave the expressway for a two-lane road bound for Agde, in the *departement* of Hérault. We easily make our way through the tangled streets of the old city, head a bit farther south to Cap d'Agde, and find our hotel. Like our hotel in Chambon-sur-Lac in the Auvergne, our inn at Agde is called Le Bellevue. Again, we find that the name is more than apt. From our cozy little balcony, our view encompasses pastel stucco houses with red-tiled roofs, agave cactus and other graceful arid-soil plants, a hilly curving shoreline, gulls bringing a shock of white to a deep blue sky, and the azure and gentle waves of the Mediterranean itself.

We have traveled from the North Sea to the south sea, from sea to shining sea, in the space of one week. It took Alex and Helmut eighteen months to make the same journey. Our transportation has been an air-conditioned car cruising along superhighways and meandering through sometimes gentle, sometimes spectacular countryside. They made the journey on a bus and then by train at the point of a gun. We've lived off the fat of the land. By the time they reached Agde, they were lucky to receive two small meals a day. Tonight we will sleep on a comfortable mattress in a fine hotel with the waves of the Mediterranean murmuring in our ears as we drift off to a peaceful slumber. They spent their two months three miles inland, sleeping on unyielding wooden planks in a barracks that was made of reinforced cardboard and was open to the wind and winter weather, in a field surrounded by barbed wire.

I'm finding it very hard to stomach the contrast.

THERE HAS BEEN A SETTLEMENT on this spot for more than twenty-five hundred years. The Greeks founded the city in the fifth century BC and named it Agathe Tyche, or "Good Fortune." Its fortune came largely from the waters; for centuries, Agde was one of the busiest fishing ports in the Mediterranean. The city's fish market is still dominated by a statue of Amphitrite, a sea goddess and the wife of Poseidon in Greek mythology. In the seventeenth century, Agde became the southern terminus of the Canal du Midi, an infrastructural wonder that connected the sea with the Atlantic Ocean one hundred fifty miles to the northwest, thus enabling travelers to save a month of travel time and to avoid the hostile Barbary pirates who lurked menacingly off the coast of Spain. Since 1697, Agde's coat of arms has featured three blue waves on a golden background, the waves representing the confluence of sea, ocean, and canal. During the last forty years, the neighboring town of Cap d'Agde has been transformed into one of the shimmering playgrounds of the Mediterranean, with many high-rise hotels on its shore and yachts moored in the safety of its slips.

As far as Alex and Helmut were concerned, the history of Agde began in early 1939, when the first of nearly five hundred thousand refugees from the Spanish Civil War began to stream across the French border. In February 1939, the French government gave the order to build six new camps to house those refugees, most of whom had fled over the cloud-topped passes of the Pyrenees in freezing weather and now found themselves homeless and penniless in a foreign land. The new camps, mostly in the southwestern regions of France, included facilities in Gurs, Le Vernet, Argelès-sur-Mer, Rivesaltes, and Agde, which received its first convoy of Spanish refugees on February 28.

Built to accommodate twenty thousand people, the Agde camp's population grew to more than twenty-four thousand by the middle of May. It was situated on what was then the outskirts of town, bordering the old Route Nationale 110, the Rue de Sète, now known as the D912. The conditions were primitive and the food scarce, but the refugees felt fortunate to no longer be in the line of Generalissimo Franco's fire. Among the inhabitants of the camp were Spanish artists who volunteered their services to paint colorful murals in the Agde City Hall and Spanish archaeologists who assisted in excavations that unearthed artifacts from the city's ancient Greek heritage.

In the summer of 1939, the French government offered the Spanish refugees three options for leaving the camp. They could join the French army and thus begin the process of becoming French citizens, they could return to Spain, or they could emigrate to Mexico. By late September, the refugees had made their choices and the Agde camp was nearly empty. But not for long. The previous year's infamous Munich Agreement had delivered a part of Czechoslovakia—the region referred to by Adolf Hitler as the Sudetenland, or South Germany—to the expanding German empire. Tens of thousands of Czech citizens fled their homes. As part of its attempt to persuade the Czech government to accede to Hitler's demands, the French government offered temporary shelter to some of those refugees. In the autumn of 1939, about five thousand displaced Czechs moved into the same barracks in Agde that had recently housed the Spanish refugees. Then in May 1940, the Agde camp's population was increased by about fifteen hundred former citizens of Belgium who, like their Czech counterparts, had been displaced by the advancing German army. But after the signing of the armistice in June and with the assistance of the International Red Cross, the refugees slowly began returning home, and by late August the Agde camp was empty once more.

So when the Statute on Jews of October 3, 1940, went into effect, and zealots such as René Bousquet began their campaign to separate undesirables from mainstream French society, the camp at Agde was fully prepared to take in this new population. The first of the *Israélites étrangers*—foreign Jews—arrived at the railroad siding in Agde in the last days of October. They were former citizens of Germany, Austria, Armenia, and Yugoslavia who had made their way to France thinking they had found a refuge from the Nazi plague that had infected their homelands. Alex and Helmut joined them on November 9, after having made the journey from Montauban in a boxcar designed for transporting cows and horses. I wonder if Alex, given his family's history with horses, ever gave thought to the tragic irony of this manner of transportation.

He and his son walked from the train station to the gates of the camp, carrying their meager luggage. Once they arrived, the travelers were divided into two groups: the women and children went in one

A scene from the interior of one of the barracks of Camp d'Agde, showing the wooden benches that served as sleeping quarters. Conditions inside the barracks were either stifling or bone-chilling and there was nothing to do. (Services des Archives, Commune d'Agde)

direction, while men and boys fourteen years of age and older were sent in another. Husbands and wives were kept apart. Alex and Helmut were assigned to Barracks No. 13 in Agde Camp No. 3, which was separated from the other camps and from the outside world by a fifteen-foot fence topped with barbed wire. The barracks were each about one hundred feet long, made of heavy cardboard to which had been added a layer of tar. The floors were slabs of concrete, the windows made of screens coated with plastic. On warm days, it was stifling inside the barracks; on cold days, it was bone-chilling.

When Alex and Helmut entered Barracks No. 13 on November 9, they were each handed a sack about three feet long and told to fill their sacks with straw from a pile in the corner of the barracks. The result was a makeshift mattress that would rest atop the wooden bench that would serve as their sleeping quarters. Their only privacy from other families was provided by a blanket hung from the low ceiling. Outside the barracks, there were a few taps that provided water for drinking and washing, but no containers for transporting water into the barracks. Latrines were concrete structures with individual spaces for standing or squatting and large petrol drums below. The latrines naturally attracted vermin and clouds of flies.

Each camp had its own kitchen where meals were served twice a day, usually a thin soup with potatoes, occasionally supplemented with brown bread. One night in late November, when Alex and Helmut had been in Agde nearly three weeks, a fire broke out in the kitchen of the women's camp. Some of the men, realizing that a fire could easily consume the other tarred-cardboard barracks, attempted to cross into the women's camp to douse the flames, but they were beaten back by the camp's guards. The fire was extinguished before it spread, but soon thereafter the women's kitchen was replaced by a brick structure.

The guards of Camp Agde, the men (and a few women) who had prevented the prisoners from crossing into the women's camp, were all French. There were no Germans barking orders in their clipped, angular language; everything was spoken in the smooth vowels and throaty consonants of the Gallic vernacular. There were no beatings, no physical intimidation, no overt violence.

There was also nothing to do. The residents of Camp Agde aimlessly wandered the confines of their enclosures every day, "vegetating," as one survivor described it. No one was killed; instead one rotted slowly.

After nearly a month of this existence, Alex characteristically decided to take matters into his own hands. He found some writing materials, sat down on his bench in his barracks, and wrote a letter, in literate and rather elegant French, to the prefect of Hérault in Montpellier. The letter, which I discovered in the holdings of the United States Holocaust Memorial Museum in Washington, D.C., is dated 5 December 1940 and displays the return address Camp 3, Barracks 13, Agde.

It is my honor to request your benevolence to help liberate myself and my son, Klaus Helmut, age 19, from the Camp in Agde.

On May 13, 1939, we boarded the steamship St. Louis, headed for Cuba, but due to a change in government we were unable to disembark in Havana, and we, along with a number

A portion of Alex's letter to the prefect of Hérault, dated December 5, 1940. "It is my honor to request your benevolence to help liberate myself and my son . . . from the Camp in Agde." (Courtesy of the United States Holocaust Memorial Museum)

of the other passengers, had to disembark on June 20, 1939, in Boulogne-sur-Mer, where the French government kindly took us in.

During the winter of 1939–1940, my son and I became gravely ill. I myself was hospitalized in Contrexéville (Vosges) at the Central Hospital, where I remained for four months. My son suffered from chronic throat infections and, at one point, from pleurisy, and the doctor ordered an operation for him (attached please find the medical certificate). [Alas, the medical certificate disappeared sometime in the last seven decades.]

The American Joint Distribution Committee deposited $500 for each of us, thus a total of $1,000, so that we would not be a burden to the state. The Committee made this commitment to subsidize our needs until our departure oversees, which I hope is not far off.

I beseech you once again to grant our freedom, as the state of our health will not enable us to spend a winter in the camp.

In the hope that you will follow up my request, Monsieur le Prefet, I send my most respectful greetings.

Alex Goldschmidt

My grandfather's letter did not go unnoticed. Apparently, the prefect looked into the matter and asked a lower official, the *sous-préfet* of the town of Béziers—about ten miles northwest of Agde—to make some inquiries. On December 16, eleven days after Alex wrote his letter, the *sous-préfet* sent a note to the prefect of Hérault on paper bearing the words *État Français,* meaning "French state," the name the Vichy government had adopted. The note read:

I have the honor to address herein the request made by Goldschmidt, Alex, who is currently interned at Camp Agde. He is soliciting the liberation of himself and his 19-year-old son Klaus.

The following information has been collected regarding the person concerned: German, resident of Martigny-les-Bains (Vosges) since July, 1939. No resources. Claimed by the *Comité d'Assistance aux Réfugiés* in Marseille (48 Rue de la Paix). The committee certifies that the American Joint Distribution Committee has made available to him and his family all the relief necessary to meet and sustain their needs.

Franz Kafka himself could not have written a more opaque, witless communiqué. Monsieur *sous-préfet* learns from the well-meaning people at CAR that the Joint has pledged some funds so that Alex and Helmut would not become, in Alex's words, "a burden to the state," and concludes that all their needs are being met. The fact that Alex and his son have "no resources" is apparently trumped by the unseen but overwhelming benevolence of the Americans. Alex's request for liberation is mentioned but neither granted nor denied. Neither is the state of the two men's health a matter for consideration, despite the undeniable fact that winter weather has descended upon Agde and its weakened internees. A letter has been received; the matter has been looked into; the bureaucracy's wheels grind on; there is nothing to be done.

A few days later, the life of Camp Agde was brightened briefly by a combined Christmas/Hannukah concert, for which a small group of local choristers entered the gates and sang carols and traditional songs. The menu of thin potato soup was supplemented by a portion of locally caught fish. For this one day, men and women were allowed to mingle, husbands and wives were reunited; for one precious day, the joy of the season was shared by the inmates of Agde.

As the year came to a close, Captain Tassard, Camp Agde's commandant, issued a status report. In a document dated 31 December 1940, the captain reported to the authorities in Vichy that the camp had 2,335 male internees, 1,520 women, 867 children, and 245 infants under three years old, for a grand total of 4,967 souls. Within a fortnight, that figure would be drastically reduced. Alex and Helmut and many hundreds of their fellow prisoners were once again loaded onto cattle cars and shipped to their next destination: a vast plain at the foot of the Pyrenees mountains and a camp called Rivesaltes.

SATURDAY, MAY 28, 2011. The morning air is fresh and sweet, with a playful breeze off the cobalt-blue billows of the Mediterranean gently tickling the red carnations on our balcony, perhaps wafting all the way from the legendary Happy Isles of Greek mythology. I awaken early and take a walk along the shell-strewn beach, trying to imagine the more than two millennia of human history these rocks and waves have witnessed. In this frame of mind, I am startled but not completely thunderstruck to behold Poseidon emerging from beneath the sea, his trident brandished aloft. It turns out to be only a local fisherman wearing a shiny black wetsuit, his spear gun clutched in one hand, a metal mesh basket full of his wriggling catch in the other.

Later, after a breakfast of croissants, jam, honey, and tea, we drive back to Agde and find the office of the municipal archives, where we have an appointment with Madame Irene Dauphin. She kindly provides us with some old photographs of the camp, a few documents—including the memo regarding Alex from the *sous-préfet*—and her genuine sympathy for my story. She also points the way to the site of Camp Agde, less than a mile away. We set off on foot.

In the small space created by the diverging Rue Paul Balmigère and the Avenue Jean Moulin, we discover a memorial to those interned at Agde. The circular floor of the memorial is paved with bricks. At the eastern side of the circle is a curved stone structure with six spaced tablets, all at roughly chest level. In the middle of the curve rises a chimney-shaped tower about fifteen feet tall, or about as high as the walls that enclosed Alex, Helmut, and the thousands of their fellow prisoners at Camp Agde.

The six tablets honor each group of people interned at the camp between 1939 and 1943: the Spanish, the Czechs, the Belgians, foreigners in general, the Jews in particular, and the first refugees from Indochina. Though I have heard stories of rampant anti-Semitism in contemporary France, we are surprised and saddened to see that, of the six tablets, only the one naming the Jews has been defaced by graffiti. But a greater shock awaits us when we translate the words on the tower. "Here stood Camp Agde," they proclaim to all who pass by. "Tens of thousands of men stayed here in their march toward freedom."

This is the legacy of Camp Agde in the minds of the local citizenry? A way station on the path to *freedom?!* Have these people not heard of the Final Solution, of the Six Million, of the goddamn Holocaust itself? I am beside myself with anger and sorrow.

We walk on slowly in the gathering heat, under a blazing sun. A street called Rue du Camp d'Agde, prettily landscaped with crimson bougainvillea, leads us to the campus of René Cassin College. René Cassin was a French jurist and human rights activist who, along with Eleanor Roosevelt, wrote the Universal Declaration of Human Rights, adopted by the United Nations in 1948. His namesake college now stands on the land once occupied by Camp Agde, one of the world's many travesties of justice that necessitated M. Cassin's declaration.

In a small clearing between a parking lot and an outdoor basketball court, we come upon two more memorials, each in the shape of a stone marker about six feet high. On one are the words, "In memory of

The memorial to Camp Agde. "Tens of thousands of men stayed here in their march toward freedom."

41 Jews deported from Camp Agde, transferred to Drancy in August, 1942, and then deported to Auschwitz on Convoy 25, August 28, 1942." "Ah, so the news did filter down here after all," I mutter to Amy.

The adjacent marker is headlined "The Just of Agde." It mentions the names of four local families who hid Jews during the early 1940s: M. Achille Bautes, M. et Mme. Joseph Joly, M. et Mme. Paul Carrausse, and M. Jean Pallares. Below these names are the familiar words of the Talmud: "Who Saves One Life Saves the Entire Universe."

I am sure that these were indeed good people. But somehow today it is not enough to mollify or impress me. "So they came up with four righteous families in Agde," I say to Amy. "Bully for them!"

We return to our car, drive into old Agde, find a café on the edge of the canal, and order a savory lunch of quiche and mineral water. The sky remains deep blue, the breeze caresses our hair, the sun sparkles on the surface of the water, the food is excellent, and we are alive and well. Yet I find that all I can think about are the desolate images of Camp Agde from Mme. Dauphin's photo collection and the insultingly obtuse words on the memorial tower.

Again I am beset by doubts concerning the journey that has brought us to this flavorful meal on this picturesque spot. Once more, I wonder whether my desire to follow in the footsteps of Alex and Helmut is not the tribute to them that I intended, but in fact a grotesque mime of a tribute, a six-week self-indulgent European tour, complete with fine food, lovely countryside, and now an extravagant sojourn by the sparkling Mediterranean. I am deeply unhappy, shaken by the day's discoveries and mourning my lost family more than ever.

We finish our meal in silence, and I add to my litany of sorrows a fear that Amy may be tiring of my doleful company. We return to our hotel, where Amy announces her desire to swim in the sea. I remain on our balcony, gazing at the scalloped waves, simultaneously enjoying the view and feeling guilty for my enjoyment. The sun slowly sets, Amy returns all aglow from her evening swim, and another soft Mediterranean night descends upon us. In my unhappy frame of mind, I go to bed and experience a memorable dream.

I am watching a play. There are actors on a stage, and I am seated in the audience. In other words, I am an observer, outside, rather than part of, the "action." The play involves an African-American family, and there is a decided civil rights component to the play's theme. The family's spiritual and moral center is embodied by the strong matriarch, a character reminiscent of Lena Younger in Lorraine Hansberry's outstanding play *A Raisin in the Sun*. But this is not *Raisin* or any play that I know.

I have been watching the play for some time and feel invested in the action and in the characters. I am anxious, in other words, to see what happens next. As I lean forward in my seat, the Lena Younger character clearly says to another character on stage, "Your grandfather would be proud of you." As she says these words, she reaches above her head and rests her hand on a rough piece of wood that in the play seems to be a judicial ruling spot of some kind. In other words, it was the place where judges rule, which in common parlance is a bench.

In my dream, a moment or two or five or ten pass slowly before I realize the significance of those words and that gesture for me. In the context of the dream, it was "just" a line in the play's script. But almost immediately after that line was spoken, I wake up and understand that the hard wooden bench suggests the benches that Alex and Helmut were forced to use as beds at Camp Agde, and that the words uttered by that woman have been meant for me.

I have no idea why those reassuring words in the play were delivered by a black woman and not spoken directly to me by Amy or a friend or even my father or brother. But I do know that those words, which I can still hear in the ringing cadences of that kind matriarchal figure, have made me feel a good deal better. I slip quietly out of bed so as not to disturb my loving wife and pad out onto the balcony, there to bask in the cold bright light of the stars and to revel in the sound of the timeless sea breaking on the ancient rocky shore.

I am sure that the blues will find me again soon enough, but for now I am deeply comforted by the thought that Alex would be proud of me for undertaking this journey. This is surely an example of the subconscious mind working in mysterious ways, but as I listen again to my black female inner voice I decide that my quest is not a sham, not a mere excuse for a grand European adventure, but indeed the result of my need to know, to witness, to reveal, and, if not to save my grandfather and uncle, perhaps to save myself.

With a last look at the stars that have witnessed centuries of human drama on this weathered coastline, I return to bed. I lightly kiss Amy's right ear, and she purrs in her sleep.

In the months since Agde, I have thought often of the dream and its many potential meanings. I consider the possibility that somehow the Greek spirit of *Agathe Tyche*, Good Fortune, has lingered in that corner of its long-departed empire. Perhaps I was not in a modern theater with a proscenium and a thrust stage, but rather seated in the sloping curves of an amphitheater attending a play by one of the original fathers of drama. In *Agamemnon*, the playwright Aeschylus assures his audience, "In our sleep, pain that cannot forget falls drop by drop upon the heart, and in our despair, against our will, comes wisdom through the awful grace of God."

As I slowly return to sleep on the shores of the wine-dark sea, I do not feel the gift of wisdom. But I am aware of a certain grace, and my heart floods with gratitude.

10

Rivesaltes

SUNDAY, MAY 29, 2011. In the morning after my transfiguring dream, on this day of rest, I perceive, for the first time on our journey, a profound desire to slow down, to pause, to delay any further discoveries of pain or sorrow or even the slightest inconvenience suffered by my uncle and grandfather on theirs. We enjoy breakfast at our ease, lingering at our table to consume with unhurried delectation the last crisp croissants accompanied by fine local honey that we spread with a leisurely knife. Checkout time at Le Bellevue is noon, and we dawdle at packing until the morning hours have all but slipped by. Even then, our bags secured in our sturdy little Meriva, we postpone our departure for still another hour, taking advantage of the hotel manager's indulgence to occupy a chaise on the rooftop deck while we indolently gaze at the wrinkled blue sea. This is not mere Sunday loafing, I tell myself, it is anxious reluctance. I am deeply aware that our next destination remains a place of infamy within the annals of French and Holocaust history, and, like Jaques' schoolboy, I find myself "creeping like snail unwillingly" toward tomorrow's appointment.

At length, we can procrastinate no longer and drive off to the west and south. Returning to the autoroute, we retrace our path to Friday's intersection with the road to Carcassonne but then continue south on the expressway toward Perpignan and Barcelona, my spirits sent soaring once more by those lyrical names on the green overhead signs. We're aware that we don't have far to travel today, so by mid-afternoon we leave the expressway for a smaller highway that hugs the Mediterranean coast and takes us through a settlement called Port Barcarès. It is just a dot on our Michelin map and we imagine a picturesque fishing village inhabited by a colorful array of grizzled watermen and their saucy voluptuous women pulling an honest yet humble existence from beneath the waves. Instead, we find an ersatz town of condos, restaurants, and docks for the outsized compensatory yachts that belong to the Beautiful People who congregate along this portion of the Côte d'Azure. Just outside the port, we come upon a "naturist" community made up of little colonies that sport such names as Eden and Aphrodite, Apollo and Odysseus. We consider taking a prurient detour to try to catch a glimpse of the inhabitants but find that our way is barred by an unsmiling, fully clothed sentry. We retreat, slightly abashed, and spend the next several miles giggling to ourselves at the unlikely prospect that we would ever want to live in such a community. It's not for us, we conclude, but *vive la différence*.

We return to the main road and are soon on the western edge of Perpignan near the city airport, where our room for the night is located. For most of our journey, I have endeavored to find charming local lodgings that reflect their particular surroundings, but tonight is an exception. Given what I imagine will be a rather grim encounter next morning, I have made reservations at a nondescript Comfort Inn, a chain motel only a few miles away from Rivesaltes. We find the room to be bland but perfectly acceptable and almost immediately drive into Perpignan for dinner and a little sightseeing.

Now the capital of the *departement* of Pyrénées Orientales, Perpignan was founded toward the beginning of the tenth century and soon came under the control of the counts of Barcelona. One of those counts, James the Conqueror, founded the kingdom of the island of Majorca in 1276 and established Perpignan as the capital city of the mainland territories of the kingdom. In the next century, the city lost nearly half its population to the Black Death, and during the following three hundred years it passed repeatedly from Spanish to French control and back again as the spoils of many wars between the two countries. Since 1659, the citizens of Perpignan have lived under the French flag, although many street signs today appear in both French and Catalan. In 1963, the Catalan surrealist painter Salvador Dali declared that the city's railway station was the exact center of the universe and acknowledged that some of his best ideas had come to him as he sat in the station's waiting room. In Dali's honor, the city has erected a sign on one of the platforms that reads *Perpignan: Centre du Monde*.

On this warm late spring afternoon, we leave our car near the thirteenth-century castle of the kings of Majorca and stroll around the high castle ramparts and through the narrow winding streets of the medieval city until we come upon an Italian restaurant in the beautiful Place de la République. We eat heartily; I find myself talking and laughing in an unusually animated manner. Mindful of my appointment in the morning, I have decided this evening to adopt as my mantra Stephen Sondheim's "Tragedy tomorrow, comedy tonight!" As we return to our motel on the edge of town, however, my spirits sag and sleep comes late.

Monday dawns cloudy and windy. We eat a hurried breakfast in the Comfort Inn's generic dining area, near a table of pilots and flight attendants who are catching a plane at the Perpignan-Rivesaltes Airport. After loading the Meriva, we set off grimly in search of the nearby camp. A memorial museum dedicated to those who were interned at Rivesaltes is in the planning stages, and I have been in e-mail contact with Elodie Montes of the museum staff. In my last message, I confirmed that I would be seeing her at about 10:00 a.m. today. Anxious to be prompt—on top of my other anxieties—I have left what I assume will be plenty of time to find the site, which, given that it will be the location of a nationally supported museum, I further assume will be clearly marked. To my vast annoyance and frustration, we discover that my assumptions are utterly wrong.

Returning to the A9 autoroute, we become stuck in Perpignan's rush-hour traffic and then are slowed by an enormous bottleneck caused by a massive construction project involving six lanes of traffic and at least as many exit ramps going off in different directions. Thanks to Amy's considerable navigational skills, we manage to get off the A9 and onto route D614, which leads us into the center of the small town of Rivesaltes. Spotting a sign reading *Musée-Mémorial du Camp de Rivesaltes*, we follow its arrow north on the D5, assuming that all will now be easy. But we then come to a traffic circle in which the D5 intersects with the D12, with no further indication of which road to follow. Over the next thirty or forty minutes, we try first one route and then the other, once following another road—the D18—which intersects with D12—but never again seeing another sign indicating that the *Musée-Mémorial* is any closer than Paris.

Frustrated beyond measure, I can barely take in the landscape, which varies between the verdant vineyards that produce the distinctive wines of the Pyrénées Orientales *departement* and arid plains that stretch to the rising uplands of the Pyrenees Mountains to the west. The scudding low clouds that obscure the higher peaks match my dark mood.

Finally we see a low building off to our right. We cannot make out what its small sign proclaims but decide that in this storm of uncertainty, we have reached a temporary port. The building proves to have nothing whatsoever to do with the camp—it's a vocational training center—but luckily the receptionist speaks English and kindly allows us to use her telephone. I reach Ms. Montes almost at once. She was expecting my call but is stuck at the museum's main office in Perpignan for the next several hours. She gives me detailed directions to the camp entrance and promises to meet me there tomorrow morning at 10:00. So Amy and I decide to push on to our destination for the next two nights, the nearby village of Prades.

But now that we know how to find the camp, my curiosity gets the better of me. We drive a few more kilometers up the D5 until we reach an almost indecipherable crossroads. To the right, a rough dirt road leads off into a tangle of unkempt undergrowth. To the left, standing forlornly by the side of the highway, are three small monuments. One pays tribute to the Spanish Republicans who were interned here after the Civil War. One is for the Gypsies. One is in memory of the Jews.

After a few moments spent gazing at the monuments, we wordlessly drive down the dirt road into a vast, empty, silent space. To our right are a half-dozen giant metal windmills, their blades revolving slowly through the humid air. We see scrubby trees that somehow take sustenance from the dusty grey clay soil. The roadway is treacherous, pocked by deep ruts. A sense of sorrowful abandonment overhangs all.

We come to the ruins of what was once the camp's main gate, two immense vertical columns supporting the horizontal. There are coils of rusted, abandoned barbed wire twisted among the undergrowth. Driving through the gate, we come upon crumbling brick barracks, most of them open to the cloudy sky. I can drive no longer; we stop and step outside the car into as bleak and desolate a landscape as I could ever imagine. There is the sound of the ever-present wind in the scrubby trees and other than that a silence as profound as might be experienced at the bottom of the ocean.

I am seized by a sadness unlike any I have felt since we landed in Europe nearly three weeks ago. Suddenly I feel an irresistible urge to flee. Amy and I share a glance, we fling ourselves back into the car, and with all speed we make our way out of the camp, head south around the perimeter of Perpignan, and drive up into the foothills of the Pyrenees toward Prades. Neither of us speaks for miles.

Finally, I decide to treat my missed connection with Elodie Montes as a reprieve, an opportunity to return to the role of carefree tourist before tomorrow's resumption of my pursuit of Alex and Helmut. Indeed, there is much to relish on the journey to Prades, as the highway snakes upward through rock formations and a red-tinged soil reminiscent of the stunning scenery of the American Southwest. Occasional herds of sheep and goats appear in well-tended upland fields and the sky slowly clears as our altitude increases. By the time we reach our destination, my spirits have risen accordingly.

A small village just thirty-five miles from the Spanish border, Prades was founded in the ninth century. Its soaring St. Peter's Church dates from the eleventh century, with important renovations in the seventeenth century giving it one of the largest and most ornate altarpieces in all France. But its innate beauty aside, there are two reasons why the rest of the world knows about Prades: the monk and mystic Thomas Merton, author of the influential autobiography *The Seven Storey Mountain*, was born here in 1915, and the great cellist Pablo Casals lived here for many years during his self-imposed exile from Spain following the defeat of the Republican forces in 1939. It is the Casals legacy that has inspired me to stay in Prades while visiting Rivesaltes. I am rarely so fulfilled as when I am on pilgrimage.

Our hotel is a lovely stone building that was built as a tannery two hundred years ago. After we check in, we stroll up a steep hill to the city's main square, which fronts the church of St. Peter. The square is neatly bounded by plane trees, the gnarled trees with the sometimes twisted trunks often painted by Van Gogh; Amy and I have actually taken to referring to them as Van Gogh trees. There are several cafés along the square. We choose one, order sandwiches and beer, and spend a peaceful hour relaxing, reviving, and reveling in the joyful fact of our good fortune to be in such a remote yet beautiful portion of the planet.

We then walk into the cool, dim interior of the church, where we admire the celebrated altarpiece. I reflect contentedly that I am in the same exalted surroundings where Maestro Casals played Bach when he put Prades on the map with his first international music festival in 1950. I imagine that I can hear the echoes of his profound performances reaching me across the decades, and my unsettling memories of this morning are temporarily banished. I am a happy pilgrim as we walk back down the hill to our hotel hand in hand.

But the next morning comes all too soon, and I head back alone to meet Ms. Montes. Amy has decided that after nearly three weeks on my schedule, she needs some time to herself, so she plans to spend the day reading and researching a project of her own by the side of the hotel's swimming pool. As I drive the thirty miles or so to my appointment, I juggle two conflicting fears. One is that Ms. Montes will stand me up, and the other is that she will appear but will have nothing of consequence to show me. To try to allay those fears and also to brighten up the cloudy day, I slip one of my favorite recordings into the Meriva's CD player: the Goldberg Variations by Bach, the second of the two commercial performances of the piece made by the great eccentric Canadian pianist Glenn Gould, released just weeks before his death, at age fifty, in 1982. In addition to being a superb pianist, Gould liked to drive, so the thought of his accompanying me on this journey down the mountain enhances my deep enjoyment of the music.

As I take the final curves on the road before arriving at the entrance to the camp, I bet myself that Ms. Montes won't show. Indeed, when I arrive at the lonely crossroads with the three memorials, I am alone in the vast emptiness. But it is only 9:50, and within five minutes, a little white Renault rounds the bend, pulls up beside me, and a trim young woman emerges holding a folder. It is Elodie Montes. Within minutes I discover, both to my satisfaction and my sorrow, that my other fear was groundless as well.

THE CAMP DE RIVESALTES had its origins in 1935, when the French army, noting that the southwest corner of the country—near the Mediterranean and so close to Spain—was strategically important, requisitioned a little more than fifteen hundred acres of land to build a military base. Roughly two-and-a-half miles long by one mile wide, the base was completed three years later and named Camp Joffre after General Joseph Joffre, a Rivesaltes native who was the commander-in-chief of French forces during the First World War. When the Spanish Republican forces were defeated in early 1939, Camp Joffre was one of several sites, along with the camp at Agde, where refugees from Spain were housed. Within a year, the camp expanded to take in other "undesirables," including refugees from Nazi Germany, Gypsies, and, especially after the *Statut des Juifs* of October 1940, Jews. In the last months of 1940, families of these undesirables were moved into the barracks originally intended for French colonial troops. Then, in early January 1941, the camp was euphemistically renamed a *centre d'hébergement*, an "accommodation center." Men, women, and children were placed in segregated barracks arranged in a series of *îlots*, or blocks, designated A through K. The foulest chapter of the history of Camp de Rivesaltes had begun.

Within a very short time, utter misery seized those interned there, due to overcrowding, filth, disease, squalor, exposure to the elements, inadequate food and medicine, and—perhaps most debilitating of all— an utter lack of any meaningful way to pass endless hours behind barbed wire in the vast empty space. Men and women had separate barracks, with an additional section of the camp set aside for mothers with children under six years of age. The barracks themselves, with concrete walls and floors and a single entrance, were each about a hundred fifty feet long and contained up to a hundred people. They slept on bunk beds, the top bunk reached by a rickety ladder, with the beds lined up against each long wall, a narrow aisle stretching between them. As was the case at Agde, the internees at Rivesaltes slept on thin mattresses filled with straw, which was rarely if ever changed. In the four corners of each barracks, there was a tiny room reserved for the very elderly, the very ill, mothers with nursing infants, and, in some cases, someone who claimed—either via election or through sheer intimidation—the title of barracks chief. The one or two windows in each barracks contained no glass; thus it was either stiflingly hot or bitterly cold, depending on the season. The camp's population continued to expand, until by May 1941, there were an estimated ninety-five hundred people representing sixteen nationalities.

Contemporary accounts of the living conditions at Rivesaltes were stark. One social worker wrote, after visiting one of the barracks, "It was dark, cold, and humid, and there was no heating. And seizing you by the throat upon entering, a bitter odor of human sweat which floats in this den which is never aired out." Another left this report: "The living quarters are very badly maintained and, with only rare exceptions, are repugnantly filthy. It is impossible to get rid of the vermin that have taken hold there, since there does not exist a systematic disinfecting mechanism. In general, the internees possess only the garment and the underwear that they wear, and the hovels in which they live make it impossible for them to properly look after their clothing."

The food, such as there was, was bad. Meals always consisted of a thin soup made with potatoes, squash, turnips, parsnips, or cabbage. Occasionally, bread was served along with the soup, but never meat. There was also corn, but not the sort of sweet corn found growing stalk by stalk in the lush fields of Iowa or Illinois. This was feed corn, usually served by French farmers to their pigs; in Rivesaltes, it was fed to the Jews. In the spring of 1941, a representative of a Jewish relief agency visited Rivesaltes and reported that "while the normal daily ration required by a human being lies between 2,000 and 2,400 calories—the essential requirement being 1,500 calories—most of the internees consume barely 800 calories." The relief worker went on to point out that, due to the cold in the barracks and the often inadequate clothing worn by the unfortunates in the camp, many of those precious calories were lost every day to the exertion of shivering.

One latrine served every three or four barracks. Like the barracks, the latrines were made of concrete. To use the latrine, a person would walk the forty or fifty yards from the barracks, climb a half-dozen steps to a platform divided into five or six spaces that offered the bare minimum of privacy, stood or squatted on two pieces of wood, and contributed to the contents of the large petrol tanks below. From the same relief worker's report of 1941: "Access to lavatories is generally difficult because of the mud surrounding them. They are so poorly maintained and so rarely disinfected that not only is there a dreadful stink but also a permanent risk of infection, especially during the hot season when flies and mosquitoes proliferate and spread contagious diseases. Rodents have appeared, which besides attacking the food reserves also carry harmful bacteria."

When the first internees arrived at the newly organized accommodation center of Rivesaltes in January 1941, they found the water pipes frozen and, thus, access to showers nonexistent. This obstacle to cleanliness persisted even with the arrival of warmer weather, as there were few washbasins and the flow of water was frequently interrupted. For weeks, those trapped within the barbed wire were only rarely able to wash themselves and even then, hastily and incompletely. Another eyewitness account declared, "Some internees have not undressed for six months. One can only imagine their present state of destitution."

The consequences of living in crowded, unhealthy living quarters with a seriously inadequate diet and almost total lack of hygiene quickly manifested themselves. Many prisoners—for that is what they were— soon fell ill. Cases of tuberculosis, dysentery, and enteritis, on top of simple malnutrition and exposure, swept through the camp. Many prisoners died in the arms of family members or, even more wretchedly, alone on their mattresses of straw. Medical facilities within the camp, not surprisingly, were insufficient. Severe cases were occasionally moved to the St. Louis Hospital in Perpignan; an exasperated social worker wrote of the institution, "although it resembles the worst medieval general hospitals, it continues to receive patients."

In August 1941, the U.S. State Department forwarded a memorandum on conditions at Rivesaltes—written by a relief worker hired by the American Jewish Congress—to a Monsieur de Chambrun of the Foreign Ministry of the Vichy government. The memo concluded, "No self-respecting zoo-keeper would allow the animals in his care to be housed under the conditions prevailing here." There is no evidence of any reply from the ministry.

Rivesaltes, it must be said, was not an extermination camp. No one there died by design of the authorities. There were no roll calls, no guard towers, no snarling police dogs, no overt brutality meted out by the French guards. There was at least one instance, reported by a survivor whose testimony was videotaped by the United States Holocaust Memorial Museum in Washington, of a coordinated sexual assault by French soldiers. This witness told of soldiers entering one of the women's barracks and going up and down the center aisle, lifting blankets bunk by bunk to decide which women to take back to their quarters. But for the most part, prisoners were not hounded, harassed, or humiliated.

They were simply left alone in that vast empty space to lean into the constant stiff winds that blew winter and summer, the mistral that stirred up the dust and dirt into little cyclones of torment in the dry season and wrinkled the puddles that covered the endless mud when it rained. They were left alone with no books or newspapers to read, no work to accomplish, no place to walk but on the well-worn path to the latrine, no place to sit but on their bunks in their crowded, uncomfortable barracks, nothing to do but wait or hope or dream increasingly threadbare dreams. Children played with stones and sticks. The days seemed endless . . . and yet they ended far too soon for many prisoners of Rivesaltes.

In August 1942, the Vichy government ordered that part of the camp at Rivesaltes be reorganized as the *Centre National de Rassemblement des Israélites*, or the National Center for the Gathering of Jews. Foreign-born Jews in the Unoccupied Zone were rounded up, brought

Barracks within the enclosure of Camp Rivesaltes, circa 1941. Today the flat sandy ground is overrun with scrubby stunted evergreens that push their way into what remains of those structures.
(Courtesy of the United States Holocaust Memorial Museum)

to Rivesaltes, and temporarily housed in blocks F, J, and K. Beginning on August 11 and continuing until October 20, nine convoys of prisoners, including both these newly "gathered" Jews and those who had been residents of Rivesaltes for the prior two-and-a-half years, were all loaded onto boxcars and cattle cars and shipped to the extermination camps of Eastern Europe.

During the years 1941 and 1942, about twenty-one thousand internees passed through Camp Rivesaltes. More than two hundred died in the camp, including fifty-one children aged one year or younger. More than twenty-three hundred were shipped to their slaughter.

In November 1942, the German army invaded the Unoccupied Zone and, finding the camp no longer useful for its murderous purposes, ordered the closing of Rivesaltes on November 25. But nearly two years later, after the liberation of France, Rivesaltes was reopened as Camp 162 to house German and Italian prisoners of war. During the following two years, nearly ten thousand inmates lived there. As proof that the harshness of the camp's climate respected no national boundaries, more than four hundred POWs died in the camp before it was closed again in 1946.

But the unhappy history of Camp Rivesaltes was far from complete. Beginning in 1954, France waged an eight-year war against the independence-minded population of Algeria, which had existed as a French colony for more than a hundred years. Within that country, there was a sizable population of Algerians, mostly Muslims, who had fought for the French in the Franco-Prussian War of 1870 and in both world wars. In the war for Algerian independence, those soldiers, known as Harkis, once more took the side of the French government, and after Algeria secured its independence in 1962, the Harkis were subject to often brutal reprisals from their newly independent countrymen. Many tens of thousands of Harkis were shot, burned alive, castrated, dragged behind trucks, and tortured in other unspeakable ways. Thousands of Harkis fled to France, thinking that the country for which they had fought would shelter them. Instead, the French government refused to recognize the right of these former soldiers to live peaceably within French society and confined more than twenty thousand Harkis behind the same barbed wire fences in Camp Rivesaltes that had imprisoned the Jews twenty years earlier.

Even in the twenty-first century, Rivesaltes has served as a prison for "undesirables." As recently as 2007, the better-preserved barracks were home to immigrants, many of them also Muslim and in the country without proper papers. The camp, constructed as a base for the French army to prepare for the defense of its homeland, has instead largely served as a place of misery and anguish for nearly eighty years.

ONE OF THE FIRST PIECES of documentary evidence from my grandfather and uncle's long, sad journey through France that found its way into my hands is a list of Rivesaltes detainees that I discovered among the holdings of the U.S. Holocaust Memorial Museum in Washington. Listed above such names as Szpitzman, Lippmann, Stern, Levy, and Wiesenfelder, Alex and Klaus Goldschmidt were among twenty men who entered the gate of Camp de Rivesaltes on January 14, 1941—the date it officially opened as an accommodation center—and were assigned to Block K, Barracks No. 21. A dossier was filled out for each of them—No. 222 for Alex and No. 223 for Klaus Helmut—listing their names, the city of their birth (misspelled in Alex's case), their nationality (German), their religion ("Israelite"), their marital status, and their profession ("salesman" and "student," respectively).

For six months, they survived the brutal cold, the never-ending mistral winds that Alex declared sapped his strength, the flies and vermin, the suffocating boredom that was only occasionally leavened by letters from his wife and children, and the wretched, inadequate food. Neither of them was particularly robust to begin with, and they both lost considerable weight during their time in Rivesaltes. Alex's weight dropped from 136 pounds to 104, Helmut's from 127 pounds to just 94. By the time spring came to the Pyrenees and the chill of their barracks gave way to oppressive heat, Alex feared that they would not live to see another winter. His apprehension was intensified by the brutal evidence of his immediate surroundings. In a letter written to my father in early 1942, Alex declared, "We saw people literally dying of hunger before our eyes."

Partly to pass the time and partly to earn a small salary that might aid them in acquiring more and better food, Helmut took a job in the camp infirmary, first as an assistant and later as a medical orderly. In that same letter, Alex reported that "part of Helmut's job was to transfer the dead— sometimes 2 or 3 a day—and carry the bodies out. These were men who, had they had some degree of nourishment, would not have died."

In his own letter to his older brother, written the following spring, Helmut recounted his days and nights in Block F, the Rivesaltes camp hospital. Given the severe deprivations he and his father faced daily during their imprisonment, I'm struck by the ironic, sometimes almost playful tone my uncle struck in his narrative. Since I never knew him, of course, his words are all I have to form an impression of his character. I must say that I find him very appealing.

First, along with two Spaniards, I was what one could best describe as a "Girl Friday" in the three barracks that served as the infirmary. Then I was "promoted" and made responsible for cleanliness. I had to make the beds of the seriously ill patients (Careful! Lice!), distribute medicine ("pill giver"), take patients' temperatures, etc. Part of my job took place in the operating room: I served as the *Infirmius*, in cases of death to help carry off the dead, which was almost a daily occurrence. I also became adept at helping with bandaging. In dealing with sick people I learned a lot, but it was truly not easy. There were two main reasons that prompted me to stay in the job: 1) I didn't want to and couldn't do without the meager pay, and 2) I saw no other way to stay out of the Jewish Tent where I visited Father every evening while he was ill. There the care and treatment were even worse. Of course, I didn't get fat in Block F either.

During those first six months of 1941, as Helmut and Alex struggled to stay alive in Rivesaltes, their dire situation was somewhat ameliorated thanks to the successful attempts of three family members to achieve what they had failed to do: attain freedom in America. The first to make the crossing were Johanna Behrens, the sister of Alex's wife, Toni, and Johanna's husband, Max Markreich. Max and Johanna emigrated to the West in 1939, spent months in a displaced persons facility in Trinidad, and finally reached safe haven in the United States in January 1941. Immediately, Max began writing letters on behalf of his relatives and some friends he had made during his time in the West Indies. He wrote to the Mizrachi Organization of America to request that a tallith (a traditional prayer shawl) and a set of prayer books, with texts in both Hebrew and English, be sent to the camp he'd recently left in Port of Spain, Trinidad. And on March 17, he wrote an impassioned letter to a New York Jewish relief organization called the National Refugee Service with regard to Alex and Helmut. "Dear Sirs," the letter begins,

Alex Goldschmidt is my brother in law, he emigrated together with his son in May 1939 to Cuba, but they could not be landed, because the emigrants on the S/S "St. Louis" got no permits for debarcation. So they returned again to Europe and my relatives came to France, where they have been placed at once in an internment camp. Since that time they changed their stay at several times, and according to a letter which I received just now from Mrs. Goldschmidt (Berlin) they are now in the camp: Ilot K, Bar. 21, Camp Rivesaltes, Pyr. Orientales.

They are all in fear of their lifes, because they will not be able to suffer the awful privations a longer while. And therefore it is necessary to send Affidavit to the American Consul in Marseille on behalf of the above named persons in order to give them an opportunity to emigrate to the States. Owing to the fact that I am a newcomer and without the necessary connexions I beg you to take care of the unfortunate people and to help them as soon as possible.

Hoping to hear from you at your earliest convenience I remain, yours very truly, Max Markreich

His letter seems to have had an effect. About five weeks later, on April 24, Max wrote to a Mr. Coleman at the National Refugee Service, "I have the pleasure to inform you that I was able to procure an affidavit on behalf of Mr. Alex Goldschmidt and his son Helmut in the Camp Rivesaltes. I hope that this fact will facilitate the endeavours to incite the raising of the passage from France to the United States in favour of both internees. Yours very truly."

The other Goldschmidt family members who managed to escape Nazi Germany and emigrate safely to the New World were my parents, Günther and Rosemarie. Thanks to their membership in the Jewish Cultural Association (the details of which I describe in *The Inextinguishable Symphony*) and thus their ability to earn a small salary, plus the intercession on their behalf of a former student of my mother's father (a violin teacher, Julian Gumpert), Günther and Rosemarie were able to book passage on a Portuguese ship called the *SS Mouzhino*, which left Lisbon on Tuesday, June 10, 1941. The ship docked at Ellis Island on June 21, and my parents were met by Lotte Breger, a schoolteacher who had raised money to help pay for their passage, and Max Markreich, who had received a letter from the American Jewish Joint Distribution Committee informing him of the date and time of the *Mouzhino's* arrival.

Within a few days, Günther and Rosemarie Goldschmidt visited the Immigration and Naturalization Service to sign their important "First Papers," documents indicating their intention to become American citizens as early as the law permitted. They also changed their names, becoming in the course of the afternoon George Gunther Goldsmith and Rosemary Goldsmith.

Thus, with close relatives on American soil and the affidavit process having begun, Alex and Helmut Goldschmidt's fortunes improved markedly. No longer were they mere "undesirables"; they were now "undesirables" with American "connexions." The French authorities reacted accordingly, and the wheels of the clumsy machinery that held them captive began slowly to turn in their favor.

The first indication that something had changed was their transfer to a new block of barracks within the confines of Rivesaltes. In early June, they left Block K and were moved to Barracks No. 43 within Block B, a portion of the camp reserved for those detainees with relatives in foreign lands and very real means to join them. From their new barracks, Alex and Helmut wrote a long letter to Günther and Rosemarie, dated June 19, 1941, two days before the young immigrants caught their first exhilarating glimpse of the Statue of Liberty. Alex was, understandably, all business; Helmut could hardly contain his enthusiasm. "Dear Children," began Alex,

> I hope that you will soon have completed your journey across the big pond and that it will have been, in spite of everything, relaxing and beautiful for you after all the strenuous see-saw days of your emigration. I wish you, with all my heart, a full measure of happiness and may all your hopes and plans be fulfilled.
>
> I don't know whether you received our airmail letter which was sent to Lisbon. It was taken to the post office on May 30th. I'll briefly repeat that, thanks to Uncle Max M.'s enterprise and his efforts on our behalf, Helmut and I now have affidavits. But I'm not quite sure whether that is enough. Yesterday I was notified by HICEM [an international organization dedicated to helping European Jews emigrate to safety] that the Joint Distribution

Committee has deposited $1,000 to cover Helmut's transportation expenses. Please tell Uncle Max as soon as possible; he is also trying to arrange for our travel costs. In case he has obtained ticket money for us, please ask him to keep it for us.

Last year, in October, when we were sent to Montauban, we lost all our baggage except for my book bag in which I had our documents and my private letters, so we don't have anything decent to wear, not even underwear or shoes. Even though I assume that before we emigrate—unless it does not happen at all because of some overwhelming event—we shall each receive from the Joint a suit, a pair of shoes, and a set of underwear; what we have now is completely useless. No tramp would consider our suit and shoes worth taking along, and it is urgently necessary, if one wants to get a job or a profession over there, to have some basic things.

The latter worries me a lot, with my meager knowledge of the language. To become completely dependent on my children would be dreadful. I know it would be a crime, after what we have gone through in the last 22 months, to await the end of the war here if there is any alternative. But since one mustn't gamble with the fate of one's family and one's own, the most intensive efforts must be made to get us over there as quickly as possible. I hope to be my old self again in a few months provided it all doesn't take too long. I am *sure* that you two are doing *everything* in your power to get affidavits for Mother and Eva *as quickly as possible*, so that I can hope to see you all once more in the not-too-distant future. It is this thought that keeps me going and will continue to keep me going.

When we sailed off on May 13, 1939, on the "St. Louis" and you waved to us for such a long time from the dock, we could not have had an inkling that our voluntary separation would become such a long and involuntary one. Please give my regards to Uncle Max and Aunt Johanna. With many good wishes and loving regards, Yours, Father.

P.S. Please send the stamps back for Helmut.

At the bottom of the second page of Alex's letter, Helmut hurriedly scribbled a few lines of his own:

Dear Rosemarie, dear Günther, I'm sure you can't imagine how very happy I was when we found out from Mother that every-thing has now worked out for you after all!! I'll continue to keep all my fingers crossed! I hope you received our letter sent to the "Mouzhino." I'll hasten to finish this so that Father's letter can go off. More soon . . . And so: Good Luck!!! And then: until we meet again!!! Love, Yours, Helmut.

Nineteen days after they sent that letter to America, on July 8, 1941, Alex and Helmut left Camp Rivesaltes. They had been spoken for; they had "connexions"; they were, it seemed, finally bound for freedom. Placed on a train heading east, they made their way to a new camp near Aix-en-Provence, a camp reserved for refugees with a promising future. I can only imagine the relief they must have felt at leaving behind that vast bleak badlands at the foot of the Pyrenees.

TUESDAY, MAY 31, 2011. What I don't have to imagine, however, is the image of those badlands themselves. They are here, all about me, as Elodie Montes guides me around the ruins of Rivesaltes. Like me, Elodie has a personal connection to this unholy place. Her grandfather was one of the many thousands of refugees from Spain who were interned here in 1939. When I learn of this essential bond that we share, I wrap her in a spontaneous and heartfelt embrace; she is no longer merely a museum curator but a kinsman of blood and grief.

In the Meriva, we drive slowly for twenty minutes along the dirt roads that wind through the vast expanse, Elodie occasionally pointing out certain landmarks: the relatively grand building that once housed the camp commandant; the Harki barracks, which still retrain a trace of the Algerian designs that some energetic Harki children painted to brighten the concrete gloom; abandoned rolls of barbed wire that lie twisted and rusting among the stunted evergreens that grow wild where

A partially reconstructed barrack in Îlot F, part of the planned Rivesaltes museum.

once there was only sand and flat desolation. She directs me to Îlot F, the former block of barracks reserved for women with young children. This barracks will soon serve as the central exhibit of the planned museum, and Elodie provides me with a brief history of the project.

In 1993, after years of abandonment during which a veil of neglect had descended over this bleak plain, the journal of a Swiss nurse who had worked on behalf of the children of Rivesaltes in 1941 and '42 was published. Four years later, Friedel Bohny-Reiter's searing words ("The moans of the tormented linger in the air. Even despair has disappeared from these aged, ashen, doleful faces.") were transformed into a documentary film, just as plans were announced to destroy the camp and erase its memory forever. The film inspired action. In 2000, the French minister of culture included Rivesaltes in a list of historic monuments to be developed, and the governing body of the *departement* of Pyrénées Orientales gave its unanimous approval to a memorial museum. Over the next decade, Holocaust historian Denis Peschanski was named to lead the overall design team, Rudy Ricciotti won a competition to serve as the architect of the memorial, funds were raised, and construction began. But progress has been slow. Elodie hints diplomatically that she suspects that the right-wing government of President Nicolas Sarkozy has dragged its feet somewhat over the issue of full funding for the memorial. Block F, a tiny portion of the vast holdings of the original camp, has been mostly cleared of its scrubby undergrowth, but that and a rebuilt barracks and latrine are the sole visible evidence that something is being built here to commemorate the brutal legacy of this place.

I did not come here to see a museum, however, but to bear witness. I ask Elodie if she knows which of these ruined remains of crumbling concrete once served as my grandfather and uncle's dwelling. She pauses, looks down at her folder of papers, and says quietly, "You mean Îlot K, Barracks 21?" Yes, I do. "We can walk there from here." From Block F, we follow a path westward for a few minutes. We come to a small road that she tells me once served as the boundary between F, the block for women and young children, and K, reserved for Jewish men. Then, after another short distance, Elodie stops before what remains of a building on our right, gently places her right hand on my left shoulder, and nods.

Like most of the ruins on this desolate plain, what was once Barracks 21 has lost its roof and much of its walls. Thorn bushes push through vestiges of windows and crowd the threshold, requiring us to step over them to enter the former interior. Within the broken walls, we stand on a floor made up of the remains of the collapsed roof, invasive weeds, and the inevitable debris and decay of decades: flakes of concrete, random little piles of earth, a shred of faded blue cloth, a small animal skeleton in a corner, some rusty nails, a broken brown bottle, scattered ribs of agave cactus plants, bits of shattered wood. Rot surrounds us.

Elodie picks her way slowly through the obstructions to what remains of the opposite wall, describing how the bunks would have been arranged on either side of the long-vanished aisle. I follow mutely, trying to comprehend that this ruin once was home to eighty, ninety, or one hundred men, two of whom were my grandfather and uncle. Elodie turns to tell me something and then, seeing the stricken look in

More than a little dazed by the bleak surroundings, I stand before what remains of Îlot K, Barracks 21, where Alex and Helmut were housed for six months in 1941.

my eyes, bows her head and starts to weep. "Oh, I . . . I am so, so sorry," she gasps. We embrace again, huddled against the chilly wind, sharing our sorrow.

We return silently to the car and I drive her back to her Renault. I thank her profusely for her time, her information, her empathy, and her kindness, and I ask if I may continue to stay in touch via e-mail. She assures me that my inquiries will always be welcome. We shake hands, possibly mutually embarrassed by our two hugs, and she drives off. I wave, stand still for a long minute, then climb slowly into the Meriva and head back along the treacherous road to Barracks 21.

I stand before what remains of the front entrance. I am alone, with only the wind for company as it sighs heavily, ruffling my hair and growing goose bumps along my arms. I close my eyes, trying my utmost to imagine this blasted heath as it was seventy years ago, when eight or nine thousand souls were crowded together in forced "accommodation," living on limited rations of nourishment and hope. My imagination fails.

I step up into the space bounded by what remains of 21's walls and discover that my legs no longer have the strength to support me. I collapse in a corner amid the rubble and find myself speaking aloud to Alex and Helmut. I tell them over and over how sorry I am for them, sorry for the cold and the heat and the wind and the rain and the hunger and thirst and the anxiety and the loneliness and the boredom and the fear and the frustration and the stink and the flies and the sickness and the sadness. I tell them how happy I am that they had each other. I tell them how I wish I could have saved them. I tell them how glad I am that I came all this way to see for myself, and how determined I am to tell their story. And I tell them that I miss them, that I miss them, oh God, that I miss them.

And then I can tell them no more, as I sit crumpled in my little corner, crying like a lost child.

Presently I compose myself, pocket a shard of ceiling as a souvenir, and, before I take my leave of this abandoned place, take out a blue ballpoint pen to scratch a graffito on what is left of a wall. "For Alex and Helmut Goldschmidt," I write, "who lived in this barracks from Jan to June 1941. I will never forget."

11

Les Milles

Sunday, June 5, 2011. I must have known. Earlier in the year, as winter melted into spring and my plans for this journey coalesced into something solid, the thought must have taken root in my subconscious that eventually I would need to set aside my concerns for Alex and Helmut for a while, lest the burden become unbearable. As it happens, my highly solicitous subconscious advised my practical conscious mind to schedule three days in warm, painter-friendly Provence following our visit to Rivesaltes, days to be spent in self-indulgent relaxation amid the sunny surroundings that inspired the likes of Cezanne and Van Gogh, Daudet and Bizet. So on some level, I must have had an inkling of how shaken I would be on the last day of May. How I knew, I have no idea. But I accept the gift with joy.

Though I had made reservations in Provence for Thursday, Friday, and Saturday nights, I left Wednesday, June 1, open, again anticipating that events in Rivesaltes might dictate how we would spend that day. My shaken state of mind upon my arrival back at our tannery hotel in Prades after my short stretch in Barracks 21 moves Amy to declare Wednesday a day solely of pleasure and exploration. So in the morning, we decide to visit Spain, neither of us ever having been there before. We drive the thirty-five miles up a winding mountain road, curling through the green and rocky Pyrenees, until we reach the frontier, which, on this clear and sunny noon, affords us an unobstructed view deep into the storied land of Cervantes, Goya, Albeniz, Velasquez, Lorca, Segovia, Picasso, Domingo, and so many more celebrated writers, artists, and musicians. Using our best high-school Spanish, we order lunch at a restaurant just inside the border in Puigcerdà, a town that has occupied this mountain top for more than eight hundred years.

That evening, after floating down the switchbacks back to Prades, we drive to the tiny village of Eus, which clings to the sides of a steep hill partially visible from our tannery. Crowned by a church dedicated to Saint Vincent, Eus exhibits an enchanting mixture of cobblestoned present and ancient past. The ruins of a medieval castle lend their ancient stones to form some of the church's walls and the walls of several adjacent private homes. On this crystal-clear evening, as the sun sets over the mountains, forming long shadows from the crumbling castle turrets, we wonder whether another sort of enchantment has been cast: we meet almost no other human beings and yet encounter literally dozens of cats as they stroll and take their leisure in the winding lanes and on narrow walls, stone staircases, tiled roofs, and enclosed patios. Perhaps, we whisper to each other, "Eus" is Catalan or Occitan for "meow." Just to be safe, we order fish for dinner.

Thursday dawns cloudy. On our way back east and north, we pay a final visit to the desolation of Camp Rivesaltes, enabling me to show Amy the site of Barracks 21 and some of the other sad landmarks I learned about from Elodie. Neither of us has any desire to linger, so well before noon we are back on the wide expanse of the A9, retracing our route from the previous Sunday. This time, however, we drive past Béziers and Montpellier, not leaving the expressway until just the other side of Nîmes, where we catch a two lane road heading east into the heart of the legendary region of Provence.

Whole books have been written about Provence, its history, cuisine, natural beauty, and the writers, poets, and painters who have lived and been inspired there. It comprises a little more than twelve thousand square miles, making it roughly the size of our home state of Maryland, although its shape is decidedly more regular than the salamander oddity of "The Old Line State." Provence was home to some of the earliest human life forms on earth; primitive stone tools from 1 million BC have been discovered on the Provençal coast. Nature-loving Celts from the Iron Age, believers in sacred woods and healing springs, took up residence in Provence, trading honey and cheese with their neighbors to the north. The great tides of civilization from Greece and Rome washed ashore in Provence, leaving behind as they receded the great city of Massalia—known to modernity as Marseille—as well as forums, arenas, and aqueducts that survive to dazzle us today. The medieval leaders of the Catholic Church so favored the land and climate of Provence that for more than one hundred years in the fourteenth and early fifteenth centuries, ten popes lived and ruled in Avignon. Provence was fought over and changed hands many times over the course of centuries, until it finally became a permanent part of France in 1481, following the death of the last Provençal ruler, Good King René, a patron and avid supporter of painters, troubadours, and tournaments.

Good King René's influence has persisted through the subsequent centuries, as artists of all stripes have flocked to Provence to paint, write, compose, and cook. Colette, Alphonse Daudet, Edith Wharton, and F. Scott Fitzgerald have written there; Georges Bizet, Charles Gounod, and Darius Milhaud have composed there. The list of painters who have set up their easels in Provence only starts with Van Gogh, Cezanne, Renoir, Monet, Matisse, Georges Braque, and Edvard Munch. And no mention of the pleasures of Provence would be complete without a gastronomic catalog including such native delights as bouillabaisse, ratatouille, the Thirteen Desserts, and the region's locally produced olives, olive oil, honey, cheese, peaches, berries, melons, and wine.

All this and Mediterranean sunshine, too, as I have been telling Amy for days, based in equal parts on research, general hearsay, and the personal testimony of my parents. My mother loved the sun. I recall her many enthusiastic tales of the times she and my father stayed in the town of Saint-Rémy-de-Provence, basking under what seemed, from her stories, to be permanently sunny skies. So I have booked three nights at a former grand château—now a hotel—just outside Saint-Rémy, anticipating abundant sunshine.

For all three days, it rarely stops raining.

However, we are not disappointed. The château's rooms and its restaurant are luxurious, restful, and deeply satisfying, particularly after the stress and sadness of Rivesaltes. We take long naps and walk the grounds of the château. We spend much of Friday exploring Saint-Rémy, renowned as the birthplace of Nostradamus and the residence, for one prolific year, of Vincent van Gogh. While committed—by choice—to the asylum of St. Paul Hospital for twelve months beginning in May 1889, Vincent produced an astonishing one hundred forty-two paintings, including portraits of his cramped but cozy bedroom at the asylum, studies of the wheat fields and olive trees he could see from his window, and *Starry Night*, lit by his own inner fire. We peer upward during our stormy nights in Saint-Rémy, hoping in vain to catch a glimpse of his vision, but we are delighted to see the descendants of the very olive trees Vincent painted, their grey-green branches tossing in the gentle wind and rain of a soft afternoon. On Friday evening, in a Saint-Rémy *brasserie*, we witness seven Provençal cardsharps gathered around a green velvet-topped table, playing an enthusiastic game of poker, a scene Vincent would have loved.

Saturday morning offers a few breaks in the clouds, so we take a scenic spin along some picturesque back roads of Provence, venturing far enough east to catch a glimpse of Mont Sainte-Victoire, the mountain Paul Cezanne captured on canvas dozens of times. By noon we are back in the Alpilles mountain range near Saint-Rémy and rain has begun falling again. Not daunted, however, we drive into the village of Maussane-les-Alpilles, find a *boulangerie* and a *fromagerie*, and enjoy a romantic repast of fresh bread and cheese huddled on the steps under the stone awning of the village church. The pain, sorrow, and endless frustrations of 1941 seem long ago and far, far away.

But Sunday morning, announcing itself with the tuneful tolling of church bells from Saint-Rémy, heralds the end of our Provençal idyll and the resumption of our grim pursuit. Luckily, we do not have far to travel today, so we linger at breakfast and take our time leaving the château. It is noon when we finally drive away from Saint-Rémy, heading east on the D99. We enjoy the rural charms of Provence for another hour or so before we rejoin the faster pace of the everyday world and speed south and east, catching another autoroute in its rush toward Aix-en-Provence, the medieval capital of the region. Our route spins us south on a bypass, and from there we drive into the small, largely unattractive town of Les Milles. We struggle to make sense of our directions and eventually find our lodgings for the next two nights, a lovely little B&B called La Gracette, presided over by our more than gracious hosts, Dana and Raphaelle. As they usher us up to our room, which opens into a round, turret-shaped bathroom, we learn a bit about pigeons and class divisions.

In medieval days, pigeons were so highly prized that only the nobility were allowed to keep them. Many a grand château boasted a separate structure, its distinctive circular shape announcing to all who beheld it that here was a dovecote, or pigeon house, a special home for those highly valued birds that only the wellborn could possess. When the revolutions of the eighteenth and nineteenth centuries tore down some of the walls separating the upper and lower classes, one of the first perquisites claimed by the new bourgeois was the right to keep pigeons. Many homes built in the following decades proudly included a rounded wing or tower to declare the owner upwardly mobile enough to possess pigeons, whether or not birds actually lived there. Our round bathroom is proof that the original owners of La Gracette had made the grade.

As evening approaches, mindful of our appointment tomorrow morning and of last Monday morning's confusion, I am determined to learn the exact location of Camp des Milles. With Raphaelle's detailed directions to guide us, in only ten minutes we are looking over a barred gate at the outlines of an immense factory, the site of the former camp. Satisfied that we'll be able to find our way back in the morning, we look for a place to have dinner. Nothing is open in the little town on this Sunday evening, so we drive toward the outskirts of Aix, confident that we'll find something. But perhaps this corner of France is subject to blue laws of which we have no knowledge; not a single open restaurant do we find. Finally, faint with hunger, we admit defeat and dine on Big Macs and fries at a McDonald's. Sacrilege though it seems at the time to consume fast food in France, we devour our dinner with relish, as well as ketchup and mustard: little packets of savory Dijon mustard at that. Far from home, we offer up silent thanks for good old American standardization.

Back at La Gracette, we speak briefly with Dana and Raphaelle, telling them about my unhappy connection with their town. They listen quietly and respectfully, their faces reflecting sincere sympathy. But I find myself soon growing weary of Raphaelle's story of her mother's utter ignorance of what went on at the factory by the railroad tracks. Fearing that I might begin to ask pointed questions I will come to regret, we make our excuses and retire upstairs to our little bedroom adjoining the pigeon house. Soon enough, I know, we will again be transported from our comfortable present into the painful past.

DECADES BEFORE CEZANNE, Van Gogh, and their fellow painters made their pilgrimages to Provence, the factory in Les Milles produced bricks and the distinctive terra-cotta tiles that adorn the roofs of many Provençal houses. But the factory had fallen into disuse by the late summer of 1939, its 160,000-square-foot, four-story structure sitting silently within its dusty seventeen-acre grounds. Within a fortnight of the beginning of the war in early September, the facilities returned to life as an internment camp for thousands of "undesirable foreigners," mostly German and Austrian refugees fleeing from the plague of Hitlerism that had infected their homelands, but also exiles from other countries who lacked the proper transit papers for legal immigration, a number of political dissidents, and former members of the International Brigades who had fought on the Republican side during the Spanish Civil War. Having come to France seeking respite from persecution in their home countries, these mostly Jewish fugitives found themselves ensnared once again.

Some were released in the early spring of 1940, but after the German army invaded and overran France in May and June, about two thousand men, again mostly refugees from German-speaking lands, were either brought to Les Milles or ordered to turn themselves in. A fact that remains a source of shame for France is that the three-year history of Camp des Milles is a uniquely French tale. No Nazi directive played a part in its initial organization or in how business was conducted there. Camp des Milles was strictly a product of the Vichy regime. The camp guards were all recruited from the local population of farmers and merchants, mostly humble apolitical people anxious only to make a little extra money by following the orders of the camp commandant, who in turn received his orders from Pierre Laval, the French minister of state. As was the case in Rivesaltes, the guards at Camp des Milles inflicted few overt acts of malice on the prisoners. The writer Lion Feuchtwanger, in his memoir, *The Devil in France*, recalled that during his time at Camp des Milles, he did not "experience or witness anything that could be described as cruelty or even as mistreatment. There was never a case of beating, of punching, of verbal abuse. The Devil in France was a friendly, polite Devil. The devilishness in his character showed itself solely in his genteel indifference to the sufferings of others."

Upward of ten thousand internees of Camp des Milles suffered from the overcrowded conditions, the lack of hygiene and decent food, and most of all from the crushing inactivity. They had no reason to get up every morning to greet another day of mindless, dull routine mixed with a constant low-level fear of what the far-off authorities in Paris had in store for them.

Within the fenced and barbed-wire enclosure of the camp, prisoners had two options: they could be either inside or outside the immense factory building that dominated the space; neither option was particularly pleasant. Out in the dusty open, there was no shade to block the blazing Provençal sun or protection from rain or the frequent winds that whipped the dust into miniature cyclones. Inside the factory was near total darkness and, depending on the season, a clammy cold or an oppressive heat. There were no windows on the ground floor, the site of the kilns where the bricks had been formed. On the bright side, since brick making requires straw, there was a generous supply of the soft fiber on hand for use as bedding material. But the straw was the only amenity offered by the camp; there were no bunks, cots, or even mattresses, just clumps of straw and the occasional blanket that a fortunate internee had either brought from home or purchased on the camp's thriving black market. The ground floor of the factory was eventually filled with the delicately negotiated and often fiercely defended sleeping quarters of hundreds of men who lay head to foot from one wall to the other. Brick dust lay everywhere and polluted the air that everyone breathed.

Detainees walked up a rickety flight of wooden steps to reach the factory's second floor. This space was more commodious, and one wall was almost entirely made of windows, which promised more light. But that promise was broken because of the authorities' fear of air raids; some of the windows were boarded up and the rest were painted dark blue to inhibit detection of any interior light. The result was perpetual twilight during the day and pitch darkness during the interminable nights. A few feeble electric light bulbs and the occasional candle provided light, but candles were used sparingly in the presence of all that straw. There were no chairs, no tables, and no benches provided, only piles and piles of old bricks. The inmates would often attempt to use the bricks to construct furniture, but without mortar it invariably collapsed. The second floor, like the first, soon became crowded with men huddling in their own small nests of straw.

Each morning the camp resounded with a bugler playing a wake-up reveille at 5:30. Twenty minutes later, the prisoners received the day's meager ration of bread, along with a tin cup of weak coffee. Around 11 a.m., the midday meal was served, consisting usually of soup made of lentils or beans, sometimes with some stringy meat of indeterminate origin. The evening meal, served at 5 p.m., was generally less robust than lunch, with a bit of cheese accompanied by the occasional sausage or sardine. Once a week, typically on Saturday or Sunday, the fare would be augmented by eggs and wine from local farms and vineyards. At 9 p.m., the bugle would sound again, directing everyone outside to return to the factory's interior. The large iron doors would slam shut behind the last man, and everyone shuffled to his wretched bed of straw. Thirty minutes later all lights were extinguished, and the prisoners faced another night in which their proximity to each other made sleep fitful at best. Inmate Harry Alexander recalled in an interview conducted by the United States Holocaust Memorial Museum, "I cried a lot, we all cried a lot, thirteen-year-old boys, old men, all of us huddling on our piles of straw in the utter darkness."

*The courtyard of
Camp des Milles, with
the former brick factory
in the background,
circa 1941.*
(©ECPAD—Collections
La documentation fran-
çaise–Raymond Brajou)

Out in the yard, there were four latrines on one end of the enclosure and three on the other. They were essentially little outhouses made of wood, each with a single hole in a plank situated only a few yards above a foul morass of human waste, which was visited constantly by swarms of flies. At all hours of the day, lines of almost a hundred men stretched from each latrine into the center of the enclosure. At night, the prisoners were restricted to four indoor latrines that were declared off-limits during the day. A prisoner's nocturnal trips to relieve himself were hindered by the darkness and the challenge of navigating among the thousands of men stretched out on the floor and then finding his way back to his own pile of straw. Thus, when the doors of the factory swung open each morning at 5:30, men would awkwardly race each other across the yard for the privilege of being first in line.

But the three meager meals and the lines to use the latrines were welcome islands in a daily ocean of boredom. There was little to do. The guards would occasionally order groups to transport a pile of bricks from one corner to another or even to dig holes and then fill them up again, but for the most part—in keeping with the overall lack of cruelty or mistreatment—there was little interaction between guards and prisoners. So men filled their idle hours in conversation, often speculating about the unknown future, and in irregular dealings with what became a bustling black market.

A prisoner needed hard currency to make transactions in the market, but if he had the money, nearly everything was for sale. Such items as clothing and blankets were available, as well as food supplies and newspapers obtained from outside the gates. A farmer came once a week to collect camp garbage such as potato peelings for his pigs, and he brought little portions of cooked pork wrapped in newspaper that he sold when the guards' backs were turned. But prisoners could also buy or sell the camp's own rations or cigarettes or a precious place in the latrine lines. Through these acts of getting and spending, the men of Camp des Milles not only improved their lot, but also managed to get through another day, twenty-four hours closer, they all hoped, to a resolution of their fates.

For everyone who made his nightly manger bed of straw in the brick factory was in some sense a member of the elite—a small, favored slice of Europe's Jewish population that was desperate to emigrate elsewhere, to escape the increasingly tangible menace threatened daily by the advance of Germany and National Socialism. In March 1941, HICEM— an international organization dedicated to helping European Jews emigrate to safety—set up an office at Camp des Milles, thus granting it the unique status of a transit camp. Camp des Milles was considered a gateway, populated only by those for whom others had spoken and obtained the necessary papers; affidavits had been signed abroad and emigration was an assumed conclusion once the final step—a visa— had been obtained. So every day passed in the crowded brickyard was, in the hopeful minds of the incarcerated, another step on the uncertain but deeply desired road to freedom.

That road led to Marseille, the bustling Mediterranean seaport town only about thirty kilometers to the south. Most journeys abroad would likely leave from Marseille, and the city was also home to many foreign consulates. So, although Camp des Milles was a detainment camp, the authorities allowed for the occasional journey to Marseille if official business was to be transacted. In order to make the trip, a prisoner had to leave the camp precisely when the factory doors opened at 5:30 a.m. and to be on the Les Milles-to-Marseille streetcar by 6:00; according to the aforementioned Harry Alexander, Jews were not allowed to board the streetcar after six o'clock. Another former prisoner, Rudolf Adler, told a Holocaust Museum interviewer that he made several trips into Marseille to visit the Chinese consulate (he and his family successfully emigrated to Shanghai) but never attempted to escape, always returning to the camp at the end of spending a long day with Chinese officials. A well-brought-up German, he put his trust in what he believed was a well-ordered system and simply waited for the wheels of justice to grind slowly in his favor.

Another aspect of life at Camp des Milles that made it markedly different from more severe work or concentration camps was the singular collection of artists and intellectuals who were housed there and their attempts to introduce a high level of artistic performance and scholarly pursuits to their fellow inmates. Among those imprisoned at the former brick factory were such figures as the surrealist painter Max Ernst, the historian Golo Mann (the son of novelist Thomas Mann), the Nobel Prize–winning physician Otto Fritz Meyerhof, composer Franz Waxman (best known in later years for writing the scores for such Hollywood films as *Sunset Boulevard* and *Rear Window*), sculptor Peter Lipman-Wulf, and writer Lion Feuchtwanger, whose memoir, *The Devil in France*, remains the most arresting account of daily life in the camp.

These and other enterprising inmates converted the factory's main brick oven, a tunnel stretching more than a hundred yards, into a cabaret that they christened *Die Katakombe*, or The Catacombs, borrowing the name from a political nightclub in 1920s Berlin. Shrouded by the literal darkness of the stone oven and the figurative gloom of their uncertain incarceration, and lit only by guttering candles and their esthetic determination, the prisoners staged plays and operas, offered lectures on topics both whimsical and practical, and sang and danced their way through many an endless night. Max Ernst gave informal talks about painting and also offered demonstrations of his unusual technique. A former dancer with the Monte Carlo ballet, Theodor Schlicker, was a transvestite who performed in The Catacombs as Thea. Scholars and teachers lectured on Shakespeare and Tolstoy and offered courses ranging from home repair to bookbinding.

Peter Lipman-Wulf wrote about his memories of those artistic and intellectual offerings: "The scenario in the flickering light, casting mysterious shadows of our bundled-up comrades, was highly dramatic, but also romantic and timeless. Every eye was hanging on the lips of the speakers and, in our enclave-like meeting grounds, one truly believed oneself to be transported back to the time of the Catacombs of ancient Rome."

But as welcome as these diversions were and as vital to the prisoners' morale, the plays, lectures, and song recitals could only do so much to alleviate the overwhelming tedium of daily life in the camp. Feuchtwanger concluded, "What I found most difficult about the camp was the fact that one could never be alone, that constantly, day and night, every act, every physical function, eating, sleeping, voiding, was performed in the presence of hundreds of men, men who were talking, shouting, moaning, weeping, laughing, feeding, smacking their lips, wiping their mouths, sweating, smelling, snoring. We did everything in the most public view, and my greatest desire was to be rid of all that throng."

MY GRANDFATHER AND UNCLE were delivered into that throng in July 1941, thanks to the affidavits obtained by Max Markreich and to the fact that my father and mother had established residency in the United States. Like their fellow detainees, Alex and Helmut hoped that their stay in Camp des Milles would be brief and that they would soon be on a boat to join Günther and Rosemarie in America. But those hopes were quickly dimmed. The U.S. Immigration Act of 1924 was restrictive from the beginning, and after war broke out in Europe in 1939, the law's annual quotas for German and Austrian citizens were no longer met. There may have been several figures in the American government who contributed to this slowdown, but history has identified the chief culprit

The factory, now a well-funded memorial museum, as seen from the railroad siding a quarter mile away.

as Breckinridge Long, a longtime friend of President Roosevelt, who in January 1940 was appointed assistant secretary of state. He became convinced that Nazi agents were attempting to infiltrate the ranks of legitimate immigrants, so he began a policy of requiring longer and longer forms to be filled out both by those hoping to come to America and by those who hoped to welcome them here. In a memo circulated to other members of the State Department in June 1940, Long wrote, "We can delay and effectively stop for a temporary period of indefinite length the number of immigrants into the United States. We could do this by simply advising our consuls to put every obstacle in the way and to require additional evidence and to resort to various administrative devises which would postpone and postpone and postpone the granting of visas."

In July 1941, just as Alex and Helmut arrived in Camp des Milles, the number of refugees allowed to immigrate to the United States was cut to about 25 percent of the quotas established by the 1924 law. Contributing to this decline was something called the Relatives Rule, a State Department regulation that required any applicant with a parent, spouse, child, or sibling remaining in Germany, Italy, or Russia to pass an extremely strict security test to obtain a visa. Also in July, the State Department began requiring a security review of all immigration applications by committees representing a number of governmental agencies, among them the State Department's Visa Division, the Immigration and Naturalization Service, the FBI, and Army and Navy Intelligence. Once that review process had been completed, the State Department sent out "advisory approvals" to its consuls abroad, who were then allowed to issue their precious visas. But by then, Long's policy of "postpone and postpone and postpone" had had its dire effect.

When they walked through the gates of Camp des Milles in July, Alex was sixty-two years old and Helmut was two months short of his twentieth birthday. They found spaces to sleep amid the straw-strewn comforts of the brick factory's second floor and within a short time became habituated to the routine of daily life at the camp. Alex found work in the camp's kitchen to earn money for such necessities as blankets and shoes, and Helmut eagerly partook of the camp's intellectual offerings.

On September 22, the day after Helmut turned twenty (and the day of Rosh Hashanah, the Jewish New Year), Alex wrote to his older son and daughter-in-law. How luxurious Günther and Rosemarie's lives in far-off New York City must have seemed to the unwilling captives of Camp des Milles. "Dear Children," the letter began.

I hope you haven't been worried about us because you haven't heard from us for some time now. But I work all day long cleaning vegetables in the kitchen and in the evening I'm dead tired and Helmut's time is completely occupied with various courses. There is a meager amount of pay for the work we do; weekly it amounts to perhaps ¾ of the cost of shoe soles and heels, and in addition to that you get a second helping of food at noon and in the evening. If one gets up every morning at 6:00, by noon one isn't in the mood for writing. On this New Year's morning I'm sitting on my bed of straw, using my blanket as a desk.

Thank you for everything that you've already done for us. Above all, for your assiduous efforts with the National Refugee

Service. Surely it is the present circumstances that are responsible for everything taking so long, and unfortunately I have recently become very skeptical about anything working out in this regard. Here in Les Milles no visas have been handed out since the introduction of the recent American immigration regulations. There are about 1,300 people here, most of whom want to go to the U.S. There are repeated delaying tactics, and the moment the U.S. enters the war everything will come to a stop.

You can imagine that we are facing our third winter in France with quite a bit of horror. The food here is probably better than it was in Rivesaltes, but it's very unbalanced and contains little fat. Nevertheless, we have gained some weight. Helmut's weight, which went from 127 pounds down to 94 pounds in Rivesaltes, is now at 113 pounds, and my weight, which went from 136 to 104 pounds, is now at 112.

I think the worst of the horror is still to come, unless quite unexpected things were to happen. One must not think about it, and so work is the best medicine. I am deeply worried, though, in case we don't get away from here before winter begins, about where we will get underwear and socks. CAR [the French committee on refugees] gave us a suit made of army material, which is warm, but no overcoats or underwear. I know that you and Uncle Max Markreich are doing everything possible to get us over there. Might personal appearances in Washington be possible?

We went to Marseille on Helmut's birthday to ask the Quakers to look into the baggage we checked at the time in Martigny-les-Bains. But probably it will all be in vain. We saw many well-dressed people on our little outing, and in honor of the day we went to eat in a simple decent restaurant. I gave Helmut some French stamps as a present. He would be very grateful to you for any stamps you can collect for him.

I hope to hear from you shortly. Many good wishes and love, Yours, Father

On the following day, September 23, Helmut wrote to his brother and sister-in-law.

Dear Rosemarie, dear Günther,

Many thanks for your perfectly beautiful and dear letters! We're already waiting for your next one. You don't know how thankful you should be to be on the other shore!! We're so glad to have you over there because it's the only way we can have a somewhat better prospect of getting there too. The bad thing is, however, that because of the new regulations no one here has received his visa. Indeed, even those who had been promised a visa by a certain date before the new decrees went into effect are still waiting for further confirmation. In addition, we're afraid that open war will be declared between the U.S. and Germany—perhaps even as soon as today—and our last chance will become invalid. In spite of all your efforts we shall probably have to put up, for better or worse, with a third—and I hope our last—wartime winter.

For a month now I have been taking a three-times-a-week book-binding course here in Les Milles, which gives me much pleasure now and may prove useful later. Please save all postage stamps you can get for me, from all countries, used as well as new ones, worthless as well as valuable ones. I had to start collecting all over again, so I need practically everything.

I think of you often and wish you all the best, especially of course that you'll be hired by an orchestra soon. That's it for today. Love, yours, Helmut

By the way, practically all the letters that arrive here have been examined by Wehrmacht Headquarters.

As it happened, Günther and Rosemarie (by now George and Rosemary) *were* hired by an orchestra, though not one anybody would recognize. Since arriving in the New World in June, they'd managed to scrape together a meager living, my mother as a domestic and my father as a worker in a factory that polished and reconditioned old zippers.

Between them, they earned twenty-six dollars a week, enough to enable them to rent their own apartment on 103rd Street near Columbus Avenue in New York City. But they continued to practice their instruments in their free time, and toward the end of the summer, they learned about a Chicago-based traveling orchestra that was looking for new recruits. The ensemble's founder and conductor, a Czech-born musician named Bohumir Kryl, was to hold auditions in New York for a tour of the Midwest and South that was scheduled to last from mid-September until shortly before Christmas.

George and Rosemary eagerly made appointments to audition for Mr. Kryl in his hotel room. They were both hired, with a combined salary of forty-five dollars a week, and on September 15, 1941, just days before Alex and Helmut wrote their letters from Camp des Milles, my father and mother went out on the road in the Kryl Orchestra's rattletrap school bus. For the next twelve weeks, they gave concerts in such towns as Springfield, Ohio; Springfield, Illinois; and Springfield, Missouri; Terre Haute and Evansville, Indiana; Knoxville and Nashville, Tennessee; Little Rock and Jonesboro, Arkansas; Monroe and Shreveport, Louisiana; and Lubbock, Amarillo, Austin, San Antonio, and Galveston, Texas. They were always on the move and, understandably from their youthful point of view, found next to no time either to write to Alex and Helmut or to write letters and fill out immigration forms on their behalf.

But Alex's brother-in-law Max Markreich continued his tireless efforts to alert any authorities he could find to the plight of these two souls caught in the snares of Camp des Milles. In the autumn of 1941, as George and Rosemary were touring with the Kryl Orchestra, Uncle Max wrote to the International Relief Association, Inc. (IRA) and to the Refugee and Immigration Division of Agudath Israel Youth Council in Brooklyn. The answers were disheartening.

From the IRA came this response: "As much as we would like to help in cases like yours we are unable to do so, firstly because we are still trying to raise sufficient funds to be able to pay for those refugees for whom we have obtained visas, and secondly our committee is pledged to help only active anti-fascist non-Communist refugees who are especially endangered."

Then, on November 3, 1941, Uncle Max heard from Agudath Israel. "Dear Mr. Markreich," the letter began:

Due to the recent decision of the Department of State in Washington, we regret to advise that all immigration work and any problems pertinent to it have come to a total standstill. Until further notice from the State Department as to the new procedures in the immigration situation we will be unable to render any additional advice and help. With Torah greetings, Harry Sherer, Refugee and Immigration Division.

As they had feared, Alex and Helmut were forced to endure a third winter in French captivity. On January 1, 1942, Alex observed his sixty-third birthday within the confines of Camp des Milles. On the following day, he penned an angry letter to the son from whom he had heard nothing all autumn, the son in whom he had invested so much hope and trust.

Dear Günther,
The day before yesterday I, at last, received your long-awaited letter. Thank you for your good wishes for my 63rd birthday; I send them back to you as 1942 New Year's wishes. I am very glad that you are doing well, above all that after all your strenuous exertions you were in good health, and I hope that you still are today. I would have written you long ago, that is after the 7th of November when my last letter was mailed, if only I had received a *single* line from you since the 5th of September. About 4 weeks ago I thought it was ridiculous, as I told Helmut that I probably would not hear from you until my birthday. Unfortunately, however, it turned out I was right.
Look, dear Günther, you write us at best one page saying that you understand our lot and implore us not to despair. If after 2½ years of internment we would indeed be on the point of despairing, which is in itself quite possible after all this disheartening, bleak time, then your nice words would change

nothing. I see nothing but words, nice words, suitable for a magazine that thinks it's giving its readers encouragement. They are the same words I heard when I came home on furlough, spoken by those who had not heard the whistle of bullets during the First World War. But that you believe you have to give us that kind of lecture really appalled me, so after thinking about it for hours the last two nights I came to the conclusion that you haven't the slightest inkling of our situation.

In June, the last month we were in Rivesaltes, after we each had lost about ⅓ of our weight, we were at a point where I thought we would not live to see the winter. Then, just in the nick of time, the affidavit from Uncle Max Markreich arrived and resulted in our transfer to Les Milles. For 4 months I worked from early until late at night as an assistant in or outside the kitchen, mostly in the broiling sun, the oldest among 25 people, until I got an infection in my right hand that lasted 6 weeks. It was not only painful but handicapped me considerably. Since the work is still done outside—and the temperature has been between 10 and 20 degrees F in the mornings—and with the meager pay of 45 fr a week, for which one can't even buy one loaf of bread, I decided not to go back to work there after my hand healed.

Recently, although the food here has become wretched, I have recuperated so that I now weigh 120 pounds, still 15–20 pounds less than in the old days. Helmut also has regained a good part of the weight he lost, but unfortunately since we left Germany he has had 10 throat infections, the last one 14 days ago. And sometime this week his tonsils are supposed to be surgically removed in neighboring Aix-en-Provence; then he will presumably be less prone to infection. We wouldn't have decided to do this if the newly arrived doctor had not recommended it as absolutely imperative. The worst thing is that we haven't any underwear or coats. When our underwear is being washed, we actually have to go to bed since we don't have a change of underwear. What was previously called de-lousing is very problematical since the disinfection cars are so old; they probably date back to World War I, so the young breed of vermin isn't even killed.

We live from one mail delivery to the next; the mail is distributed at 2:00 PM and if you receive nothing one day then you hope for something the next day. So when I realized you hadn't sent us any news between September 9th and November 30th, you can understand why I was *very* sad about that. And your birthday letter could have been written by any stranger since there is no personal information about you in it except for telling me what states you played in! Helmut is just as sad about all this as I am. It is the first very serious disappointment I have experienced in one of my children.

Well. Yesterday morning Helmut, who is still my best comrade as he has been from the start, gave me half a day's ration— c. 110 grams—of bread, an orange, and a fountain pen bought with the pay he received for work he performed in the spring in Rivesaltes as a medical assistant. The pen is very simple, no golden penpoint, but it will last a few years. He was very dear and made the day really festive. On January 1st, 1941, we slept on wooden cots without straw in Agde; in 1940, in Sionne, with the temperature 10 below zero F, we slept in a large room on stones and litter; this year we sleep in a room of an old brick factory. Still, it's better than the two previous years!

For today, with love, yours, Father

One week later, on January 8, two days after Rosemary's twenty-fifth birthday, Helmut added his words of reproach to his father's indictment. "Dear Günther," he wrote,

I don't really know how to go about writing this. That is to say, would it be better to write candidly or should I hold back my thoughts and feelings? But since I assume you're still the same person you used to be, I won't force myself to hold anything back. I am so glad that you two have already hit it off so well in social and artistic matters as well as in material things. Of course I know that your touring was enormously strenuous and I know, too, that on the material side, even though you are earning good money, it's not enough to put anything aside. But your letter, well, it wasn't an appropriate New Year's and birthday letter for your Father and Brother! You don't write anything about what must have been very satisfying experiences for you—nothing about your work, nothing about the country and people and the many impressions that you formed in the New World. No, you don't seem to realize how a prisoner waits for letters from those close to him! I don't wish to complain, for I know that at this time there are millions of people who would be grateful to have an existence like the one we have here for the duration of the war. In addition, our situation has improved. We are less hungry and more optimistic. But being called martyrs of trampled justice without having done anything to build up a new justice because one is merely a passive victim is little consolation, because we want to live—to live in the full meaning of the word. That kind of "hero-ization" seems terribly ironic to us, just as it would seem a mockery to a soldier who receives a gleaming Knight's Cross for having his legs frozen off.

After a quarter year in which you made us wait in vain for mail, we are very disappointed with your letter. It contained almost nothing except excuses, even though we did not complain to you about anything. In spite of your being so overworked, it is almost unnatural that you found no time to write us. I hope you understand this letter in its proper sense and that perhaps by now you will already have found the time and peace and quiet to let us participate differently in your life. After all, right after your arrival in New York along with Max Markreich you demonstrated that where there is a will there is a way!

I do hope that it is not now too late. It seems that cases that have already been approved in Washington now have to be checked over if the visa has not yet been issued. Even the consulate here in Marseille doesn't know what they require now. I'm afraid that because of the new regulations immigration for us has in effect been blocked. So for the moment I believe more in a European miracle than an American one. Of course, as always, I hope that we will soon see each other again—for many reasons! But at the moment, I don't believe it will happen.

There isn't much news to report about us. Ever since the war began I have had 8–12 more or less serious sore throats, and so I am going to have a tonsil operation next week. I will be glad to be freed at last from these constant infections. Rosemarie, I thought of you on your birthday and I send you many good wishes. I hope your own personal wishes as well as ours will be fulfilled! All the best! Best regards to both of you.

Yours, Helmut

Write to us, don't keep us waiting!! And don't forget to put interesting stamps on your letters!

By this time, my father and mother were back in New York City, their tour with Bohumir Kryl having ended precipitously a month earlier. On December 7, 1941, as the Kryl bus was approaching Brownsville, Texas, on U.S. Highway 77, federal police ordered it to halt and demanded that the passengers identify themselves. George and Rosemary still had their German passports with them, documents that prominently displayed the sign of the swastika. The two were immediately taken into custody, and the police phoned Washington to determine whether they had just nabbed a couple of German spies posing as musicians. Not until the following morning did the Immigration Office cable Brownsville and clear their names.

That night, Mr. Kryl announced that he had run out of money and the rest of the tour was canceled. Furthermore, he said, the bus was staying with him and the musicians were all responsible for finding their own way home. George and Rosemary, not wanting to spend their modest recent savings on transportation, decided to hitchhike. With their instruments under their arms and their thumbs in the air, thanks to the kindness of strangers they covered the two thousand miles between south Texas and New York City in time to return to their little apartment on 103rd Street a few days before Christmas.

A few weeks later, they received those searing letters from Les Milles. It is true that their peripatetic existence of the previous months must have made regular correspondence difficult, but his father and brother's accusations of indifference and selfishness must have caused my father to feel the deepest wounds of guilt, sorrow, and remorse. Spurred into action, he, too, was able to procure an affidavit on behalf of Alex and Helmut. He sent that welcome news, along with the sum of twenty-five dollars, to Camp des Milles. On March 21, 1942, Alex wrote a grateful and hopeful letter back.

Dear Günther and dear Rosemarie, thank you for doing as much as you could to get that affidavit. I hope that the documents are now complete and have arrived at the State Department in Washington. The main thing now is that the visas be granted; they say the first visa since December was granted yesterday in Marseille. If the State Department will actually send us the visas or notify the Consul, I would ask to be telegraphically informed so that I can get the necessary ship bookings. It would be a deliverance for us.

We two are well although we have had to suffer through a severe winter, without coats, without being able to change or wash our underwear which is in rags. Helmut had several episodes of sore throat again and was supposed to go to a hospital in Aix-en-Provence in the middle of January to have his tonsils removed. After 4 days of observation in the hospital, he was sent back and the operation was postponed to a warmer season. Otherwise our lives follow their accustomed path; in addition to the constant worry about our loved ones, we now have to concentrate on keeping ourselves healthy. Besides its poor quality the food here is absolutely insufficient in quantity, so that if you couldn't get some extra food you'd go downhill fast. For months, both at noon *and* in the evening, there was only soup, white beets or red beets or Jerusalem artichokes or sweet potatoes, and each variety was served by itself for a very long time. In the final analysis, if we had not been able to occasionally get some additional food thanks to our meager earnings we would not have survived this period of internment which by now has lasted more than 30 months—unfortunately many others did not.

Today, except for the early morning hours, we are having a hot Sunday. I am writing this letter outdoors. On the whole the climate here is good, whereas in Rivesaltes in the Pyrenees there were storms; the Mistral virtually saps your strength. I will bless the day that brings us freedom again. At my age, every month spent under the current conditions shortens one's life, and it is time that the portals to freedom be opened for us, so that we're not all used up before it finally comes to pass. Therefore, do everything you can to get us out.

For today then, with love and in the hope that we'll be seeing each other again soon, Yours, Father.

Helmut added some lines of his own to his father's letter:

The emigration problem looked dismal until a few days ago: not a single person under the German quota has received a visa since the middle of December. Now in the last few days the reports that have come from over there, much like yours, sound more favorable. And today they said that as of yesterday visas for the German quota were again being issued in Marseille. I hope that in the meantime our second affidavit has reached Washington and has been approved. If so, then it no longer seems completely impossible for us to be able to get to America. Perhaps you're right, and a miracle will happen when one least expects it. That would be wonderful! If only we knew that Mother is safe and if only we could be certain that one day, in the not-too-distant future, we would be reunited with her. Because Eva is working, she and Eva seem to be somewhat protected from deportation; whereas she thinks that unfortunately the danger to your mother, dear Rosemarie, is greater.

The most unpleasant aspect of our present existence is the fact that primitive things like eating, washing, etc., turn into problems that must be solved repeatedly and that therefore take much more time than one would wish. And yet I try to make as much use of the time of my "imprisonment" which would otherwise be lost. So I am taking part in various courses, language courses (Spanish among others), an electro course. In addition I work in the camp's primitive book bindery and attend various lectures—one about the development of European Intellectual History "From Homer to Goethe," one about U.S. History, etc. I am very sad that you have not received the letter we sent in early November; in it were detailed reports about the cultural events in the camp such as concerts, lectures, performances, etc. At the moment I'm reading Shakespeare plays. After having read Othello and Macbeth I am now reading King Lear, and with growing admiration Tolstoy's War & Peace.

Warmly, yours, Helmut

In the early spring of 1942, my parents were employed for the first time in the United States as legitimate professional musicians when they were hired by the Southern Symphony Orchestra of Columbia, South Carolina. The engagement was for several weeks in May and June, when the orchestra gave outdoor concerts in a festival setting. They wrote excitedly of their plans to Alex and Helmut, but when they took the train from New York to Columbia, they did not get off in Washington to knock on the doors of congressional offices on Capitol Hill, where fateful decisions about visas were being made every day. Instead, when they arrived in Columbia, they sent the captives fifty dollars. In the middle of May, they received a letter from Helmut that hinted at all the bureaucratic obstacles he and his father faced as they worked at their release.

Dear Günther, dear Rosemarie, many thanks for your kind and interesting letter. I'm sure you want to know right away what our current emigration prospects are, and so I will begin with that. The authorizations received from Washington, even for those under the German quota, are slowly increasing in number. Thus one day we might also be among them. In any case, we are obtaining the necessary documents so that in case of a "Convocation" we don't lose any time. We have already received the police certificates of good conduct from Martigny-les-Bains and Montauban, but we are still waiting for the extract from the police records for which we have already paid the Vichy fees. 'Wait!' continues to be our slogan.

When we received your letter I was lying in the infirmary, silent as a fish. A very capable young specialist from here removed my tonsils on April 24th. For a couple of days I was not allowed to speak or eat anything except ice. But in the meantime I've recovered quite well, which I owe in large part to the Quakers, who saw to it that I had canned milk and sugar. I am glad that it's finally been done!

I can understand why you are happy to have made such a good start with the Southern Symphony Orchestra, but I am also very curious to hear about your other activities. The things you write about Negroes in the southern states is very interesting. I can well understand that it would seem strange. Here in southern France one also sees quite a few Negroes who seem to enjoy equal rights socially. Besides the many altogether smart-looking black soldiers, one sees various colored people with fine facial features and hands who often seem to be involved in a variety of intellectual professions. As for my personal attitude toward Negroes and other colored people, I have always tried to see primarily the human being in every homo sapiens. I must admit that it has always been especially unpleasant for me when, as a 'captive,' I had to obey a black guard. But perhaps that is also a natural reminder of an ever-present national consciousness.

However things stand, we have to be thankful at least to be here, where to be sure we're not safe and where we are concentrated in camps, but without being subjected to anti-Semitism or persecution. What a lot we'll have to tell one another once we're all sitting around the same table again!! How much longer? Sometimes I think it will all be over sooner than we generally suppose, at least in Europe. But I can't understand why you spent two days in Philadelphia at the invitation of a former colleague, whereas you didn't even take two hours to see the beautiful city of Washington! We hear again and again that something can actually be accomplished there through the personal intervention of relatives. Possibly those involved had ways and means you don't have. But the chance that you could have interested someone in our case was surely not so remote that a stay of more than two hours would not have been worthwhile. You have to admit this is true and you must understand that we were very disappointed!

There's still a lot I could write you, to say nothing about the things one can only say face to face! I don't want us to have to go through another winter under these conditions, especially when I think of Father, but there have been frequent periods when he had even less resistance than he has now. Please let us hear from you regularly. We wait so anxiously for word from you, and the days when we receive good news are always the most beautiful! Love, yours, Helmut

In early June, George and Rosemary returned to New York. Almost immediately, George wrote to Washington, requesting a meeting with an immigration official to discuss the case of his relatives in France. Within ten days, he received a reply, informing him that an appointment had been arranged for the second week in November. On June 7, Max Markreich again petitioned the Refugee and Immigration Division of Agudath Israel. In filling out yet another lengthy form, he wrote on the line marked "Destination in United States and Purpose of Entrance": "New York, later Middle West. Beginning of a new life."

A few days later, my father received another envelope from Les Milles that contained letters from both Alex and Helmut, dated June 9, 1942.

Dear Günther and Rosemarie,

Your description of the city of Columbia, its landscape and people, interested me very much. It reminded me somewhat of the novel "Gone With the Wind," which of course takes place for the most part in and around Atlanta (Georgia). Fortunately, I can report to you that we are both well. Helmut has recovered from his tonsil operation and has recuperated. For about 4 weeks now he has been working 5 days a week in the Quaker kitchen which was recently set up for about ⅓ of the camp inmates. His bonus, on top of the basic portion of food, benefits me too. For about the same time I have been on barrack room duty for about 60 people living in our room, for which I get a small payment with which I can buy about 1 kilogram of dried peas a week. I pick up and distribute meals and bread (more than 38 stops) and receive a food bonus, although in many cases it's scarcely worthwhile but still does make a difference. After having been so worn down at the beginning of spring, I now feel better and weigh, dressed, about 120 pounds. That's still far too little but I hope to be able to catch up again. If I can't gain more weight, I don't think I will be able to live through a fourth winter.

About 8 days ago we received 2,150 Francs through the Quaker office in Marseille, without any indication of who the sender was. Since I assume you are responsible, I thank you *very, very much*. With the money we bought, because it was urgently necessary, a suitcase, a pair of used shoes for Helmut, and a hat for me—for I haven't had one for two years.

Dear Günther, I don't wish to sound ungrateful for this gift, but it occurs to me again that if you really knew our situation you would have helped us even more long ago. You had decent engagements for months, and if you had put away 50 cents for us every day during that time it would have helped us immensely. You surely want us to come over; but if I am no longer able to support Mother and myself because of ill health and lack of strength, then I don't want to become a burden to my children. You have seen to it that we received another affidavit, for which we are grateful. But if you had personally gone to the State Department Immigration Office on your way through Washington in May, we would probably have had our visas long ago and perhaps we'd be in the same position as others on whose behalf personal efforts were made.

I have described our situation for you several times. This will be the last time. If you don't move heaven and earth to help us, that's up to you, but it will be on your conscience. It won't be long before Helmut, who is still growing, will no longer be able to exist under the present conditions without permanent damage—this is a fact, and no words need be wasted on it. I find it very touching: often he has literally divided his last piece of bread with me. I have been very frank today, and I would regret it if you were angry with me, but an honest word can also be binding rather than divisive.

In the last few days we have had hot weather here; the vermin plague, in particular fleas and bedbugs, has become very severe. Helmut, undaunted, continues to work at the big cooking kettles in spite of the heat. Today he had a day off and slept almost all afternoon after going to his book-binding course in the morning. It has been reliably reported that those over 60 will be released if 9,000 francs are deposited for their livelihood. But I want to stay with Helmut in the hope that the hour of freedom will ring for us in the not-too-distant future. For today, many loving regards and good wishes. Yours, Father

On the back of the first sheet of Alex's letter were these lines from Helmut:

Dear Rosemarie and dear Günther,

Since Father has already reported to you in detail, I just want to add my warm regards and good wishes. I'm sure we'll get a letter from you in the next few days; we're eagerly waiting for it! Perhaps we shall receive the long-awaited Visa! Father is counting on it. Oh, what stories we could tell you then!! I'm sure I don't have to emphasize that Father and I help each other out wherever we can and on the whole we are good friends.

That's all for today. Next time I'll write more! Yours, Helmut

If everything suddenly works out, we could arrive at *your* place a few weeks after this letter reaches you!

It would be the last letter from his father and brother that my father would receive.

For some months, French Minister of State Pierre Laval had made no secret of his distaste for the so-called "undesirables," the foreign refugees, most of them Jews, who had made their way into France since the persecutions in Germany and Austria in 1938 and the massive German defeat of the Low Countries in 1940. In a memo sent to French diplomats, Laval declared that "the population of Hebrew stock has reached an excessive proportion"; they "form a manifestly dangerous element" who "engage in the black market and in Gaullist and communist propaganda, constituting for us a source of trouble to which we must put an end." "The only way to conjure away this danger," Laval concluded, was "to repatriate these individuals to Eastern Europe, their country of origin."

The French conjuring began on *Jeudi noir*, Black Thursday, July 16, 1942. On that day and the next, the police in Paris rounded up more than thirteen thousand Jewish men, women, and children who were not yet French citizens and took them to a number of assembly points. These included police stations, gymnasiums, schools, and—most infamously—the indoor bicycle track called the Winter Velodrome, *Vélodrome d'Hiver*, or the *Vél d'Hiv*. From there, these undesirables, each allowed no more than two suitcases, were sent off on packed trains to the East.

Within a few weeks, it became apparent that all the hopes marshaled for months by the inmates of the camps within what was still referred to as Unoccupied France had been hanging on the thinnest of threads, and that the thread was now to be severed. In early August, Joseph Schwartz of the American Jewish Joint Distribution Committee cabled to the Joint headquarters in New York from his post in Lisbon the ominous news that all exit visas for Jews had been suspended. On August 6, James Bernstein, the European director of HIAS, the Hebrew Sheltering and Immigrant Aid Society of America, sent the following cable to New York:

FOREIGN OFFICE ORDERED ALL VISAS PREVIOUSLY GRANTED CANCELLED STOP NEW APPLICATIONS MUST GO THROUGH FOREIGN OFFICE NOT PREFEC- TURE AS FORMERLY STOP SITUATION REFUGEES UNOCCUPIED FRANCE TRAGIC STOP

The Vichy government had begun the process of delivering about ten thousand foreign Jews into the hands of the Nazis, most of them from the *Centres National de Rassemblement des Israélites*, the National Centers for the Gathering of Jews. Two of these *centres* were Rivesaltes and Les Milles. On August 5, René Bousquet, the secretary general of the French police and the man whose friendship with Emil Poult had brought Alex and Helmut to Montauban two years earlier, sent a confidential memo to all local authorities in the Unoccupied Zone in which he outlined detailed instructions for the operation. The dispatch forbade the deportation of Jews of more than sixty years of age.

Nevertheless, on the afternoon of Monday, August 10, both Alex and Helmut were among more than 270 Jews—those whose last names began with the letters *A* through *G*—who were ordered to assemble under the hot sun in the courtyard of Camp des Milles. They were then marched about a quarter mile to a railroad siding and loaded into boxcars. An eyewitness reported, "They were cattle cars, strewn with bunches of straw. In each car, a jug of water and a bucket to serve as a toilet." Another witness, Pastor Henri Manen, wrote in his journal, "All around me the police are ghostly pale. One of them will say to me the next day, 'I have been in the colonies, I have been in China, I have seen massacres, war, famines. I have seen nothing as horrible as this.'"

The cars' doors were sealed tight, with so many men in each car that it was impossible to do anything but stand packed together. The train stayed motionless all night in the stifling August heat. The next morning, August 11, the train rolled north to—in the words of author and Holocaust historian Susan Zuccotti—"a camp in a town on the outskirts of Paris that was soon to become a familiar and dreaded word in Jewish households: Drancy."

MONDAY, JUNE 6, 2011. The Provençal sun, so elusive during our days of rest in Saint-Rémy, shines brightly this morning out of a deep blue sky. At 10:00 a.m., we drive up to the gates of Camp des Milles and, after giving our names to a guard, are waved through to a parking area adjacent to a bustling building site. Like Rivesaltes, Camp des Milles is being transformed into a memorial museum; unlike Rivesaltes, it enjoys substantial government and corporate support, with a glossy brochure boasting words of encouragement from Elie Wiesel. Last week, Rivesaltes was a vast, empty, lonely expanse; today at Camp des Milles, it is hard to avoid workers in hard hats and bright yellow vests as they swarm through the courtyard and the interior of the old brick factory.

I pause as I get out of the car and gaze silently for a long minute at this hulking building, essentially unchanged from when Alex wrote his last letter to my father almost sixty-nine years ago. He existed here as a prisoner for thirteen hellish months. I have come here at my leisure. Yet again, I find the contrast to be nearly unbearable.

A pretty young woman on the staff of the *Fondation du Camp Des Milles*, Katell Gouin, comes out to greet us, followed soon after by Odette Boyer, the director of the memorial project. They will take us on a tour of the factory and the proposed museum. As a prelude, they hand each of us a hard hat and a fluorescent vest like those worn by the construction workers and ask us to select a pair of steel-tipped boots to wear as we make our way through the rubble-strewn site. Katell carries a flashlight. Properly outfitted, we walk across the courtyard and into the dark interior of the brick factory.

We pause to allow our eyes, so recently splashed with sun, to become adjusted to the gloom. I use that time to once again try to transport myself into the past, to experience this place as my relatives did when it both sheltered and confined them seven decades ago. We set off single file down a corridor until Katell shines her flashlight above our heads to an archway on which we can make out Greek-style masks of tragedy and comedy flanking the words *Die Katakombe*. These decorations are what remain of the little theater devised by the internees in the factory's main brick oven. Katell tells us that there were additional designs on the theater's interior walls, probably some paintings by Max Ernst, but that they were destroyed when The Catacombs was reconverted to a brick oven after the war.

We walk another few yards to the workshop where bricks were once molded, a high-ceilinged space where the camp's courses and lectures were offered. Here, I reflect, Uncle Helmut studied bookbinding, learned about Homer and Goethe, and discussed Macbeth, for whom in his agony life became "but a walking shadow," an image that must have held particular resonance for Helmut in this twilit world of flickering candles. Katell directs our attention to four smaller ovens, which served as sleeping quarters for some of the camp's inmates, and I find myself thinking about the awful irony of these poor unfortunates coming to an early familiarity with ovens. We then climb the wooden stairs to the factory's second floor, where hundreds of men—Alex and Helmut among them—made their humble beds of straw night after endless night. Which corner was theirs, I wonder, what little portion of this dim dusty expanse did they claim as their refuge when they returned after a day working in the kitchen or wandering the courtyard to lie on their backs and gaze at the blue painted windows as they hoped against hope for their liberation? I lean wearily against a concrete pillar and gratefully feel Amy's comforting hand in mine.

Katell again leads the way as we clump back downstairs and emerge, blinking, into the brilliant sunshine. We trade in our work boots for our own shoes, return our vests and hard hats, and follow Katell into a separate building that once served as the guards' dining room and today is known as the Room of Murals, a reminder both humorous and poignant of the notable array of artists who were imprisoned here. Each of the room's four walls displays colorful frescos rendered lovingly and in great detail, the subject of which is food, bounteous food.

The Banquet of Nations, one of the remarkable frescos painted by one of Camp des Milles's inmates more than seventy years ago, now on display in the museum's Room of Murals.

One painting depicts a procession of blue-skinned figures bearing plates that groan under the weight of immense sausages, cheeses, artichokes, and succulent fish, while others carry overflowing barrels of wine. Another wall features the words *"Si vos assiettes ne sont pas très garnies, puissant nos dessins vous calmer l'appétit,"* or "If your plates are not very full, may our drawings calm your appetite." The most imposing painting, called *The Banquet of Nations*, offers a droll echo of Leonardo da Vinci's *Last Supper*, with men representing many nationalities dining on dishes from their various homelands: an Italian with a forkful of spaghetti, a Chinese man eating rice with chopsticks, an Inuit consuming blubber, an Indian in a turban swallowing fire, an Englishman in the guise of Henry the Eighth about to enjoy a plate of roast beef. *The Banquet's* painter was soon to be murdered in Auschwitz.

At this point, Katell concludes our tour by leading Amy and me out of the gates of Camp des Milles and along a roughly quarter-mile path to a railroad siding containing a single boxcar from a 1940s-era train. I am intensely aware that at this moment, for all my figurative travels

The single boxcar that stands at the railway siding at the museum, representing the trains that transported roughly two thousand prisoners to Drancy in the summer and fall of 1942.

these past weeks in the footsteps of Alex and Helmut, I am quite literally walking the same Via Dolorosa they followed on August 10, 1942. Did they know their fate, I ask myself numbly. As if reading my mind, Katell points back to the factory and tells us that during those terrible days in August and September when about two thousand people were shipped to Drancy, dozens of inmates, who could clearly see the teeming siding from their vantage point, chose to jump to their deaths from the factory's top floor rather than join the majority.

Katell swings open the door to the boxcar and we step inside. It's a bright warm day, but probably no more than seventy-five degrees. Even so, it is stiflingly hot within the car, and we are only three. I try to imagine what it would feel like to be among more than a hundred people jammed together with the door sealed shut, the boxcar standing still all night before beginning its journey northward. And my grandfather and uncle among the damned.

Fearing that I might sink to my knees and start to weep, I stumble out the door and back onto the safety of the siding. My mind suddenly rings with those words of warning and remonstrance sent by Alex and Helmut to my father in the New World: "I think the worst of the horror is still to come." "It is almost unnatural that you found no time to write us." "Do everything you can to get us out." "I can't understand why you spent two days in Philadelphia but couldn't spend two hours in Washington." "If you don't move heaven and earth to help us, that's up to you, but it will be on your conscience."

Those words resound like curses, and I clasp my head in my hands and stagger down the siding to a low iron fence, trying to squeeze them from my memory. I am suddenly furious with my father for his inattention and neglect, and then a moment later, awash in pity for the unbearable guilt he must have carried to his dying breath. Trying to think of anything else, I recall Helmut's repeated requests for stamps . . . and then remember how my father helped me start my own stamp collection when I was a boy, how he would often come home from work with little clear plastic packages of commemorative stamps from faraway lands like New Zealand, Egypt, or Togo. Was he trying, in a feeble way, to redeem himself?

At that moment, in that terrible place, I feel my father's guilt bore into me. It hurts like a shard of jagged glass rasped against my flesh. But excruciating as it is, I realize to my shock that it is also painfully familiar. I know this feeling, I tell myself, as well as I know my reflection in any mirror. And I have known this feeling for as long as I can remember. It has brought me here, far too late for me to do any good. My father failed to save his father and his brother. I have failed to save my grandfather and my uncle. This is my inheritance: failure, sorrow, and guilt.

Amy is once more at my side, and hand in hand we begin a measured walk back to the old brick factory. But our steps only heighten my grief, as I reflect that Alex and Helmut were not afforded the choice of walking this path *away* from the boxcar. I am reminded of the passage in *Catcher in the Rye* when Holden Caulfield recalls his brother Allie's funeral and then savagely says that it began to rain and all the mourners hurried off "someplace swanky for lunch," leaving Allie alone in his grave. I tell myself that there is nothing I can do to alter this unspeakable history and that it will do no one any good if I rend my garments or sleep every night on a bed of nails out in the rain. But I feel such helplessness and exhaustion in the face of so much cruelty, ugliness, and depravity. All I can do, I conclude, is to resume the journey, to keep on following my relatives until the end. And then to tell their story.

We bid farewell to Katell and wish her well, along with her colleagues, and return to the Meriva. I avert my eyes from those of Alex and Helmut as they gaze accusingly at me from their place above the rearview mirror, and we drive slowly away.

On September 10, 2012, exactly seventy years after the last train left Les Milles bound for Drancy, the memorial museum was dedicated and officially opened by French Prime Minister Jean-Marc Ayrault.

12

Drancy

Tuesday, June 7, 2011. There is something about a long drive in an automobile that comforts the spirit. Long before the internal combustion engine, Herman Melville's Ishmael warmed the damp, drizzly November in his soul by taking to the sea. In our day, Jack Kerouac understood that all he really needed for solace was "a wheel in his hand and four on the road." This morning, we back Jack. As I steer our little Meriva northward along the French autoroute system, my blues of yesterday seem to recede further with each passing mile. The hum of the tires, the pleasant vibration of the steering wheel, the unfamiliar landscape unfolding before us, and the mellifluous names on the road signs as they flash past all contribute to a sense of adventure and possibility, the best rebuke to the feelings of futility and dread that enshrouded us in the shadow of the brick factory. Although the next stop on our itinerary is the sad suburb of Drancy, we will get there by way of one of the jewels of our civilization, the sparkling city of Paris. On this bright morning, on the move, we are happy once more.

Having learned from the letter Alex wrote in Agde about his stay in the Central Hospital in Contrexéville, I have decided to pay a return visit to that charming little city on our way to Paris. Under sunny skies, we speed north as far as Lyon and then bear to the northeast. By late afternoon, we reach Contrexéville and decide to spend another night at the Inn of the Twelve Apostles. Its proprietor, a garrulous native of Italy who has called Contrexéville home for decades, is surprised and pleased to see us again. After a long day on the road, we are more than happy to avail ourselves of his hospitality.

Early the next morning, we pay a call on the town's *Mairie*, or city hall, where we make inquiries regarding the existence of a Central Hospital in the winter of 1939–1940, the months Alex mentioned in his letter. A helpful young woman named Audrey Hestin tells us that there was no community hospital in Contrexéville during that period, but that one of the town's hotels had been temporarily converted into a military hospital in the months following the start of the war. She suggests we visit the national military archives, which are located in Vincennes, just outside Paris, to see if theyt have any record of Alex's convalescence. Before we leave town, we pay a call on the building that once housed the hotel in question. Now a professional school that in-structs its students in hair design and restaurant and hotel management, the four-story structure looks across the main thoroughfare to the trees and fountains of the thermal park. We spend a few minutes walking through the halls, as I wonder which of the rooms might have sheltered Alex with a mattress and warm blankets, the last actual bed he would ever enjoy.

We then return to the road, making our unhurried way along a pastoral byway through the town of Chaumont, where we again buy some crusty bread and flavorful *fromage* for a pastoral lunch in a green field. Soon after, we say our farewells to the leisurely pace of the country-side, as we merge into the steady stream of traffic on an autoroute bound for Paris. We spend that night in a forgettable motel in what amounts to a truck stop on the distant outskirts of the capital city and arise on Thursday morning filled with the excitement of knowing that this very day we will see the legendary City of Light.

Thanks to more extraordinary navigating by Amy, we drive safely through the traffic-choked Parisian bypass to the remarkable Château de Vincennes, just east of the metropolis. Dating back to the fourteenth century and built largely by King Charles V, the castle featured the tallest fortified tower in all of medieval Europe. It was a lavish residence for French royalty for centuries, until Versailles became the favored location in the years leading up to the Revolution. The château was later converted to a state prison, whose most famous inmate was the Marquis de Sade. In recent years, it has housed the archives of the French military. After walking slowly through the cobblestoned courtyard, admiring the architectural glories of the old castle, we present ourselves at the *Service historique de la défense* and pose our question. Once again, we are disappointed. The French armed forces have no record of a military hospital in Contrexéville and no record of coming into contact with Alex Goldschmidt in the winter of 1940. I resign myself, for now, to never learning the details of how my grandfather spent the winter after being expelled from his relatively Edenic existence in Martigny-les-Bains.

Fortunately, the Château de Vincennes is a relatively short drive, even in midday Parisian traffic, from our hotel, located on the Rue de Faubourg Saint-Antoine in the 11th *arrondissement*. We squeeze the Meriva down an impossibly narrow passageway to a spot in an underground garage, check in, and immediately make arrangements to meet my cousin Deborah Philips and her partner, Garry Whannel. Actually, to be absolutely genealogically correct, Deborah and I are second cousins once removed, on my mother's side. Both my mother, Rosemary, and Deborah's father, Klaus, grew up in the German city of Düsseldorf. They were close to the same age, but the generations were somehow scrambled and it was Klaus's mother who was Rosemary's first cousin. Since my family is so small—and because I like Deborah and her sister, Claudia, so much—I've always operated on the shorthand assumption that we're simply cousins and left it at that.

Deborah grew up in London, but her father often traveled to Paris on business and frequently took Deborah along, resulting in Deborah's long-standing love affair with Paris and her near fluency in French. A few years ago, Deborah, a professor of literature and cultural history at the University of Brighton, purchased a small *pied-à-terre* in Paris, and she and Garry spend several weeks every year in France. They have offered to show Amy and me the town. We are delighted.

For four days, they squire us around the city of which Victor Hugo wrote, "Nothing is more fantastic. Nothing is more tragic. Nothing is more sublime." We discover that nothing can compare to seeing Paris by foot and Métro, as Deborah and Garry lead us on a walking tour that encompasses the Champs Elysées and the Place de la Concorde, the Seine with its bridges and bookstalls where Gene Kelly and Leslie Caron danced in *An American in Paris*, the Pompidou Center, the Opera, the Musée d'Orsay, the Jardin des Tuileries, the Cathedral of Notre Dame, and the cathedral of books and ideas that is Shakespeare and Company. One afternoon when Amy and Deborah go shopping, I make my solitary way to the Père Lachaise Cemetery and visit the graves of Chopin and Bizet, Poulenc and Cherubini, Balzac and Sarah Bernhardt, Delacroix and Molière, Edith Piaf and Jim Morrison and Oscar Wilde. At night, Deborah and Garry introduce us to the finest out-of-the-way restaurants they have discovered on their personal culinary journey and also, at my request, join us for a meal at *Le Boeuf sur le Toit*, that hangout of artists and their hangers-on during the dancing decade of the 1920s. We agree wholeheartedly with Thomas Jefferson, who declared that "a walk about Paris will provide lessons in history, beauty, and the very point of life."

We also stop at the Shoah Museum to see its Wall of Names, erected in tribute to the Jews who were sent to the East, a wall that includes the engraved names of Alex and Helmut Goldschmidt. We break away from the crowds surrounding Notre Dame to visit a sheltered spot on the eastern tip of the Île de la Cité, the *Mémorial des Martyrs de la Déportation*. A guard allows us to descend a steep flight of concrete steps that leads us nearly to the level of the Seine, although vertical bars of concrete impede our view of the water flowing gently by. The focal point of the memorial is a crypt illuminated by two hundred thousand little pieces of glass—one for each of the deported souls—that somehow sparkle in the gloom. So close to the life-giving river and to the soaring majesty of the cathedral, we are nonetheless isolated and cut off from the city's bustling humanity. So, too, were the victims this somber place remembers so tenderly.

By Saturday, we are ready to fulfill the purpose of this pleasure tour of Paris, the decidedly unpleasant side trip to the suburb of Drancy. We are to be joined on this journey by a recent acquaintance I made at the beginning of the year due to an unexpected e-mail.

Over the Christmas holidays of 2010, I heard from the publisher of *The Inextinguishable Symphony* that an Ingrid Janssen had written to me from an address in Paris. In January, we began a correspondence and I learned that she is a few years younger than me, that she was born in Oldenburg, and that her father, like mine, was born in 1913. She wrote that she had discovered my book and learned some things about her hometown that both fascinated and dismayed her. Now she lives in Paris with her husband, working as a television and documentary film producer. When I told her about our visit to Paris and its grim purpose, she and her husband Jacques offered to drive us to Drancy.

So on Saturday morning, we meet Ingrid and Jacques in the lobby of our hotel. They are a striking couple, both tall and trim, she with shaggy blond hair, he with receding grey hair and a close-cropped beard. Both wear fashionable leather jackets. We climb into their Saab and off we go, Jacques at the wheel, winding our way along wide boulevards and increasingly narrow streets as we approach the northeastern suburbs. The shops are now less chic, the cafés and small electronics outlets we pass often identify themselves with signs in Arabic, Farsi, and Turkish. Our conversation, sparse to begin with, falls nearly silent.

Jacques pulls the car to the curb and announces solemnly, "Here we are." We emerge and walk slowly across the busy street to stare up at a deeply moving memorial sculpture created by Shelomo Selinger in 1976. Made of weathered pink granite, the sculpture comprises ten anguished human figures flanked by two curved surfaces on which are carved passages in Hebrew and French. On the left is a brief description of the murderous legacy of the Drancy camp. On the right is a quotation from the Book of Lamentations: "Is it nothing to you, all you who pass by? Behold, and see if there be any sorrow like unto my sorrow."

IT WAS DESIGNED TO BE A QUIET REFUGE from the hurly-burly of urban life. Architects Marcel Lods and Eugène Beaudouin conceived a modernist plan that featured some of the first high-rise apartments in all of France, embracing a tree-lined courtyard of grass and ample flower beds. According to its architects, peace would reign within this horseshoe design of gentle residential living, and to prove it they bestowed upon their creation the name *La Cité de la Muette*, or "The Silent City."

Shortly after the armistice of June 1940, the German invaders confiscated the entire complex and, surrounding the Silent City with barbed wire, converted it first into a police barracks and then into a detention center for holding Jews and other undesirables. But it was the French police who marked the most notorious use of the Drancy camp by conducting a series of raids throughout Paris in late August 1941 and incarcerating more than four thousand Jews within the apartment complex that had been designed to accommodate about seven hundred people. For nearly two years, the Drancy camp was guarded entirely by French *gendarmes*, who exhibited an appalling disregard for the abject suffering of the inmates. Food was scarce, hygiene was nonexistent, and there was no defense against the onset of cold weather. A prisoner who managed to scribble a note to relatives described the conditions at the camp in three short, brutal phrases: "Filth of a coal mine. Straw mattress full of lice and bedbugs. Horrid overcrowding." By early November 1941, more than thirty inmates had died, and even the German military authorities were moved to order about eight hundred prisoners released for health reasons. Following the *Vél d'Hiv* roundup the following summer, more than seven thousand souls—men, women, and children—were crowded into the seven highrise apartment buildings. From the top floors, it was possible to see the skyline of Paris a few miles to the south, a view dominated by La Basilique du Sacré Coeur in Montmartre. But true civilization was miles and miles away.

Beginning on June 22, 1942, convoys of trains began departing from Le Bourget station, about a five-minute bus ride from the Drancy camp, heading for the extermination centers of Eastern Europe. At first, the orders from Berlin prohibited the deportation of children under fourteen, so mothers, fathers, and older siblings were frequently separated from their younger family members. Bewildered and terrified, children as young as five or six years old were forced to wave goodbye to their parents and then try to survive the horrors of Drancy on their

"Behold, and see if there be any sorrow like unto my sorrow." The memorial sculpture by Shelomo Selinger that stands at the entrance to The Silent City.

own. A story began circulating that soon the children would be joyfully reunited with their families at a mysterious place called Pitchipoi. In early August, orders from Berlin allowing deportations of young children having now arrived, the journeys to Pitchipoi could commence.

By the time the last convoy left for the East, on July 31, 1944, nearly sixty-five thousand Jews had been deported from Drancy. Approximately sixty-one thousand were shipped to Auschwitz, another thirty-seven hundred to the Sobibor extermination camp. Fewer than two thousand survived.

Alex and Helmut Goldschmidt arrived at Drancy on Thursday, August 13, 1942. They did not stay long. Almost immediately after their arrival in the apartment complex, on the morning of Friday, August 14, they were ordered onto a bus for the brief ride to Le Bourget. Once there, they were again loaded onto cattle cars along with nine hundred eighty-nine other Jewish prisoners, of whom about one hundred were children under fourteen. It was Convoy Nineteen, the first of the transports from Drancy that included young children bound for the happy land of Pitchipoi.

SATURDAY, JUNE 11, 2011. Behind the Selinger sculpture, a railroad track intersects with a second track, on which a single boxcar stands, representing the thousands of cars that departed from this place during those two hellish years, each car filled to capacity with human beings, their journey made all the more unspeakable, if such a thing is possible, by the fact that some of the passengers on those trains were little children who were eagerly looking forward to a reunion with the parents who had been torn from their grasp a few weeks earlier and who by now had probably disappeared up the chimneys of the smoking crematoria hundreds of miles to the East. I scan the ground for a stone to hurl at the boxcar in front of me, but on either side of the pathway is only a well-tended lawn, and on the edge of the lawn a trimmed hedge, and, overhead, a French flag that flaps softly in a gentle breeze. There are no weapons at my disposal. And what good would it do, anyhow?

On the other side of the memorial lies the Silent City, looking pretty much as it did on that August day in 1942 when Alex and Helmut passed through. Here is the horseshoe-shaped apartment complex and here is the little tree-lined park in the center. "Who in God's name would *want* to live here?" I ask Amy, Ingrid, and Jacques. They shake their heads, although Jacques points out that, by the look of things, it's a fairly poor neighborhood and the inhabitants may not have too many choices of low-cost housing in greater Paris. It's true: the complex has the look and feel of many "urban renewal" projects of 1960s America, and it's probable that many of those who call this place home would prefer living elsewhere. But what a ghastly history to come home to every evening.

For the next ten minutes or so we walk slowly around the horseshoe, sometimes looking closely at doors leading into the apartment buildings themselves, once to note a small plaque that someone has affixed to a wall in memory of the French poet and painter Max Jacob, who died here in the Drancy camp in March 1944. I find it next to impossible to believe that I am standing where my grandfather and uncle stood in the midst of their agony sixty-nine years ago, and I feel that familiar numbing sadness that I have come here much, much too late to help them. I say nothing but hold tightly to Amy's hand as we walk. When we complete our circular journey and stand once more in the shadow of the boxcar, I am overcome and hold my wife tightly as I weep.

After a minute, I lift my blurry eyes to the sculpture and find myself whispering, "No . . . there is no sorrow like unto my sorrow."

I turn then to apologize to Ingrid and Jacques for my emotions and see them in an identical embrace. Ingrid, through her tears, says to me, "Do you know why I tried to get in touch with you last year?" I shake my head and after a long pause, she begins to speak.

"I was born in Oldenburg, but I left after high school in 1973. When I lived there, nobody ever spoke about the Jewish history of Oldenburg. Oh, we learned about 'History,' what had happened in Berlin and Munich and Nuremburg, but it was taught to us as something abstract, something that had happened far away and had nothing, nothing to do with us. And so I never connected this 'History' to my personal environment."

Ingrid turns away and seems to be regarding the French flag as it defines the suddenly brisker wind that swirls over our heads. When she resumes her story, her voice is harder, colder.

"Then I read your book and learned what had happened in my home town on the Crystal Night. Something made me write 'Juden+Oldenburg' in my Google browser and then I discovered more of the dark part of my hometown, things I had never heard about or imagined had happened so close by."

She turns to me, starts to speak, but then looks away again.

"The next time I went home to Oldenburg to see my father—he was born in 1913, so he was twenty-five in 1938—I asked him about Crystal Night. Where was he? What did he do that night? What did he know about the march through the town of the arrested Jewish men? He must remember! The newspaper must have written about it! What happened? What? *What?*"

Ingrid, suddenly aware of her raised voice, lowers her head and thrusts her hands into the pockets of her leather jacket. When she speaks again, there is weariness in her tone, as if she has said these words to herself many times before.

"His answer was like so many answers I have heard from him over the years, from him and from others . . . evasive, secretive, silent. I couldn't get him to the point. He didn't listen to me. He didn't want to listen."

She takes a deep breath, and when she starts up again, the words tumble forth in a rush.

"Then he told me about a school friend, a friend named Alex Goldschmidt, who escaped to America. He said they were both musicians and played together in his former school orchestra. And he told me—I was so very surprised when he told me—about a meeting in Oldenburg in the late '60s with former inhabitants of the city who had been thrown out by the Nazis. He went to this meeting in hopes of finding Alex, but he was informed that Alex didn't have the money to come back to Germany to attend this meeting."

"But Alex could never have come to that meeting in Oldenburg in the late '60s. He got on a train here in Drancy in 1942 and never came back. He never came back!"

Ingrid looks at me with infinite sadness. "My father was like so many Germans of his era. He was a Nazi. He was a soldier and a Nazi. Did he try to embellish the past? Did he confuse your grandfather with your father? He never mentioned Günther, only Alex Goldschmidt. When I read your book, I was struck by the similarities with your father, that he was a musician, that his parents had a clothing store in the central city, that he was the one who escaped to America.

"My father died in 2009, so there will be no answers to my questions. I will never know if he really knew your family. That is why I wrote to you. If you miss pieces of a puzzle, even if you know that some pieces are lost forever, you always try to find the pieces next to them in hopes of getting an idea of the whole picture."

Ingrid takes a step toward me and takes hold of both my hands.

"My father was a Nazi. It is . . . so hard . . . for me to see that he didn't feel concerned for the destiny of his high school friend when he needed it so much. Was it just curiosity after the war when he tried to find him at that meeting? Was it also guilt? I will never understand, but I am still asking."

She looks to the ground, and when she raises her head again, I see that tears have returned to her eyes.

"Martin . . . Amy . . . I am sorry. I am sorry. I am so sorry."

We embrace, a child of victims and a child of a perpetrator, holding each other in this terrible place, this Silent City that muffles with the decades the deafening cries of the dead. Ingrid's sorrow is not like my sorrow. But it is sorrow, deep and genuine.

"Thank you," I whisper to her. "Thank you for bringing me here. And thank you for your tears."

13

Auschwitz

Monday, June 13, 2011. We have been in Europe for over a month. Each time we've begun a new leg of our journey, whether starting out for Sachsenhagen or heading south to Agde, I have contemplated that destination with a combination of moderate trepidation and the eagerness of discovery. Not so today. As we drive east, I am aware of nothing but pure dread coursing through me.

It took the trains from Drancy three days to reach the Polish city of Oswiecim. We will make it in two. Fully cognizant—once more—of the profound differences between our luxurious mode of travel and that endured by Alex and Helmut, I am terrified at the prospect of reaching this final destination. These feelings stem in part from my realization that, unlike all the other places we've visited during the past four and a half weeks, where my relatives always had a future, we are speeding ever closer to the end of their hopes and the end of their lives. But I'm also aware of a large reservoir of irrational fear that I am carrying with me, the terrors birthed in childhood of late-night knocks on the door, of shadowy yet somehow corporeal figures called "Nazis" who meant me harm, who would stop at nothing to do to me what they had done to my grandparents, uncle, aunt, and to millions of other innocent people. It occurs to me with frightful clarity that I have borne these fears all my life, and now here I am driving directly toward the epicenter of that murderous campaign of cruelty, hopelessness, and loss. "No. Stop. Turn around. Flee. *They're going to kill you, too!"* These and countless other foolish warnings flood my thoughts. But I drive onward, ever onward, toward the East.

There is one saving grace to our journey, which I discover as I look over the map this morning in our Paris hotel. Based on my calculations, it's about fifteen hundred kilometers to Oswiecim, and it should take us about fourteen hours to drive there. Searching for a place to spend tonight, I notice that almost exactly halfway to Oswiecim—about seven hundred fifty kilometers from Paris—lies the town of Eisenach, the birthplace of our favorite composer, Johann Sebastian Bach. It occurs to us both that a pilgrimage to Eisenach would be a good way to cushion the blow that will strike us in Poland. And I reflect, not for the first time, on what seems to me the perfect karmic balance represented by the fact that Germany has brought forth both Bach—not to mention Beethoven, Brahms, Goethe, and Schiller—and the Holocaust.

We are very fortunate that today is Whit Monday, a holiday that reduces Paris traffic considerably. So after squeezing our Meriva through the narrow passageway from the underground garage, nearly shearing off the car's right outside mirror in the process, we escape the maw of the city's fearsome congestion in mere minutes. Mindful of the distance we need to travel these next two days, we stick to expressways.

As we purr along, I attempt to explain to Amy my deep reaction to what Ingrid told us in Drancy on Saturday. I had never before personally met a German citizen with direct ties to the Nazis who had expressed any grief, remorse, or even simple sadness for what happened to my family. Ingrid's tears were a gift.

Then we both note Ingrid's mention of her father's possible feelings of guilt over the loss of his high school acquaintance—whether that young man's name was Alex or Günther—and wonder if Ingrid herself feels a sense of inherited guilt. Here was a paradox . . . she seems to feel guilty because of her father's actions and I feel guilty because of my father's inactions, and yet our families were on opposite sides in the drama that enfolded them. How can we both feel guilty? The only answer we can imagine is that the crimes committed by the Third Reich were so monstrous that both the perpetrators and the victims have been forever sullied and stained. The two sides are not equal in guilt, of course. But the oceans of tears on both sides are deep and seemingly inexhaustible.

We turn northeast toward Mainz and Wiesbaden and realize, as we circumnavigate Frankfurt, that we traveled this road back on May 11, during the initial part of our journey. We head north, travel northeast again to Bad Hersfeld, and then settle on a due easterly direction on Germany's A4. As the afternoon shadows begin to lengthen, we turn off the expressway and drive slowly and joyfully down a gentle incline into Eisenach, where our hero Johann Sebastian was born on March 21, 1685.

To the south of the city stretch the canopied hills of the Thuringian Forest and, looming over Eisenach from its perch on a twelve-hundred-foot crag, is the legendary Wartburg Castle, the foundations of which were erected in the eleventh century. Martin Luther attended school in Eisenach as a youth and later returned as a heretic. Declared an outlaw by the Holy Roman Emperor in 1521, Luther took shelter in Wartburg Castle, where he translated the New Testament from Greek into vernacular German. Today the house where Luther lived during his school days is a popular tourist attraction.

The prolific composer Georg Philip Telemann also lived in Eisenach, and a house around the corner from the Luther residence bears a plaque in Telemann's honor. But what makes this place a must-see destination for classical music lovers is that Eisenach was the birthplace of Bach, whose music, Goethe observed, "is as if the eternal harmony were communing with itself, as might have happened in God's bosom shortly before the creation of the world." In 1884, a statue of Bach in his choir robe and wig was unveiled here; twenty-two years later, a Bach museum opened in a six-hundred-year-old house near the site of the Master's birth.

After checking into our hotel, we walk the few blocks to the Bach Haus, a bright yellow building that seems to radiate more than a little of Goethe's "eternal harmony." It is past 6 p.m. and the museum is closed, but we are content to gaze in awe at the house and grounds and to take pictures of each other at the base of the Bach statue in a little park across the way. It is a perfect evening, just days from the summer solstice, and we sing the Gloria movement of Bach's prodigious B-Minor Mass as we stroll through the cobblestoned streets of the old city. We come to the central market square, which is dominated by the facade of the Church of St. George and a sixteenth-century gilded fountain also dedicated to St. George, the town's patron and protector. We find an open ice cream shop, and, sitting on a marble bench, we eat our ice cream and listen to the play of the fountain's waters and the sounding of the church's chimes every quarter hour, as darkness slowly falls on a scene of utter peace and tranquility. As I drift off to sleep a few hours later, I hug that image tight, knowing what the immediate future will bring.

Tuesday dawns cloudy; saying little, we pack up the car and return to the autobahn, heading east once more. Our route takes us about fifty miles south of Leipzig, where Bach served as cantor of St. Thomas Church and wrote some of his most glorious music, and just north of Dresden, where Saxon kings collected exquisite porcelain, Friedrich Schiller wrote his "Ode to Joy," and at least twenty-five thousand civilians were killed during the Allied firebombing of the city in February 1945.

In the early afternoon, we pass the city of Görlitz and shortly thereafter enter Poland. As we cross the frontier, black-and-white images of September 1, 1939, courtesy of too many hours watching the History Channel, come crowding into my imagination. Much faster even than a *Blitzkrieg* tank, we speed east and then southeast past Legnica, Wrocław, and Opole. At Katowice, we leave the expressway as it continues on to Kraków and head south to the city of Tychy. It is now evening and we are only about fifteen kilometers from Oswiecim. Nothing on earth could persuade me to spend a night in that godforsaken town, so we find a hotel in Tychy to await the morrow.

I am nervous, short-tempered, and doubtless bad company. But after sitting silently for ten minutes in the hotel's dining room, waiting for what turns out to be a very flavorful meal known locally as *bigos*, or hunter's stew, my dear wife engages me in a passionate conversation about LeBron James. I am, alas, one of the many pitiable fans of James' spurned team, the Cleveland Cavaliers, whom he abandoned the previous summer so that he could "take his talents to South Beach" and play for the Miami Heat. But two nights ago Miami was defeated by Dallas in the deciding game of the NBA Finals and we Cleveland fans are overflowing with *schadenfreude*. Forgetting for a while why I am here in this hotel in Tychy, I give Amy the gift of my analysis of LeBron's shortcomings in big games. She knows me well, one of the many reasons I love her. Tonight I appreciate her ploy to the depths of my being.

I sleep better than I expect to, but in the morning I am more unsettled than ever. It is warm and humid, and shortly after 9:00 we start down highway 44, heading southeast. The countryside is flat and green, with few trees. We could almost be in Iowa, I think to myself. But we are not in Iowa. We are in Poland, coming ever nearer to one of the most hideous places on earth. My mouth is dry, my palms are wet, and my heart is racing. *"Turn back, turn back, turn back"* are the words my brain fashions to match the rhythm of our tires on the rough road. But my right foot remains firmly affixed to our little Meriva's gas pedal, and before I am ready for it, we pass through a traffic circle and a black road sign announces that we have arrived in Oswiecim, the end of the line.

IT SITS AT THE CONFLUENCE OF TWO RIVERS, the Vistula and the Sola, and on the imaginary border that divides the German and the Slavic peoples. Its history goes back at least as far as 1178, and for most of the intervening years, it has repeatedly switched its allegiances to reflect the ever-changing political and military administration of the region. In the fourteenth century, the town was part of the Holy Roman Empire and its official language was German. A hundred years later, the Hussite wars brought it under Bohemian rule, and its citizens were expected to speak Czech. During the sixteenth century, both its rulers and language were Polish. In the eighteenth century, Oswiecim became one of the Austrian possessions of the Hapsburg Empire; once again its official language was German and its name was changed to Auschwitz. As late as 1918, one of the honorifics of the Hapsburg emperor was "Duke of Auschwitz." With the collapse of the monarchy, the town reverted to Polish rule and its name to Oswiecim, but the rulers of the new "Thousand Year Reich" in 1933 were determined to reclaim the region for the revived glory of the German *Volk*. Adolf Hitler had two primary social, ethnic, and military goals: the destruction of the Jewish "race" and the acquisition of *Lebensraum*, or an unfettered space in which to live, in Eastern Europe. Those goals, he hoped, would both be realized in Auschwitz.

The origins of a camp in Oswiecim go back to the time of the *Sachsengänger*, or "people on their way to Saxony." At the end of the nineteenth century and the beginning of the twentieth, a wave of emigration to the west brought workers from Russia and Poland to the German frontier, where they lived until they found employment in Prussia, Saxony, or the other German states. In 1917, a camp consisting of twenty-two brick houses and ninety wooden barracks was built on the outskirts of Oswiecim for the use of these itinerant workers. Twenty-three years later, the Nazis constructed their concentration camp on the site of the *Sachsengänger* facility.

On September 1, 1939, on the first day of the Second World War, the German air force bombed Oswiecim. One week later, the market square was renamed Adolf Hitler Platz and the town's name reverted to Auschwitz. The Nazis intended to achieve *Lebensraum* in Poland through a policy euphemistically identified years later as "ethnic cleansing," whereby Jews and Poles were to be expelled and people of true German descent were to be imported. Thus, within a few months, Auschwitz was Polish no more, but an essential part of the German Reich.

By the spring of 1940, there were already six concentration camps operating on German soil: Dachau, Sachsenhausen, Buchenwald, Flossenbürg, Mauthausen, and Ravensbrück. But Heinrich Himmler, head of the SS, envisioned a more advanced, more efficient mode of murder and began seeking a suitable site at which to launch his new program. He dispatched inspectors to Auschwitz to render a report. On its debit side was the current condition of the former *Sachsengänger* camp, which was rundown and stood on swampy land that was a breeding ground for malaria-carrying mosquitoes. But on the plus side were two factors: a camp was already in place and the town was a railway junction that could be easily accessed by German trains but also shut off from the outside world. In April, Auschwitz was selected from among several other possible sites, and construction began immediately to transform the old itinerant workers' camp into what would become the most far-reaching extermination camp of the Third Reich.

In early May, Himmler appointed Rudolf Höss, who had served as second in command at the Sachsenhausen camp when Alex was a prisoner there in the weeks after *Kristallnacht*, to be the commandant of Auschwitz, and on June 14, 1940, the camp opened for business. Although Auschwitz is infamous as the epicenter of the Holocaust, its first inmates were not Jews but rather Polish political prisoners. More than seven hundred Poles, mostly students and soldiers, entered Auschwitz on that first day, followed six days later by three hundred felons from nearby Kraków. In August and September, two more transports of more than three thousand prisoners from Warsaw jails were sent to Auschwitz, most to assist in its further construction.

Again, at first the considerable majority of the inmates of Auschwitz were not Jews but Poles who had been persecuted and then arrested for belonging to suspect political organizations or for being involved in the Polish resistance to the Nazi invaders. For nearly two years, most of those unfortunate enough to pass through the iron gates of Auschwitz, which were decorated with the cynical slogan *Arbeit Macht Frei* ("Work Makes You Free"), were dissident doctors, clerics, students, teachers, and scientists. During that time, mass murder had yet to be unleashed upon the inmates; death was caused rather by hunger, disease, overwork, and the brutality of the SS.

To describe life, such as it was, within the barbed wire and electrified fences of Auschwitz, is to exhaust such adjectives as harsh, cruel, savage, barbaric, and sadistic. Upon arrival at the camp, each prisoner was issued a number that replaced his or her name, a number that was tattooed onto the forearm. Prisoners had their heads shaved and, to replace their clothes, were given coarse canvas striped shirts and pants and poorly fitting wooden shoes. They slept, often six to a wooden bunk that had been designed for three, on sacks filled with straw. They were fed weak tea or coffee in the morning, a watery soup of nettles or parsnips for lunch, and moldy bread for the evening meal. A daily ration of food amounted to no more than seven hundred calories. Days began at 4:30 a.m. during spring and summer, an hour later in the depths of winter. Work in the camp's gravel pits, brick ovens, or lumberyard occupied most prisoners' time, generally twelve hours a day, and woe to anyone who fell ill from malnutrition or exhaustion; an inability to work led to physical punishment or on-the-spot execution. Other offenses such as a missing shirt button, a lost cap, or a misplaced shoe were punished with solitary confinement in a tiny cell that required the prisoner to stand for hours at a time. Other miscreants would be hanged by their wrists with their arms tied behind their backs, resulting in dislocated shoulders. Still others were placed in subterranean cells with no windows and with so little air that the prisoner would gradually suffocate. Particularly sadistic guards would secure a lighted candle to the wall above the prisoner's head to hasten the loss of breathable oxygen.

Auschwitz was by no means the only Nazi concentration camp in which so-called medical research was conducted. But many Nazi doctors regarded it as the preferred place in which to conduct experiments on human beings. The Bayer chemical company, which had invented aspirin in 1897, purchased prisoners to be used as guinea pigs in the testing of new drugs. Dr. Carl Clauberg, a gynecologist from Upper Silesia, attempted to permanently close the uteruses of women prisoners through the use of experimental chemicals. Dr. Horst Schumann murdered hundreds of mentally and physically handicapped prisoners in the service of what was termed a "euthanasia" program; he also used x-rays to sterilize both male and female inmates. Professor Johann Kremer, in the name of an experiment to study the effects of hunger in humans, literally starved his subjects to death in the last five months of 1942. Other prisoners were injected with diseases, including malaria and syphilis, their sufferings duly noted in the doctors' notebooks.

The most infamous doctor at Auschwitz, SS-Hauptsturmführer Josef Mengele, thirty-two years old when he arrived at the camp, earned the nickname the "Angel of Death" for his grisly experiments. His specialty was twins—how they were alike and how they differed. Using more than a thousand sets of twins, most of them young children, he would induce gangrene and other diseases into one twin, wait for him or her to die, and then murder the other twin, to compare autopsies.

Each prisoner was identified by a number tattooed on the forearm and by a colored triangle known as a *Winkel*, sewn on his or her shirt and trouser leg. Red triangles identified the wearer as a political prisoner, green a common criminal, black an "antisocial" offender such as a prostitute or drug addict, blue a foreign laborer, brown a Gypsy, purple a Jehovah's Witness, pink a homosexual, and yellow a Jew.

Eventually, yellow would become the primary color in the grim rainbow of Auschwitz. Although the camp had begun primarily as a prison for Polish enemies of the German invaders, within eighteen months it was deemed ready to assume its role in what came to be known as the Final Solution of the Jewish Problem.

Beginning with the Civil Service Law of April 7, 1933—the ordinance that provided the legal justification for the expulsion of Jews from government jobs, police and fire stations, post offices, libraries, and all state-run cultural institutions across Germany—a myriad of judicial solutions to what was termed the Jewish Problem had been devised and implemented. By late 1941, it had become common knowledge in the upper strata of the German government that Chancellor Hitler had decided upon a Final Solution to the problem; it fell to one Reinhard Heydrich to see that the plan would be carried out smoothly and efficiently.

Herr Heydrich was the director of the Head Office of Reich Security (RSHA), the duty of which was to fight all "enemies of the Reich," both within and without the German border. He called a meeting for December 9, 1941, that was to include representatives of all the significant branches of the Nazi Party apparatus, from the departments of the interior, justice, and the foreign office to the head of the Gestapo. But two days before the meeting was to convene, on December 7, the Japanese air force launched its secret attack on American forces at Pearl Harbor. By virtue of its treaty with Japan, Germany was obliged to declare war on the United States. As a result, Heydrich postponed the conference until January 20, 1942, and named as its venue a villa at 56–58 Am Grossen Wannsee, a quiet residential street on the banks of

Lake Wannsee, on the western outskirts of Berlin. The gathering is now remembered as the Wannsee Conference.

Thanks to the careful notes taken that day by Adolf Eichmann, Heydrich's right-hand man, we know that Heydrich made Hitler's aims perfectly clear. "Under proper guidance," he declared, "in the course of the final solution the Jews are to be allocated for appropriate labor in the East. Able-bodied Jews, separated according to sex, will be taken in large work columns to these areas for work on roads, in the course of which action doubtless a large portion will be eliminated by natural causes. The possible final remnant will, since it will undoubtedly consist of the most resistant portion, have to be treated accordingly, because it is the product of natural selection and would, if released, act as the seed of a new Jewish revival." In the course of the "practical execution of the final solution," Heydrich concluded, "Europe would be combed through from west to east." There was no ambiguity. This Final Solution called for the systematic extermination of the Jewish population from the continent.

There had already been mass deportations and executions of Jews before the Wannsee Conference convened. Beginning in September and October 1941, Jews in Germany, particularly in large cities, were loaded onto trains, shipped to occupied Poland and Latvia, and shot. But lethal as these actions were, they were judged to be too messy, impractical, and inefficient by the Nazi masterminds, who also took into account the strained nerves of the German soldiers who were charged with pulling the triggers. Himmler issued orders to explore alternative methods, and explosives and poison gas were tried out on Jews and undesirables deemed mentally handicapped. In the words of historian Sybille Steinbacher, the Nazi regime became determined "to find a means of murder that was as efficient as it was discreet and anonymous, and which minimized the psychological burden on those carrying out the executions."

Thus, a series of mass extermination camps came into existence in the aftermath of Wannsee. The names of these camps resound hollowly in the history of the twentieth century like the tolling of a funeral bell: Chełmno, Belzec, Sobibor, Treblinka, Majdanek, and Birkenau.

Brzezinka, which means "birch forest" in Polish, was a small village about two kilometers from the site of the Auschwitz camp. Cleared of its native population by the Nazis, it became the site of the camp known as Auschwitz II or by its German name, Birkenau. Poison gas had been used on prisoners in Auschwitz I as early as September 1941, when about nine hundred Soviet prisoners of war were murdered in the camp's infamous Block 11, known as the "punishment block." But it was in Birkenau that the Nazis perfected techniques that enabled them to commit murder on a massive scale using technological advances that had been developed to an exacting degree in the service of genocide.

Skilled as they were in exploiting propaganda and euphemism, the authorities at Birkenau referred to the first two gas chambers simply as "the little red house" for a simple structure made of bricks, and "the little white house" for a building with a whitewashed exterior. Beginning in late March 1942, trains from all over Europe began to pull onto the one-way track that led beneath an elevated watchtower to its terminus in an open field. When the trains stopped moving, guards opened the doors of the cattle cars and roughly removed the terrified inhabitants, those who had survived the days-long journeys from Germany, Hungary, Austria, or France. The victims were first separated according to sex and then marched past a phalanx of soldiers and camp doctors, who in those minutes of terror and confusion acted as angels of life and death. If the doctor determined that a new arrival was young and fit enough for work, a wave of his hand to the right would send that prisoner to a barracks to begin his brutal incarceration at Auschwitz I or II. Generally, no more than about a quarter of each convoy was allowed to live. The most wretched of the newcomers, the old, the very young, the sick, the weak, were dispatched to the left, to the little houses.

At the entrance to the houses, the victims were told that they would be showered and deloused in preparation for their life in this work camp. Guards would sometimes welcome them with an elaborate speech. They promised hot soup and coffee after the shower; they requested that their charges remove their clothes and hang them on a hook, making sure to remember the number of the hook so that there would be no confusion when they retrieved their clothes after their shower. Then the naked prisoners would be ordered into the houses. The little red house could hold around eight hundred people; the white house's capacity was around twelve hundred.

When the rooms were full, the airtight doors were closed and fastened. Then SS men stationed near small holes in the roof and in two of the walls would dump in pellets of a cyanide-based pesticide known by its trademark name, Zyklon-B. Panic ensued within, and the condemned would hurl themselves against the unyielding doors where, in the words of an eyewitness, "they piled up in one blue clammy blood-spattered pyramid, clawing and mauling each other even in death." To muffle the agonized screams of the victims, the SS would sometimes order motorcycle engines started and gunned, although it is unclear whose sensibilities they were protecting.

After about twenty or thirty minutes, all would fall silent within the little houses. The doors would be opened, and the *Sonderkommandos*, Jewish prisoners who were promised extra food and their ultimate freedom as payment for this horrific detail, would enter wearing gas masks and rubber boots. Gerald Reitlinger, in his study of the Final Solution, wrote, "Their first task was to remove the blood and defecations before dragging the dead bodies apart with nooses and hooks, the prelude to the ghastly search for gold and the removal of teeth and hair which were regarded by the Germans as strategic materials." Gold fillings were collected, melted down, and turned into ingots for eventual delivery to the Reichsbank. The victims' hair was spun into a fine thread and used to make rope, stuff mattresses, and manufacture felt.

The looted corpses of the murdered were taken to the crematorium of Auschwitz I, tossed into mass graves and covered with quicklime, or simply burned in a nearby field. The ashes from the incinerated bodies were usually dumped into the dark waters of the Vistula and Sola. But they were often sold to a local fertilizer company as human bone meal or used at the camp as insulation for buildings and paving material for the surrounding roads.

By the end of 1942, the little red and white houses were deemed inadequate for the task of murdering Jews on a mass scale, so plans were developed for the construction of higher-capacity crematoria.

By June 1943, Birkenau boasted four fully functional gas chambers that each could execute up to two thousand people a day. These new buildings were not only state-of-the-art killing centers but also landmarks in the cruel and cynical art of deception. The ruse that victims were about to undergo nothing more taxing than a cleansing shower was underscored by freshly painted signs in German, French, Hungarian, and Greek that pointed the way to the "bathroom" and the "disinfection room," and offered cheerful slogans such as "Through cleanliness to freedom." The gas chambers themselves were outfitted with dummy shower heads, and guards would distribute soap and towels to their naked charges before locking the airtight doors behind them.

The new facilities featured special double-paned glass peepholes through which the guards could watch their victims' death agonies and high-powered ventilators that sucked out the lethal remnants of the Zyklon-B from the chamber before the *Sonderkommandos* ventured in to clean up. The new crematoria also included built-in incineration rooms to enable more convenient access for the disposal of the corpses. Bodies could now be hoisted via elevator to one of the five ovens that were kept busy night and day.

During the Nuremberg trials of Nazi war criminals, correspondence from the corporations vying for concentration camp building contracts was introduced as evidence. One such business, the firm of C. H. Kori, made its case by pointing out that it had already furnished the Reich with four furnaces for the Dachau camp. Its letter continued: "Following our verbal discussion regarding the delivery of equipment of simple construction for the burning of bodies, we are submitting plans for our perfected ovens which operate with coal and which have hitherto given full satisfaction. We suggest two crematoria furnaces for the building planned, but we advise you to make further inquiries to make sure that two ovens will be sufficient for your requirements. We guarantee the effectiveness of the cremation ovens as well as their durability, the use of the best material, and our faultless workmanship."

The skill and workmanship of the Kori company, as well as the efforts of such businesses as I. A. Topf and Sons of Erfurt, Huta Structural and Foundation Engineering from nearby Katowice, the Silesian construction firm Lenz & Company, and the chemical giant I. G. Farben, which held the patent for Zyklon-B, proved to be as effective as promised. Engineers and designers who a few years earlier had conceived of medical innovations and advancements in the technology of highway construction now set their minds to the task of ever more potent and efficient engines of death.

Their handiwork, though planned to be carried out in secrecy, was not and could not be hidden. Also testifying at Nuremberg was Commandant Rudolf Höss, who declared, "Of course the foul and nauseating stench from the continuous burning of bodies permeated the entire area and all of the people living in the surrounding communities knew that exterminations were going on at Auschwitz."

In July 1944, Soviet troops began what would become their victorious advance to the west, pushing back German lines of defense as they went. They liberated the Majdanek death camp in eastern Poland and then crossed the Vistula River about two hundred kilometers from Auschwitz. The Nazis used the next six months attempting to erase from history all record of their crimes at Auschwitz. In July, about 155,000 prisoners were held there; by the beginning of 1945, about half that number had been transported to concentration camps in the West, among them Dachau, Buchenwald, Sachsenhausen, and Bergen-Belsen.

During the month of October, about forty thousand people were murdered in the gas chambers of Birkenau. In November, Himmler ordered the executions to stop. In the fields of Birkenau where bodies had been burned, the trenches and other low-lying areas that had been filled with bones and ashes were cleared, leveled, and covered over with turf. The crematorium at Auschwitz was redesigned and changed into an air-raid bunker. And in January 1945, the gas chambers of Birkenau were dynamited.

On January 17, 1945, the SS issued orders calling for the immediate execution of all remaining prisoners in the Auschwitz camps, but in the chaos of the Nazi retreat, those orders were ignored. Instead, Auschwitz and Birkenau were evacuated and nearly sixty thousand prisoners were forced to accompany the Nazi army as it fled to the west. Many thousands perished in the cold and bitter conditions; anyone who couldn't keep up, fell, or tried to rest or run away was shot. A little more than forty thousand prisoners survived the death march and were then interned in other camps to await their eventual liberation.

Back at Auschwitz, the final ten days of the camp's existence saw a frenzied attempt to destroy the carefully tended records of the murderers. Files, dossiers, death certificates, and other papers were burned. The x-ray machine that had been used for Horst Schumann's experiments was removed and sent west. On January 21, the last of the sentries were ordered down from the camp's watchtowers. Before they fled, the retreating Nazi soldiers set fire to the main facility; six days later, only six of the thirty barracks remained.

On Saturday afternoon, January 27, 1945, soldiers from the 60th Army of the Soviet Union's First Ukrainian Front came upon the smoking remains of Auschwitz and Birkenau. They discovered around six hundred corpses and more than seven thousand emaciated survivors, prisoners who had been deemed too weak to accompany the death march. The fleeing Nazis also left behind clothing stolen from their murdered victims, including nearly 350,000 men's suits and more than 830,000 women's dresses and other apparel. In a warehouse near the main camp, the Soviet soldiers discovered more than seven and a half tons of human hair. Researchers estimated that it came from the shaved heads of about 140,000 women.

Since the Nazis destroyed so many records and files as they prepared their hasty evacuation from Auschwitz, arriving at an exact number of human beings murdered there has proven to be a difficult task. Based on testimony from survivors and perpetrators and the work of latter-day scholars, the figure of 1.1 million to 1.5 million people seems accurate. About 90 percent of those gassed, at least 950,000, were Jews. It has been estimated that about 75,000 non-Jewish Poles and 20,000 Roma, or Gypsies, were also gassed. About 200,000 people died of starvation, disease, or overwork.

In June 1942, Polish teacher Antoni Dobrowolski, who was working for the Polish underground, was arrested by the Gestapo and sent to Auschwitz. On October 21, 2012, Dobrowolski died. He was 108, the oldest known survivor of Auschwitz.

ON OR ABOUT MONDAY, AUGUST 17, 1942, Convoy Nineteen, the train from Drancy bearing my grandfather, my uncle, and 989 other Jewish prisoners rolled slowly beneath the guard tower at Birkenau and came to a halt, its piston-applied brakes moaning on the iron wheels. The box-cars' doors slid open and the 991 inhabitants, after three days packed together in darkness, emerged blinking into the unfamiliar sunshine. They were ordered onto the well-trampled grass and dirt of the siding and marched before the row of doctors and soldiers who had gathered under the open summer sky to render judgment. In the next few minutes, 875 of the 991 were pronounced too old or weak for work on behalf of the Reich. These 875 souls were sent down the path to the left, toward the guards who ushered them into one or the other of the little brick houses under the pretense of a shower and, afterward, a nourishing bowl of soup. Each of the 875 had led lives of happiness, sorrow, adventure, wonder, frustration, boredom, generosity, peevishness, hope. One of those 875 had been born into a well-to-do family of horse dealers, had fought for his country in the Great War, had run a successful women's clothing store where he'd acquired a reputation for kindness and honesty, had been arrested for the crime of his religious heritage, and had spent the last forty months engaged in a futile attempt to escape his pursuers and achieve a life of freedom for his family. His name was Alex Goldschmidt, he was my grandfather, and on that day he was murdered in one of the gas chambers of Birkenau. He was sixty-three years old.

Of the 991 passengers in Convoy Nineteen, 116 survived the selec-tion process conducted on the dusty siding by the railway terminus and were sent off to the right to be stripped, shaved, tattooed, and assigned a barracks at Auschwitz. Of those 116, only one would still be alive at the time of the camp's liberation in 1945. Another of the 116 was a young man born to a wealthy merchant, a young man whose school years had been marked by no particular academic achievement but who had risen to his feet in an impulsive act of bravado and defiance that would be remembered and admired many decades hence, a young man who had spent the last 15 percent of his life as a refugee and a prisoner but who had utilized part of that time tending the sick, learning the skills of animal husbandry and bookbinding, and reading the plays of William Shakespeare, and nearly all of that time being his father's constant companion and close friend. His name was Klaus Helmut Goldschmidt, he was my uncle, and on that day he was tattooed with the number 59305 and assigned to Barracks 7 in Auschwitz.

Barracks 7 was the site of what was called the *Mauerschule*, or bricklayers' school, where relatively healthy young men were taught the craft of fashioning and laying bricks. All the main buildings of Auschwitz were made of bricks, so the camp authorities deemed it necessary to have a constant supply of skilled workers. The students of the bricklayers' school had a remotely easier existence than the other inmates of Auschwitz in that their food rations were of slightly better quality and their place of work—the school—was on the second floor of Barracks 7. While other prisoners had to work outdoors in all weather, often marching hundreds of yards to get to their construction sites, all the bricklayers had to do was climb a flight of stairs.

But if Helmut had drawn a relatively plum assignment, he did not have long to enjoy it. On October 7, fifty-one days after he had entered the iron gates of Auschwitz under the archway proclaiming that work would make him free, he was sent to Barracks 20, one of the camp's hospitals. According to a plaque affixed in a room of the barracks by the curators of the Auschwitz memorial, "Prisoners who suffered from infectious diseases, mainly typhus, stayed in Block 20. In this room, in the years 1941 to 1943, prisoners were killed by lethal injections of phenol into the heart. Prisoners selected from the camp hospital or prisoners sentenced to death by the camp Gestapo were killed here. In one such special procedure, 121 Polish and Jewish boys were killed in this room. Corpses were put in the opposite room, from where they were transported to Crematorium 1. Almost every day a few dozen prisoners were killed by lethal injections in the camp."

Two days after he entered Barracks 20, on October 9, 1942, Helmut died. The official cause of death was listed as typhus, but there is every chance that he was one of the prisoners who was murdered by lethal injection. Helmut Goldschmidt was twenty-one years old.

WEDNESDAY, JUNE 15, 2011. *"My God, it's a theme park!"*

After all the miles and all the anticipation and all my fears of the past two days, these are the words I growl to Amy as we enter the crowded parking lot of the Auschwitz-Birkenau Memorial Museum in Oswiecim. There are at least a half-dozen tour buses and milling crowds of tourists, among them a group of older Japanese men and women, many of them with multiple cameras hanging from their necks, and high school classes from Tel Aviv and Far Rockaway, Long Island, some of the kids solemn and attentive and some of them hanging back, sneaking a smoke.

"Welcome to Holocaust World 3-D!" I continue, as we squeeze into a parking space. "It's the emotional roller-coaster of a lifetime! Thrills! Chills! You'll never forget to Never Forget! (Tattoos sold separately . . . striped pajamas not included . . . Zyklon-B no longer in stock.)" Amy smiles at me indulgently, then kisses me to shut me up. I can't explain to her the source of my confused feelings. On the one hand, I think it's very much a Good Thing that so many people have traveled so far to tour this memorial and to learn the details of the horrors that were perpetrated here. On the other hand, I'm put off by all the eagerness to gawk. It's as if we're rubbernecking at the smoldering wreckage of a colossal accident along the highway of Western civilization. I want everyone to just move along.

There is no admission fee to enter the Auschwitz camp, but there is a charge to join any of the several tours that depart regularly from the museum's entranceway, tours conducted in English, French, German, Italian, Polish, and Japanese. Even though we are not joining a tour group, we find ourselves caught in the swirl of humanity packed into a hallway. Three or four security guards size us up and then one of them waves us through turnstiles onto a gravel path. After perhaps fifty yards, we turn right and walk beneath the notorious iron gate bearing the words *Arbeit Macht Frei*. Somehow, I think, it shouldn't be so easy.

We ring the bell at Barracks 24, which today houses the archivists who work in the Office for Information On Former Prisoners. We are buzzed in and meet Piotr Supinski, a helpful young man who confirms the date of Helmut's death and tells me the details of his time in Barracks 7 and 20. Piotr speaks slowly and softly in perfect English;

it comes to me that he regards me, respectfully, as grieving next of kin. His kindness moves me deeply, and suddenly all my parking lot cynicism dries up and blows harmlessly away.

Amy and I leave the archives and, hand in hand, join the quiet throngs strolling along the well-kept gravel paths from barracks to barracks. We seek out Barracks 7, where Helmut lived for a few weeks with his fellow bricklayers, and then make our way with unwilling steps to Barracks 20. Here is where my uncle died, and here is where I have determined to tell him goodbye. But I realize that I have forgotten his picture in the car.

I am in no mood to face the crowds back in the entrance hall, but there is nothing to do but walk back to the parking lot and detach the photos of Alex and Helmut from their position above the Meriva's rearview mirror, where they have kept us company during our long journey. I anticipate an uncomfortable wait standing in line to get back into the camp, but something remarkable happens. The people in the halls, tourists and security personnel alike, take one look at the photos I am carrying and, without a word, shrink back and give us room to pass. Everyone seems to know why I am carrying pictures of these people and their relationship both to me and to this hideous place. My path back into Auschwitz is made free and clear.

One of the rooms in Barracks 20 is dimly lit and a small trough of earth-colored gravel lines the base of each wall. I borrow a small pair of nail scissors from Amy and slowly and carefully separate Helmut's photo from Alex's. I then kneel by one of the gravel borders, kiss Helmut's seventeen-year-old face, softly say, "I love you," and place the photo onto the gravel, where it leans against the wall. This is the loving burial my sweet uncle never had, and as I bow my head, my tears drip onto the tiny crushed stone. "*Ruhe ruhig, mein liebe Helmut,*" I whisper. "Rest in peace."

In silence, we walk slowly back to the parking lot and then drive the two kilometers to Birkenau. Here there are fewer cars and only a single tour bus. The remains of the camp seem vast in comparison to the tidy Auschwitz memorial. At Auschwitz there are many small brick buildings connected by well-groomed gravel paths; here there are only

Barracks 20 at Auschwitz, where Uncle Helmut died, either of typhus or of a deliberate lethal injection, and where I left his photograph.

a handful of wooden barracks slowly rotting in the wind and weather of the Polish countryside, surrounded by large empty fields of tall grasses that bend in the breeze of this warm June day. The Auschwitz camp is alive with visitors crunching along the paths, snatches of their varied languages competing for attention. Birkenau is all sad silence; conversations are hushed and muted; what sounds there are come largely from nature: the wind sighing in the grass, the occasional bird song, crickets.

A memorial plaque, on which visitors have placed many small stones, reads, "Forever let this place be a cry of despair and a warning to humanity, where the Nazis murdered about one and a half million men, women, and children, mostly Jews, from various countries of Europe. Auschwitz-Birkenau, 1940–1945."

The parking area abuts the elevated guard tower that straddles a single railway line; together the tower and track form one of the indelible images of the Holocaust. Amy and I walk inside the gates of Birkenau to stand in the shadow of the tower at the approximate point where the selections were made, where Alex and Helmut were separated by the wave of a Nazi doctor's hand.

They were father and son, they had been constant companions for more than three years, becoming each other's best friend, on sea and then on land, in Boulogne-sur-Mer and Martigny-les-Bains, in Sionne and Montauban, Agde and Rivesaltes and Les Milles, and finally on those terrible trains to Drancy and then to this very spot. And then, in the blink of an eye, Alex was sent to the left and Helmut was sent to the right. Did they know what was in store for each of them? Were they permitted a last embrace, a final handclasp, anything at all? Did father cry out to son, son to father? Could they have heard each other over the wail of humanity at the scene of this unspeakable crime?

I am gasping for breath, my legs suddenly too weak to support me, and I very nearly collapse, but Amy gathers me in her arms and we rock together back and forth, back and forth, until my heartbeat returns to normal and my eyes can see again.

When I have regained my strength, we slowly walk several hundred yards to the site of two of the crematoria, both of which were nearly destroyed by the retreating German army in January 1945, as they sought to cover up their deeds. Today the crematoria are harmless holes in the ground, bordered by low brick walls and crumbling concrete. From a nearby field, I pluck three little wildflowers, one yellow, one purple, one white, and then jump lightly down into what remains of one of the crematorium's foundations. I place my grandfather's photo on the ground, leaning it against the bricks, and then lay the flowers beneath the photo. "Goodbye, Alex," I whisper, "I love you so much. *Ruhe ruhig.*" Amy hugs me again, and I hold her as I weep.

Then I dry my eyes, take a final look at the photo and the flowers and climb up out of the grave. It is time, I tell myself. It is now time to let go.

For the next ten or twenty minutes, we sit with our backs against a tree, taking refuge in its shade against what has become quite a warm and humid day. We face away from the ruined crematoria and toward the boundaries of Birkenau. The barbed wire enclosing the camp is

Alex's "burial site" in the ruined foundations of one of the crematoria in Birkenau.

affixed to concrete pillars that curve inward gracefully as they crest, and I am reminded of a fragment of a poem written by a young prisoner who was held here seventy years ago. Zofia Grochowalska Abramovicz also noticed those graceful curves strung with wire and called them "the harps of Birkenau," writing that the wind made the cruel wires vibrate and utter pleasing sounds. What a sweet soul Zofia must have possessed, I think, to find a little beauty amid such cruelty and ugliness.

I close my eyes and hear the wind whispering and rustling in the green leaves overhead and imagine that I hear a thin and distant melody in the ghostly strings of Zofia's harps. Then a cow moos and a rooster crows from a nearby farm and I realize that life is everywhere. Birkenau's instruments of death are indeed in ruins, and they can no longer harm me. Alex and Helmut's journey, painful and hopeless as it turned out to be, ended here. I need to acknowledge that it ended, that they died here, but also that I am alive, that I have survived. Having followed

A few of the graceful harps of Birkenau.

in Alex's wake for so long, now that I have come to the spot where he died I must resolve, for the rest of the time that I'm given, to live life to the fullest.

"C'mon," I say to Amy, "let's get the hell out of here."

We drive away from Oswiecim toward a few days of rest in the Swiss Alps. After weathering a long, construction-induced traffic jam on the Polish-Czech border, we head west on a clear stretch of open road in the beautiful Czech countryside, toward a glorious sunset. I have brought along a recording of the Mass in B Minor by Johann Sebastian Bach, whose birthplace we visited two days ago, and as the Meriva purrs along, we listen to the Mass's last two movements.

Dame Janet Baker, one of my favorite artists, sings *Agnus Dei, qui tollis peccata mundi, miserere nobis.* ("O Lamb of God, who takes away the sins of the world, have mercy on us.") It occurs to me that it would have to be a lamb of immense strength and fortitude to take away all of the sins committed at Auschwitz. Perhaps, I think, it is an impossible task; perhaps some sins will outlast us all.

But then comes Bach's final magnificent chorus on the words *Dona nobis pacem* ("Grant us peace"). The music soars, carrying voice and spirit ever upward. If anything can restore my abiding faith in the human animal, this glorious creation can, and does. My dear wife and traveling companion sings along with me, and I think to myself, "Let my journey grant Alex and Helmut peace. Let them rest in the earth and sky of Poland forevermore. And may it grant me peace as well."

14

Coming Home

"Journeys end in lovers meeting."

That song from *Twelfth Night*—"It Was A Lover and His Lass"—sounded through my mind as we made the trans-Atlantic crossing on the solstice, June 21, and flew back to the States. From the haunted, death-soaked soil of Auschwitz, we had driven south and west to the clear, bracing air of the Swiss Alps to spend our last days in Europe amid the old-world luxury of a grand hotel. Amy's Uncle Jim, a professor and diplomat, loved to stay at the Hotel Waldhaus in Sils-Maria, an inn that has been owned and operated by the same family since 1908, and we came in remembrance of him. Three days of Alpine hiking and gourmet dining did much to restore our bodies and souls. On the morning of the longest day of the year, we returned our faithful little Meriva to the rental agency. Its odometer now read 20,177; in our six weeks on the road, we had driven 9,214 kilometers, or 5,725 miles, nearly twice the width of the United States.

On the plane ride back to Washington, I reflected that those six weeks seemed to have lasted a long, long time and yet to have passed in the blink of an eye. I recalled that before I left, I had feared both that I would be unable to uncover much information about Alex and Helmut's lives and that the trip would feel more of a mockery of Alex and Helmut's suffering than a tribute to them. Looking down on the world from thirty-six thousand feet, I decided that those fears had not been realized.

I had learned a great deal, factually, from the archives in Bückeburg and Helmut's school records in Oldenburg; from the newspaper clippings in Boulogne and the saga of Adolphe Poult and René Bousquet in Montauban. And I learned a lot, viscerally, at Barracks 21 in Rivesaltes and Barracks 7 and 20 in Auschwitz.

How deeply moving it had been to stand where Alex and Helmut had stood, to see what they saw, to feel just a bit of what they felt, if not the danger and terror they experienced. I recalled walking the docks of Boulogne, imagining how hopeful they must have felt as their ship pulled into what must have finally seemed like a safe harbor. Driving through the smiling countryside of the Vosges, I again had imagined their hope as they saw the lovely fields and hillsides that might have become their new home. The ruins of the Hotel International in Martigny-les-Bains had sharply reminded me of the futility of that hope. Peering through the locked gates of the Poult factory gave me the first inklings of what they must have felt as prisoners and enemies of the Vichy state. And, oh, the bleak, windswept emptiness of Rivesaltes! It was there that their hope must have begun to die. The catacombs of Camp des Milles had given me the sense of being buried alive; the view of the boxcar from the brick factory's second floor was chilling in the June heat. And though I learned nothing of their final moments together on the railroad siding of Birkenau, I now had that terrible place forever fixed in my inner eye.

Dozing in my seat, lulled by the hum of the engines, I felt comforted by those thoughts and eager to begin setting them down. But Shake-speare's confident declaration kept occurring to me and giving me pause. *Journeys end in lovers meeting.* I patted Amy's arm and told myself that I had traveled with my lover these past six weeks; how then could I meet her when our plane landed at Dulles Airport? Closing my eyes, I thought, "Old Will can't be right about everything."

As it happened, however, my journey was not quite at its end. What actually greeted me upon our arrival was what Winston Churchill called his "black dog"—a shroud of depression that descended on me over the next several weeks as I found it difficult to shake off the sadness brought on by those hours in Auschwitz. Perhaps it was merely the routine of daily life following the exciting days of discovery on the road. But I was also constantly conscious of one overwhelming and incontrovertible fact: impossible though it was, I had failed to save Alex and Helmut, those six weeks and fifty-seven hundred miles notwithstanding. Auschwitz was the punch line to their story after all. The bad guys had won and my family had lost; never mind my good intentions, I had been no more successful in preventing the murders than my father had been. That, at least, is how it seemed to me during the long summer days. The hopes I had felt as I drove away from Poland were proving difficult to sustain.

With the coming of autumn, however, I did my best to chase away the black dog by beginning to write the story of our journey through Europe. By recollecting the details of my discoveries in the tranquility and safety of our home office, surrounded by an untidy pile of notes, books, maps, and photos, I began to think of the trip as a pilgrimage and an act of love that might, in some mystical manner unknown to me, reach my relatives and grant them a measure of the peace I so wished for them. I began to think that by setting down the story so that others could learn about it, I was fulfilling my long-held desire to place flowers on their graves, blooms that had the potential of lasting far longer than the little yellow, purple, and white wildflowers I had buried along with Alex's photo in the ruins of the crematorium in Birkenau.

As autumn descended into winter and then as the light slowly began its cherished return, three happy things happened that, together, managed to all but banish the black dog from my door forever.

It has been nearly twenty years since I first met my friend Tamara and we made the astounding discovery that her aunt had known my parents in Berlin in 1940. My father had often regaled me with tales of how he and my mother had defied the Nazi curfews by sneaking out after dark to play chamber music with a small group of friends, and when he did he would mention Gerti Totschek, who wasn't a musician herself but who had always been the life of those perilous parties. Gerti's younger sister, Ursula, managed to escape Germany via the *Kindertransport*, the British rescue mission that saved nearly ten thousand Jewish children from Germany, Austria, Czechoslovakia, and Poland.

Ursula became Tamara's mother, and it was a source of great joy for Tamara and me to learn that her Aunt Gerti had played such an important role in my parents' lives in those far-off dangerous days.

So Tamara and I already had forged an important bond. But then in the autumn of 2011, she gathered together a group of eight friends, all of whom were children of German, Austrian, or Czech survivors of the Holocaust. Most of their parents had been participants in the *Kindertransport*, and all of us were bound together by our unique ancestry. We began meeting monthly to share potluck suppers and talk endlessly about our common heritage and what it meant to us to be the second generation of Holocaust survivors. A frequent topic of discussion was fear and guilt: how, despite our sheltered, upper-middle-class upbringings, we had all been, and in many cases were still, subject to an irrational fear of that knock on the door in the middle of the night and a belief that we were somehow responsible for what had happened years before our birth. At one of our first gatherings, I was struck by a story Vicki told. At age seven or eight, she fell off her bicycle and scraped one of her legs. She limped painfully home and then crept upstairs to the bathroom to clean the blood from her leg in solitude. Somehow, without her parents ever saying a word to her, she had absorbed the understanding that something terrible had happened to them, and something even worse to their parents, and that a skinned leg paled in comparison. "I knew—at that age!—that I had no right to complain about something so piddling," Vicki confessed, shaking her head. "Nothing that happened to me could ever amount to the pain my family had suffered, so I had better just learn to deal with my petty problems on my own."

Learning that my guilt and fears were not unique to me was therapy of the most comforting kind, and the monthly meetings of what I have come to call the Tamara Group have had a profoundly healing effect for which I remain deeply grateful.

The next happy occurrence to befall me is one I have already mentioned. In February 2012, I quite unexpectedly heard from a cousin I didn't know I had, Steven Behrens, of Cheshire, England. Steven and I share a common great-great-grandfather, Elkan Simon Behrens, father of the Bremen coffee importer Ludwig Behrens and grandfather of Toni Behrens, who married my grandfather Alex. Thanks to Steven's prodigious genealogical research, I learned some key facts relating to Alex and Helmut's whereabouts in the winter of 1939–1940, as well as some details of their transfer from Rivesaltes to Camp des Milles. As important as that knowledge was in filling in the gaps of this story, it was also extremely gratifying to learn that my small damaged family was larger and healthier than I'd realized. Steven and I began making vague plans to meet in person one day, plans that soon came into sharper focus thanks to the third happy event.

As winter melted into the warm spring of 2012, I heard from my friends Hilu and Roland Neidhardt in Oldenburg that Carsten and Monica Meyerbohlen were still considering placing a plaque on the side of my grandfather's house on Gartenstrasse. But Roland wrote, with sorrow, that Carsten had been visited by an unruly black dog of his own. He was apparently having a very difficult time confronting the knowledge that he and his wife had been living contentedly in the beautiful home that had been seized from Alex Goldschmidt, and he was finding it difficult to design the memorial plaque that he deeply wished to display.

Looking up from the computer screen after reading Roland's news, I was struck by the similarity of my long-held and enervating rhetorical question—"How do I have the right to feel true and lasting happiness when my grandfather was murdered in Auschwitz?"—to what seemed to be Carsten's current quandary—"How can I go on living in this lovely house that was forcibly taken away from a man who would end up in Auschwitz?" He had bought the property only ten years ago, with no knowledge of its former owners, yet he could find little comfort in the awareness that he had no complicity in the crime that eventually delivered the house into his hands.

I recalled that initially I had felt a deep ambivalence at the Meyerbohlens' offer of a plaque. In the months since, I had continued to turn the matter over in my mind, never quite arriving at a satisfactory decision. On the one hand, I thought, this was a generous offer by Carsten and Monica; they were under no obligation whatsoever to let the world know about the history of the house they had legally bought. The plaque would tell one small story of the countless acts of cruelty and violence visited upon the Jewish citizens of Oldenburg. Perhaps it would be the first of many; perhaps this decision by the Meyerbohlens would inspire other families to erect similar monuments throughout the city. It could mark an important new chapter in my ancestral home.

But, I argued to myself, does this let Oldenburg off the hook too easily? Would this single plaque enable the town elders to briskly wash their hands of the matter, to say to themselves, "There, that's done . . . problem solved. Our collective conscience has now been washed clean"? Can a small piece of plexiglass, no matter how elegant or eloquent, make up for what I lost, for what Oldenburg lost, for what Germany and all the civilized world lost?

Am I being played for a sucker?

I was never more grateful for the emotional and rational resources of the members of the Tamara Group. I didn't have to explain the complexity or the ambiguity of the issue to them. They understood the question at hand and the deeper general questions of loss and guilt and the possibility of reconciliation, all too well. After many nights of discussion, I came away convinced that some tangible notice of what had happened to my family was far better than nothing at all. I wrote to Carsten and Monica to tell them that I was aware of the issues they were wrestling with, that I was deeply grateful for their offer, and that I hoped plans for the plaque could move forward. I sent them a couplet from a poem by Emily Dickinson that I'd discovered, words that I thought would be perfect for inclusion in whatever memorial they might choose.

So it was with a great deal of satisfaction that I received notice from the Meyerbohlens in early June that they had settled both on a design for the plaque and on a date for its unveiling, September 27. Throughout the summer months, I looked back on the days Amy and I had spent in Germany and France and looked forward to what I now realized would be the end of the journey, when in some small way I would reclaim the family home.

I wrote to my newfound cousin, Steven, and to my long-cherished cousin Deborah, to invite them to join us for the ceremony. To my delight, they both declared their eagerness to attend.

About a week before our departure for Oldenburg, I met with the Tamara Group for our monthly get-together. "What should I say?" I asked them. "How do I strike a balance between expressing gratitude for this important gesture and making a strong statement on behalf of my murdered family?" We considered various ideas for hours, sitting around a wooden table on Tamara's deck, eating, drinking, and occasionally laughing as the early autumn dusk deepened into a warm, breezy night.

"I'm sure you'll find the right words," Anne assured me. "Just make sure you remind everyone why you're there." I nodded, profoundly grateful for such simple, direct, and important advice.

WEDNESDAY, SEPTEMBER 26, 2012. A cool, damp day in Bremen, forty miles or so from Oldenburg. Amy and I stand in the midst of the bustling central railroad station, peering discreetly into the faces of strangers, searching for Cousin Steven.

Sentimentally recalling my many twilight conversations with my father in his last months, I had decided to travel to Oldenburg via Amsterdam. We arrived in Oldenburg yesterday, welcomed warmly, as ever, by Roland and Hilu. This morning Amy and I drove to Bremen, where we have arranged to meet Steven and his wife, Helen, who yesterday flew to Hamburg from their home in Cheshire and this morning have taken the train to Bremen. We have arranged to meet under the station's big departure-and-arrivals board shortly after their train arrives at 10:42. For some reason, however, we have not exchanged photographs, so I have no idea who among the hundreds of hurrying passengers walking briskly past us is my cousin.

But then a man pulling a wheeled suitcase, a jacket over his arm, pauses a few steps away. He is about my height, with less hair but also less girth. Our eyes meet, we both raise our eyebrows and nearly simultaneously exclaim, "Steven?" "Martin?" His broad smile must mirror my own, and we embrace. Needless but jolly introductions follow, as I present Amy to Steven and Helen. There has doubtless been many a happy scene in this station over the years, as friends and lovers meet, but at this moment, I am willing to bet that ours is among the most joyful. My little family has just increased by two.

I search for a family resemblance as the four of us walk out to the car, chatting a mile a minute. I peer avidly into Steven's friendly face, not sure at first but immensely pleased at the opportunity for future discovery.

The four of us spend a delightful day in Bremen, first as tourists—as I show my family what I know of such famous sights as the beautiful eleventh-century Bremen Cathedral, the sixteen-foot-tall statue of the medieval hero Roland, and the sculpture of the Bremen Town Musicians—and then as ancestral sleuths. We walk along the handsome city boulevard known as Am Wall in search of the home of my great-grandfather Ludwig Behrens, the son of our common great-great-grandfather Elkan. We find the address, but the area was heavily bombed during the Second World War and the street is now lined with commercial ventures and office buildings. We then drive to a residential area in the eastern part of the city in search of the graves of Ludwig and his wife, Jeanette. We find the cemetery that we're looking for, but as it is Yom Kippur, the Day of Atonement, the gates are bolted shut. The detective work and close reading of maps, hurrying down strange streets in search of what turn out to be blind alleys, serve to bring us closer together. By the time we drive back to Oldenburg in late afternoon, Amy and I feel as though we have known Steven and Helen for years rather than mere hours. I am very happy.

At dinner that evening at the Neidhardts, we are again joined by the Lutheran minister Dietgard Jacoby, whom I am eager to introduce to my English cousins. Looking forward to tomorrow's unveiling at the house on Gartenstrasse, Roland and Dietgard tell me the somewhat awkward story of previous attempts to commemorate the persecution of the Jews of Oldenburg. In dozens of other cities across Germany, it has become common in the past two decades or so to place what are called *Stolpersteine*, or Stumble Stones, in the streets. Often simple cobblestones covered in brass, the *Stolpersteine* are laid in the roadway outside houses that once belonged to Jewish families, inset with their names, their birthdates, and the dates and sites of their murders. Literally thousands of these stones have been placed in German cities from Aachen to Zittau, but up until now, there have been none in Oldenburg. "Why not?" is my logical question.

Roland and Dietgard exchange long looks before answering. The "blame" seems to be somewhat equally shared by reactionary elements in the Oldenburg establishment, who have gone in for the sort of historical airbrushing decried by Roland during my last visit, and—somewhat surprisingly, it seems to me at first—the local Jewish community. Most of Oldenburg's Jews are fairly recent Russian émigrés and, led by their New York-trained rabbi, they have declared that these stones, at ground level where they are both literally underfoot and subject to such indignities as being urinated upon by passing dogs, are not fitting or dignified memorials to the murdered. As a result, other than the maintained ruins of the synagogue on Peterstrasse that was burned to the ground on *Kristallnacht* in 1938, there is no public commemoration of the fate of the Jews of Oldenburg. So the plaque on Gartenstrasse will break new ground tomorrow, as my father's hometown slowly begins to join the ranks of German cities trying to come to terms with the unspeakable legacy of the Third Reich by creating lasting memorials.

But what, finally, is the best way to accomplish these attempts at remembrance? Can something so monstrous ever be adequately memorialized? Is it even possible? The German philosopher Theodor Adorno famously declared, "To write poetry after Auschwitz is barbaric," implying that the only justified response is sorrowful silence. To that end, Dietgard mentions the Square of Invisible Witnesses in the German city of Saarbrücken.

Between 1990 and 1993, a German art teacher and his students surreptitiously removed 2,146 cobblestones from the public square in front of the Provincial Parliament building in Saarbrücken and replaced them with similar stones so that the originals would not be missed. They chose the number 2,146 because it represents the number of Jewish cemeteries that were desecrated during the Nazi era. The "vandals" engraved the original stones with the names and locations of the cemeteries and then reinstalled the stones with the engraved sides facing down, to remain in the square as silent indictments of Nazi brutality.

The citizens of Saarbrücken were thus unaware that they were walking on anything more remarkable than an ordinary cobblestoned square ... until the artist came forward and confessed what he and his students had done. Perhaps surprisingly, the Saarbrücken City Council then retroactively commissioned this already completed memorial, giving it its official blessing. Today, to the uninitiated eye the Square of Invisible Witnesses is just an ordinary cityscape.

As we sit before a cozy fire after dinner, we debate the effectiveness of such memorials. Dietgard finds the Saarbrücken square to be a powerful and poetic monument, in keeping with her belief in the hidden energy of the unseen. Roland, a more practical sort, thinks that it allows the citizens of Saarbrücken to ignore the horror as they blithely make their daily way over the buried testimonials of the silent stones. Feeling hopelessly noncommittal, I find myself agreeing wholeheartedly with whoever is speaking at any given moment. But I find it remarkable, and not for the first time, that Germany continues to have this lively debate over the best way to remember its criminal past when, too often it seems, my country continues to give only lip service to the issues of slavery and the slaughter of our Native population.

Around 9:00 p.m., we drive Steven and Helen to their hotel, and then Amy, Roland, and I set off for the airport to pick up my cousin Deborah. With her arrival, my family bolstered by yet another loving and supportive member, I feel fully ready for the unveiling on Gartenstrasse.

Thursday, September 27, is another cool and cloudy day, with intermittent showers. In the late morning, Amy and I meet Deborah, Steven, and Helen at their hotel and then spend several hours on a walking tour of the town. We first pay a visit to 34 Gartenstrasse, and I proudly show my cousins what I can from the sidewalk, pointing out the obvious grandeur of the place and such hidden details as the former location of my father's chicken run at the side of the house. I am very aware of something new; on the side of the house facing the street, there is a patch of blue cloth covering what I know to be the memorial plaque.

From the house, we stroll down Gartenstrasse and enter the beautiful Schlossgarten. I lead the way to the quiet corner of the park where, sixteen months ago, we scattered my father's ashes. It begins to rain softly and, unfurling umbrellas, we walk through the park admiring the flower beds, ponds, and gently curving paths. I tell my cousins about my father's sweet memories of the Schlossgarten; I tell them that in his final years, as he struggled with a clouded mind, he spoke lovingly of these cherished surroundings and his memories seemed to bring him peace. They nod, and I feel how deeply they understand.

Leaving the park, my tour takes us next to the Altes Gymnasium, where I show them the memorial to Helmut and his fellow students. We then enter the narrow streets of the old city, and I lead the way to the corner of Achternstrasse and Schüttingstrasse, where Alex once had his store. I am aware of a flood of pride within me and realize that I am sharing with my family a sense that, in some profound way, this is my home and they are helping me reclaim it after a very long and difficult time.

We enjoy a warm lunch in a cozy little restaurant, then agree to meet again in the lobby of their hotel that evening. At the appointed time, with Roland and Hilu joining us, we all walk solemnly to what I still think of as my grandfather's house. The ceremony is about to begin.

Carsten and Monica Meyerbohlen stand in the front garden of 34 Gartenstrasse, greeting the thirty or forty invited guests, who arrive in twos and threes. Farschid Ali Zahedi is here with his cameras. It is overcast and cool but the afternoon rain has moved off to the east, leaving behind a few shimmering drops in the leaves of the beech trees and on the rosebush that has been nurtured these past months by the last of my father's ashes. Carsten grasps my hand firmly in a welcoming grip, but I imagine that I see some lingering pain in his eyes. I realize that he may be entering into the evening with his own feelings of ambivalence. My eyes return to the blue cloth on the front of the house and I notice that a small spotlight is trained on it.

We file slowly up the front stairs, pass through the entrance hallway past the library and dining room, and turn into the grand high-ceilinged living room. Much of its furniture has been moved to the perimeter and the space filled with folding chairs. Steven, Deborah, and I take places in the front row, with Amy and Helen seated directly behind us. I crane my neck to discover that the room is full to overflowing, with many people standing against the walls. As the murmur of voices slowly falls silent, Dietgard Jacoby hurries in and gives me a sad smile. I return her smile and pat my chest above my heart to show my appreciation for her presence.

Oldenburg's deputy mayor, Germaid Eilers-Dörfler, rises and extends a greeting from the city's Mayor Gerd Schwandner. She declares that this is no ordinary gathering and asks rhetorically why there have been no other gatherings of this type, since, as she notes solemnly, "We have, after all, had reason and opportunity enough." She acknowledges that the Free State of Oldenburg was the first state in the German Reich to deliver power to the Nazis and that "an ominous signal was sent out from here that would prove to be irreversible."

Frau Eilers-Dörfler decries the "state machinery of hatred that released unimaginable forces of evil" in Germany. She mentions the destruction of November 9, 1938, the forced march of the Jews through Oldenburg on the following day, and the even worse indignities that were inflicted upon them in the following years. She declares, "The immeasurable suffering experienced by our Jewish fellow citizens in their everyday lives and then in concentration and extermination camps weighed heavily on those who endured this suffering and on those who felt deeply ashamed of it."

At this moment, Deborah leans close to me and hisses in my ear, "How *dare* she! How dare she compare the suffering of the Jews with the guilt of the Germans! We all know who suffered more, and it's not even close!"

I look at my cousin and nod my head in agreement about what, indeed, seems an utterly obtuse remark. But then the deputy mayor speaks of the slow rebuilding of Jewish life in Oldenburg and of how "durable reconciliation is not grounded in repressing history but rather through courage and enlightenment, knowledge, and honesty." She insists that reconciliation cannot merely be abstract but must be concrete and tangible. "Numbers, even horrifyingly large numbers," she says, "hardly affect us. It is the fates of individuals that stir us inside. And the fate of the Goldschmidt family gives us an opportunity to feel with real empathy what this episode in our nation's history has inflicted on humanity. We can see the exclusion, humiliation, heartache, and murder.

"Erecting a plaque on this house," she concludes, "to remember Alex Goldschmidt and his family here, could not be more appropriate. Our warmest thanks for this privately sponsored initiative go to you, dear Mr. and Mrs. Meyerbohlen, on behalf of the City of Oldenburg."

There is sustained applause from the witnesses. Carsten stands. In a low voice, in German, he speaks of the pleasure that accompanied his and Monica's purchase of this splendid house a decade ago, happiness that turned to anguish when they learned of the circumstances that led to its availability. He recounts meeting me and Amy last year, how the idea of a memorial plaque first occurred to him, how we have stayed in touch, and how gratified he is that this day has arrived and that we have traveled so far to attend this evening's ceremony.

At that point, Carsten pauses, then falls silent, then sits. Monica stands and invites everyone outside for the unveiling. But before anyone can move, Roland Neidhardt stands and says loudly, "I think we should now hear from Alex Goldschmidt's grandson."

After a beat, Monica turns to me with a broad smile and exclaims, "Yes, of course! Ladies and gentlemen, Martin Goldsmith, from Washington." Polite applause. I stand, smile at Roland, take a long look around this opulent room in my grandfather's magnificent house, smile at Amy, Steven, Helen, and Deborah, and begin to speak, trying to express the many thoughts and feelings I have carried with me since this long journey began.

"Thank you, Monica. Thank you, Carsten. And special thanks to four people whom I have known for more than ten years, who have become dear friends: Farschid Ali Zahedi, Dietgard Jacoby, and Roland and Hiltrud Neidhardt. Thank you all so much.

"We are here tonight for many reasons. We are here, in this beautiful house, because my grandfather, Alex Goldschmidt, who had fought in the trenches of the First World War on behalf of the German Reich and who was awarded the Iron Cross for his efforts, returned to Oldenburg and his *Haus der Mode*, and worked hard enough and was fortunate enough to be able to afford to purchase this house in 1919. We are here because Alex and his wife Toni brought up four children in this house, their daughters Bertha and Eva and their sons Helmut and Günther, my father, who so loved running out the front door and scampering down Gartenstrasse to the entrance of the Schlossgarten, where he would play and dream for many a happy hour.

"We are here because in 1932, officials from the newly elected Nazi Party—as noted by the deputy mayor—forced my grandfather to sell this house to one of them for a criminally low price. For the next six years, Alex and Toni moved several times, each time to smaller and cheaper lodgings.

"We are here because on the night of November 9, 1938, my grandfather was arrested during the violence of *Kristallnacht*, and because the next morning he was marched through town along with forty-two of his fellow Jews to the Oldenburg prison, and because the next day he was sent to the Sachsenhausen concentration camp, where he remained for nearly a month.

"We are here tonight because my grandfather Alex and my uncle Helmut attempted to flee Nazi Germany on board the refugee ship *St. Louis*, which sailed away from Hamburg on May 13, 1939, bound for Cuba. We are here because the *St. Louis* was not allowed to land in Cuba, nor in the United States, nor in Canada. We are here because the *St. Louis* sailed back to Europe, because my grandfather and uncle were allowed to disembark in France, and because they then spent the next three years in refugee centers and internment camps in Martigny-les-Bains and Montauban and Agde and Rivesaltes and Les Milles."

At this point, I am forced to stop and dry my eyes and take a deep breath, which does little to prevent my voice from cracking.

"We are here tonight because in August of 1942, Alex and Helmut were forced into cattle cars and shipped first to Drancy and then to Auschwitz, where they were murdered, executed for the crime of being born Jews. We are here because my grandmother Toni and my aunt Eva were sent to Riga to be executed for the same crime."

I lower my shimmering eyes to the floor for several moments. I am aware of a profound silence in the room. I wonder for an instant if the deputy mayor, the Meyerbohlens, and nearly everyone else is regretting having given me a chance to speak. When I raise my eyes again, I see through the blur the tear-streaked face of Dietgard. I smile at her with gratitude and continue.

"We are here in my grandfather's former house for all those reasons. But we are also here because of so many kind and wonderful people in Oldenburg who have made me and my wife and my extended family—Steven and Helen and Deborah, who have traveled here from England—feel so welcome; people like Farschid and Dietgard and Roland and Hilu and many, many others.

"And we are here because Carsten and Monica decided to make a brave declaration by affixing a tangible statement of remembrance to this beautiful house . . . to their beautiful house. They did not have to do this, yet they have chosen to do it. They are among the people of Oldenburg who have made me and my family feel welcome, to feel as though we belong here and that when we pass within the boundaries of this city we are coming home.

"Thank you, Carsten and Monica. Thank you for having the courage to remember."

I pause again and once more take in the sight of this lovely room. I imagine for a moment how it might have looked on a September evening ninety years ago, in 1922, when my father was nearly nine and my uncle had just experienced his first birthday. Again I feel my eyes begin to overflow, but this time I am smiling broadly. I resume.

"I feel bound to tell you all that when Carsten and Monica first mentioned their idea to me, I wasn't sure how I felt about it. And I must also admit that I have been both sad and sometimes deeply angry about what happened to my family and about the process that forced them from this house. I have felt that way often, in fact. And I must tell you that I have felt guilty about what happened, as irrational as that may seem to you, considering that this all happened years before I was born. So I want to make sure that I share with you a brief story before we go outside.

"The story is of two Buddhist monks, an older man and a younger man, who are traveling many miles on foot to their monastery. It has been raining heavily and when they come to the bank of a river, they find that the bridge has been washed away. Standing on the bank is a young woman. 'Please, sirs,' she says to the monks, 'I need to get to the other side of the river to feed my children their evening meal. Will you be so kind as to carry me across?' The younger monk begins to explain that their order does not allow them to come into physical contact with women, but the older monk stoops, gestures to his companion to do the same, and then invites the woman to climb onto their shoulders. She does so, and the two monks then wade across the river, transporting her safely to the other side. She jumps to the ground, thanks them profusely, and the two monks continue their journey.

"That evening, as the shadows are beginning to lengthen, the younger monk says, 'Master, I continue to be somewhat troubled by our encounter along the river bank. We have made certain holy vows, and one of them is that we do not touch women under any circumstances. And yet you broke your vow and caused me to break mine. Why, Master?'

"The older monk stops walking and, turning to his young companion with a smile filled with kindness, says, 'I set that woman down upon the river bank many hours ago now. Why are you still carrying her?'"

I pause and see Roland nod his head slowly as he reaches for Hilu's hand.

"I have carried the burden of guilt and anger and sorrow for many years now," I say. "It may have served a purpose, but this evening, in this place, before you kind people, I vow to set it down. Or at least, to try my best."

I sit then, closing my eyes. Amy kisses the back of my neck, Deborah grips one of my hands and Steven the other. Loud applause fills the living room of my grandfather's house.

We then file out the front door into a misty evening. Carsten appears at my side. He is smiling broadly with the clear evidence of tears in his eyes. "Thank you," he whispers. "Thank you so much for your beautiful words. You have given me permission to set down my burden also."

At a signal from Monica, Carsten and I both grasp a long piece of string that is connected to the blue cloth on the front of the house. We pull gently and the cloth falls away to reveal the memorial plaque. The crowd cheers and Carsten and I shake hands.

Carsten Meyerbohlen and I shake hands moments after the unveiling of the memorial plaque at 34 Gartenstrasse.

The plexiglass plaque has been designed by Carsten himself. Against an image of the house in winter, there appear the words, in German:

From 1919 until 1932 this was the private house of the respected citizen Alex Goldschmidt. With the forced sale of this house to the National Socialists, the sorrowful journey of this Jewish family began. Alex Goldschmidt and his son Helmut in the Auschwitz concentration camp, and his wife Toni and daughter Eva in the Riga ghetto, were murdered in 1942.

Below that, in English, are the lines from the poem by Emily Dickinson that I suggested for the plaque:

Remembrance has a rear and front,
'Tis something like a house.

Amy hugs and kisses me. She, who has been with me every step of this long journey, is crying. Then Deborah appears, sobbing, and I hold her tightly as she tries to speak. "They had so much," she manages finally. "Oh, and they lost so much." And then my newfound cousin Steven, whom I realize in this moment I love like family, is also by my side, also in tears, and we all wrap our arms around one another, sharing our bottomless sorrow and our heady triumph at having survived the evil efforts of our enemies and our pleasure at this written proof of our family's existence on the wall above our heads and our great joy at having come so far to find one another.

Journeys end in lovers meeting.

We repair to the Neidhardts' comfortable home—Amy, Steven, Helen, Deborah, Farschid, Dietgard, Carsten, Monica, and about a dozen other people who are friends of the Neidhardts or the Meyerbohlens. Hilu has prepared a delicious stew and there is amply flowing beer, wine, and mineral water. There is music and laughter and animated conversation. Everyone seems to think that the evening has been a roaring success, and everyone's spirits are high. It feels like a party, like an exuberant gathering after a solemn occasion. I suddenly decide, with apologies to the Irish, that this is a wake. Alex's wake.

I stand, a bit unsteadily, and find a spoon to clink against my glass, commanding the room's attention. "Pardon this brief interruption," I say, perhaps a few decibels louder than necessary. "I would like to propose a toast. There are many people who warrant toasting tonight, and I'm the right man to do it, since I'm more than a little toasted myself." I laugh, and if my laughter lasts a bit longer than it should, no one seems to mind.

"To my grandfather!" I exclaim, lifting my glass high. "To Alex!" And from all corners of the room comes the hearty reply, "To Alex!"

I notice Pastor Dietgard sitting in a corner next to an empty chair and, a trifle straight-linishly, I walk over and join her. Turning to her with an enormous smile, I ask what she thought of the ceremony on Gartenstrasse. She is smiling, too, but there is also a look of wonder on her angelic face, as if she has witnessed something truly remarkable. When she speaks, her voice is so tender and soft that I have to lean close to hear her words above the room's cheerful din.

"Tonight," she says, "was like a birth, the birth of a star whose light we cannot see for hundreds of years." Dietgard hugs me and whispers in my ear, "Alex was with us at the birth."

"Thank you," I breathe. If I have ever felt this deeply happy before, I cannot remember it.

An hour or so later, the last of the guests take their leave. Alex's wake is at an end. Amy retires to bed and I drive Steven, Helen, and Deborah back to their hotel. I then leave the car in the hotel parking lot and walk down the road to Gartenstrasse. The clouds have cleared away, and there are now dozens and dozens of stars winking above the canopy of trees that lines the boulevard. Standing in front of the gate of my grandfather's house, I gaze with enormous pride and satisfaction and happiness at the plaque on the wall. I reflect that, while there will probably always remain a reservoir of sadness within me over what happened to my family, my feelings of guilt and shame have largely vanished. The end of my journey has borne a new beginning.

I think of Dietgard's declaration that tonight saw the birth of a new star, one that will join the galaxy I am seeing now above my head. And I am reminded of Juliet's wish for her beloved Romeo: "And when he shall die, take him and cut him out in little stars, and he will make the face of heaven so fine that all the world will be in love with night." Tonight the light I see reflected from the plaque seems to promise a kind of immortality for my lost family. Alex and Helmut, Toni and Eva, and all of us have come home, and we are safe and happy.

And so, dear Reader, should your travels take you to Oldenburg, I invite you to pay a visit to 34 Gartenstrasse and look up, with a smile and not a tear, at the shining stars.

DIES WAR VON 1919 BIS 1932 DAS PRIVATHAUS DES ANGESEHENEN BÜRGERS ALEX GOLDSCHMIDT.

MIT DEM DURCH NATIONALSOZIALISTEN GENÖTIGTEN VERKAUF DES HAUSES BEGANN DER LEIDENSWEG DER JÜDISCHEN FAMILIE.

ALEX GOLDSCHMIDT UND SEIN SOHN HELMUT WURDEN IM KONZENTRATIONSLAGER IN AUSCHWITZ, SEINE EHEFRAU TONI UND SEINE TOCHTER EVA IM GETTO VON RIGA IM JAHRE 1942 ERMORDET.

"REMEMBRANCE HAS A REAR AND FRONT, 'TIS SOMETHING LIKE A HOUSE."

EMILY DICKINSON

Acknowledgments

A journey both metaphorical and practical, such as the one I've described in this book, cannot even be conceived, much less realized, without some extraordinary assistance. I'm eager to express my deep and profound thanks to the many wonderful people who offered their help and guidance along the way.

The United States Holocaust Memorial Museum in Washington, D.C., is an invaluable resource, both for its countless documents and, especially, for its staff of archivists and researchers. Many thanks to Michlean Amir, Diane Afoumado, Marc Masurovsky, and Scott Miller; one of the USHMM's indefatigable European-based investigators, Peggy Frankston; and photo archivists Judith Cohen, Nancy Hartman, and Caroline Waddell.

I learned an immense amount of detail regarding the voyage of the *St. Louis* and the negotiations surrounding her return to Europe within the archives of the American Jewish Joint Distribution Committee in New York City. Staff researcher Misha Mitsel made my visit to the Joint particularly rewarding.

A special word of thanks to Herbert Karliner of Miami for sharing his memories of being a twelve-year-old passenger on board the *St. Louis*.

Singular thanks to Vicki Caron, the Diane and Thomas Mann Professor of Modern Jewish Studies at Cornell University, for generously providing me with a valuable article about the agricultural camp at Martigny-les-Bains and for passing on her vast knowledge of resources in Paris.

And my deepest thanks to three superb translators who enabled me to make sense of the many shards of evidence and remembrance I collected along the way: Alice Kelley, Christa Dub, and Margot Dembo. *Merci* and *vielen Dank!*

Once we landed in Europe, our path was made infinitely smoother and much more pleasant and worthwhile thanks to the following people: Anne and Theodor Beckmann, Erika Sembdner, Rita Schewe, and Oliver Glissmann in Sachsenhagen; and Hiltrud and Roland Neidhardt, Farschid Ali Zahedi, Dietgard Jacoby, Joerg Witte, Ottheinrich Hestermann, Annemarie Boyken, Anneliese Wehrmann, and Monica and Carsten Meyerbohlen in Oldenburg.

In France we received gracious assistance from Maurice Flamangin in Boulogne-sur-Mer; Madame Gerard Liliane and Julien Duvaux in Martigny-les-Bains; Monique and Jean-Claude Drouilhet in Montauban; Irene Dauphin in Agde; Elodie Montes and Marianne Petit in Rivesaltes; Odette Boyer and Katell Gouin in Les Milles; and Ingrid Janssen, Caroline Didi, and the archivists of the Museum of the Shoah in Paris. Thanks also to Piotr Supinski at the Memorial Museum of Auschwitz-Birkenau.

I'd like to take a moment for a posthumous note of thanks to Bob Silverstein, my former agent, who succumbed to cancer in October 2012. Bob was a reliable source of cheer and encouragement and I'll always remember our jolly dinner in Paris. Sincere thanks also to Bob's sister-in-law, Zohra Belkadi, who unearthed a number of valuable leads from her home in Lyon.

A hearty thank you to my new agent, Jim Levine, for believing in this project enough to take me on as a client and for finding *Alex's Wake* a home at Da Capo Press. Many, many thanks to Da Capo's executive editor, Bob Pigeon, for his incredible enthusiasm, bracing humor, and perceptive work in shaping the manuscript. Thanks also to publisher John Radziewicz, project editor Mark Corsey, marketers Kevin Hanover and Sean Maher, publicist extraordinaire Lissa Warren, and the rest of the magnificent Da Capo team. And a spirited *go raibh maith agat* to the McShea Institute for Irish Studies.

Closer to home, I'd like to thank Tamara Meyer for organizing and maintaining her monthly gatherings of second generation Jews. Warm thanks to the group—Vicki Killian, Anne Masters, Roy Kahn, Julie Litten, Carol Schaengold, Paul Meyer, and Diane Castiglione—for being a source of comfort as we continue to try to understand What It All Means. Special thanks to Vicki and three dear friends, Glen and Lauren Howard and Robert Aubry Davis, for reading early drafts of the manuscript and making so many valuable suggestions.

My profound appreciation and love to my new-found family members, Helen and Steven Behrens, and my cousin of long standing, Deborah Philips, for making the journey to Oldenburg and participating in the ceremony on Gartenstrasse.

Finally, and very simply, I could never have undertaken this journey without my wife and traveling companion, Amy Roach. The words "thank you" have never seemed so inadequate. YVOB

Bibliography

Breitman, Richard, and Allan J. Lichtman. *FDR and the Jews*. Cambridge: Harvard University Press, 2013.

Caron, Vicki. *Uneasy Asylum: France and the Jewish Refugee Crisis, 1933–1942.* Palo Alto: Stanford University Press, 1999.

Dawidowicz, Lucy S. *The War Against the Jews, 1933–1945.* New York: Bantam, 1975.

Feuchtwanger, Lion. *The Devil in France: My Encounter with Him in the Summer of 1940.* Trans. Elisabeth Abbott. New York: Viking, 1941.

Friedlander, Saul. *Nazi Germany and the Jews, Vol. 1: The Years of Persecution, 1933–1939.* New York: HarperCollins, 1997.

Gellman, Irwin F. "The St. Louis Tragedy." In *American Jewish Historical Quarterly.* December 1971.

Gilbert, Martin. *The Holocaust: A History of the Jews of Europe During the Second World War.* New York: Henry Holt, 1985.

Goodwin, Doris Kearns. *No Ordinary Time: Franklin and Eleanor Roosevelt: The Home Front in World War II.* New York: Simon & Schuster, 1994.

Gutman, Israel, ed. *Encyclopedia of the Holocaust.* New York: Macmillan, 1995.

Lipman-Wulf, Peter. *Period of Internment: Letters and Drawings from Les Milles, 1939–1940.* Sag Harbor: Canio's Editions, 1993.

Morse, Arthur D. *While Six Million Died: A Chronicle of American Apathy.* New York: Random House, 1968.

Ogilvie, Sarah A., and Scott Miller. *Refuge Denied: The St. Louis Passengers and the Holocaust.* Madison: University of Wisconsin Press, 2006.

Paxton, Robert O. *Vichy France: Old Guard and New Order, 1940–1944.* New York: Knopf, 1972.

Peschanski, Denis. *La France des Camps: L'internement, 1938–1946.* Paris: Gallimard, 2002.

Schaap, Klaus. "Der Novemberpogrom von 1938." In *Die Geschichte der Oldenburger Juden und ihrer Vernichtung.* Ed. Udo Elerd and Ewald Gaessler. Oldenburg: Isensee Verlag, 1988.

Shirer, William L. *The Rise and Fall of the Third Reich: A History of Nazi Germany.* New York: Simon & Schuster, 1959.

Steinbacher, Sybille. *Auschwitz: A History.* Trans. Shaun Whiteside. London: Penguin Books, 2005.

Thomas, Gordon, and Max Morgan Witts. *Voyage of the Damned.* New York: Amereon, Ltd., 1974.

Werkstattfilm, ed. *Ein offenes Geheimnis: 'Arisierung' in Alltag und Wirtschaft in Oldenburg 1933–1945.* Oldenburg: Isensee Verlag, 2001.

Zuccotti, Susan. *The Holocaust, the French, and the Jews.* Lincoln: University of Nebraska Press, 1999.

Index